Royal Witches

Royal Witches

FROM JOAN OF NAVARRE TO ELIZABETH WOODVILLE

GEMMA HOLLMAN

For Mr Hough and Ms Robinson
for encouraging my love of history

Thorowowt a pales as I can passe,
I hard a lady make gret mone,
And ever she syked and sayd, 'Alas!
Alle wordly joy ys from me gone;
And alle my frendes from me can fle;
Alas! I am fulle woo begon;
Alle women may be ware by me'.

The Lament of the Duchess of Gloucester, late fifteenth century

Cover illustration: Engraving from Ebenezer Sibly's *A Key to Physic, and the Occult Sciences*, 1796. (Alamy)

First published 2019

The History Press
97 St George's Place, Cheltenham,
Gloucestershire, GL50 3QB
www.thehistorypress.co.uk

British Library Cataloguing in Publication Data.
A catalogue record for this book is available from the British Library.

ISBN 978 0 7509 8940 4

Typesetting and origination by The History Press
Printed and bound in Great Britain by TJ International Ltd.

CONTENTS

ACKNOWLEDGEMENTS

WRITING A BOOK is a huge task, and as such there are always many people to thank in its production. My first thanks must go to Dr Sethina Watson at the University of York, who first introduced me during my undergraduate degree to the plethora of amazing women in medieval society. I was intrigued to learn not only how powerful women at court could be, but how under-studied they were and sometimes difficult to trace. It inspired me to go down this particular route of research. My thanks also extend to Dr Jeremy Goldberg, who helped foster my idea to study royal witches and supported me as I developed the idea in its infancy as a Master's dissertation.

Huge thanks go to my mother Bernadette, who supported me financially during the writing of the book, and without whom it would not have been possible. Thanks must also go to all of my friends and family who encouraged me to put pen to paper, read over first drafts, and gave me great feedback and overall support. This includes, but is not limited to, my father Ross, Aaron, Ella, Ann, Jill, Cat, Fiona, Harriet, Lorraine and, most specially, to my partner Conor for being my rock through the process. Thank you for keeping me sane during this period. Thanks finally go to Chrissy and the rest of the team at The History Press for being so enthusiastic about my idea and giving me an opportunity to bring it to public light.

AUTHOR'S NOTES

LANGUAGE IN THE medieval period was ever changing, just like it is today. In a time prior to the printing press or dictionaries, spellings varied greatly from source to source. This extended to names, and often no two sources will spell a name the same way. That applies also to the people in this book. For ease of reading, I have used the generally accepted modern, anglicised versions of names, and at times translated quotations to modern English. Where appropriate, however, I have included quotations with contemporary spelling, for it can give us a better connection to the past to read the language how it was spoken. Fifteenth-century England is also notorious for a great repetition of names, which can make reading exceedingly confusing. For this reason, I have used first names for those closest to the women, their family members, to make it more personal – it is how they would have known each other. For the political players around them, however, I have largely stuck with their titles or surnames to help the reader make an easier distinction between people.

INTRODUCTION

THE FIFTEENTH CENTURY is an extremely popular period for writers of both fiction and non-fiction. It saw the height of the English empire in France, the glory days of the Battle of Agincourt, the trial and burning of Joan of Arc, the fall of the English empire, the turbulent civil war years of the Wars of the Roses, the probable murder of the Princes in the Tower, the Battle of Bosworth, and finally the foundation of the Tudor dynasty of which England – and the world – is still so fond.

And yet, in among this rich history, the royal women who were so instrumental to these dynasties are almost forgotten. It is only really during accounts of the Wars of the Roses that historians seem to remember the presence of these women, and that is only because their role cannot be ignored; Margaret of Anjou, in particular, led the fight on behalf of her husband King Henry VI who, by this point, was almost entirely incapacitated by his mental illness.

This book focuses on four women who were part of the royal family during this century. The first is Queen Joan of Navarre, who came to England at the start of the century when she married King Henry IV. Next is Eleanor Cobham who, in 1428, married Humphrey, Duke of Gloucester, who was one of Henry's sons and thus a Prince of England. Humphrey's brother, John, Duke of Bedford, married the next woman in this book, Jacquetta of Luxembourg. Jacquetta's second husband was the knight Richard Woodville, with whom she had the final woman in the book, Elizabeth Woodville. Elizabeth Woodville eventually married King Edward IV and became queen.

Despite their crucial role in government and politics, Elizabeth Woodville is the only woman of the four to have an entire book dedicated to her. The other three have usually appeared as footnotes in the history of men, mentioned only for the children they gave birth to, or for how they led to the downfall of the men they were connected to. This book is the first ever volume to be dedicated solely to these four women, and to link their stories together. All four came from different countries and different levels of society, and none were born into the English royal family. Despite this, they were linked by one incredible thread: they were all accused of using witchcraft to manipulate the king to their will, be it through love or death. When the stories of the mass witch hunts and hysteria of the early modern period are so well known, many are astonished to find that two centuries earlier these accusations were hitting the highest echelons of English society. What is even more astonishing is how very few have ever heard of these accusations.

The fifteenth century saw changes and instability in English politics that had not been seen for a long time. At the turn of the century, a new king, Henry IV, was sitting on the throne after the usurpation of the previous king, Richard II. The wars with France were renewed, and the accession of the 9-month-old King Henry VI, alongside the resulting extended regency, meant that factions grew at court with conflict and in-fighting rife. This was only exacerbated by the civil wars in the second half of the century, and the fact that there were four different Kings of England between 1483 and 1485.

With so much turmoil going on in English politics in these 100 years, it was inevitable that this conflict would next extend to female members of the royal family and nobility. Women were wives, mothers, sisters and daughters to the men who were ruling and, as women, they were inherently vulnerable. Generally, they could not command armies and garner military support in the same way as their male contemporaries (although, as always, there were exceptions to the rule) and their lack of any official roles in the machinations of government meant they were always at risk. While men could be protected by their power and status, confident that they could muster military support to defend them when needed, women did not have the same opportunities. While, in reality, they wielded vast power at court, being able to influence on a personal level, and having their own wealth and power they could call upon to get things done, their lack of official capacity simultaneously made them weak and strong.

For the period that this book covers, the women's most relevant aspects were their relationships to the men around them. When rivals at court wanted to dispose of a competing male they often looked to the women in their lives. It was much easier to take down a woman than a man. Reputation was intertwined in this period, and if a family member had acted questionably then one's own loyalty could be called into question.

In a world where women held no official position at court, it was difficult to find a legitimate reason to attack them. The idea of accusing them of witchcraft was therefore an easy option. It required very little proof, and was incredibly difficult to disprove as it was inherently a covert act performed in private. This was a century in which ideas about witchcraft and magic were developing and solidifying, and the cases against these four women contributed greatly to this, but they were also shaped by the world around them.

The accusations were made for different reasons, but they all had a political basis. It has never properly been recognised how all four of these cases were completely intertwined. They span just under seventy years, and in this time each of these women knew and was related to at least one of the others. After each case the accusers learnt valuable lessons for next time, and we can see how each accusation shaped the next. These women were, at various times, the most powerful women in the entire country, but this was not enough to protect them.

The thing that has been most striking while researching for this book is how two-dimensional the depictions of these women are in the limited writings about them. As they almost always appear as a few side pages in biographies of the men of the time, they never come across as real-life people. They are caricatured villains, driven by greed or a thirst for power, being ruthless in their climbing of the social ladder. If they are not the villain, then they are the saint: Joan is the loving mother who had her children torn from her arms in order to protect them by marrying again; Elizabeth was the virtuous woman who agreed to marry the king in order to protect her chastity and her children, who spent many years in sanctuary in order to protect more of her children, then who tragically also had her children torn from her arms and, this time, murdered.

The narrative of these women is one of centuries of propaganda, changing values and lack of research. Time has often not been taken to see who these women really were, and the lack of sources only contributes to this. But these women were real, complex people, with multiple motives and conflicting feelings. None of them were wholly good or wholly bad. As with any human being, they were a shade of grey. Wherever possible, therefore, a middle ground has been sought among the conflicting accounts of their behaviour where the real person comes through.

The hope is that this book can serve to bring these women to the forefront of their time, where they so rightly deserve to be. All were fascinating women who shaped the world around them. This book aims not only to contribute significantly to the gaps in historiography, creating hitherto unavailable biographies, but also to bring these stories to the public attention. The life of each individual woman is a fascinating story in a century where nothing was certain, and allegiances could change overnight. They found themselves at the centre of some of the biggest scandals of the age which have reverberated across the centuries, now to be retold here. These are the royal witches.

I

MAGIC IN THE LATE MEDIEVAL PERIOD

BEFORE EXPLORING THE lives of the four women contained in this book, it is necessary to take a moment to explore what exactly people in the fifteenth century believed about magic and sorcery. These women are defined as royal witches, but what exactly was a witch? This century was one of huge change, in terms of politics, technology and world view. At the start of the century, there was no singularly defined 'witch', but by the end, handbooks were circulating to help law enforcement recognise who could be a witch practising evil magic.

The previous century, courts on the Continent had been awash with intrigues. Even within the court of the Pope, there had been political accusations of sorcery against rival factions.[1] Closer to home, the French court had been falling apart due to the insanity of King Charles VI. Charles had delusions that made him believe he was made of glass, or disconnected from the world around him, and this meant there was no strong, stable ruler. Court factions began to take over, and this meant conspiracy in order to displace rivals. The king's brother, the Duke of Orléans, dominated as the head of one faction. However, his wife Valentina Visconti came under suspicion of witchcraft, for Charles' mental illness would often calm when she was present.[2] When combined with her husband's power, her guilt was seemingly clear. England had lagged behind the Continent in terms of accusations of magic at court, but as the fifteenth century began, the precedents from elsewhere in Europe made it a tempting weapon.

The lines between magic, science and religion were blurred and ever changing. To modern minds the distinctions seem far clearer, but this was a very different time. Today, the practice of astrology is often seen as a bit of fun, or a load of nonsense, but to many medieval minds it was an absolute science. This does not mean that people blindly believed it – many scholars argued that the stars could hardly guide human fates, particularly when you could have twins who led very different lives.[3] However, there was a huge section of society who believed that the cosmos could inform humans of when was an appropriate time to take a certain action. Big events such as a wedding or a battle would go more favourably if they took place under the right phase of the moon or the planets. This was so prevailing that doctors were expected to understand astrology in order to treat their patients effectively. One manuscript from 1395 instructed doctors that they should not bleed a limb if the moon was in the wrong sign.[4]

When astrology was usually considered a science, it is no surprise then that other practices which could be viewed as magic were also explored as a scientific discipline. Alchemy was the idea that with the right ingredients and conditions, one could transform one material (for example lead) into another (such as gold). Again, instead of being a fanciful notion, many people believed that this was possible. In the early 1400s, an English prince, the Duke of Bedford, employed alchemists in France to find the alchemical formula to make gold so that he could pay his soldiers, the royal purse being low.[5]

Even at the highest level of society, then, disciplines which could be considered delving into the realm of magic were being approved of and considered intellectually. However, these disciplines were not free from suspicion, and it could be a very fine line between science and magic. The astrologer making predictions for medicine could also use astrological charts for magic. Certain spells needed to be done at particular celestially important times of day or year, and these charts would help track them.[6] They could also be used for treasonous acts, such as predicting the death of the king. The scientific man delving into astrology, therefore, was always vulnerable to attack.

At the start of the fourteenth century, there were beginning to emerge two separate strands of magic; that done by laymen, and that done by the elite. It was recognised that there was a clear difference between an old medicine woman in a rural village using herbs and charms for small spells and an educated university man using magical tomes to try and summon the dead. As the century progressed, the elite, demonic witchcraft took on the name 'nigromancy', often known today as necromancy. It was believed that by using nigromancy, people could conjure the spirits of the dead in order to ask them questions or to learn about the future.[7] Sometimes, however, the strict definition of nigromancy was lost, and it was used as a general term to describe evil magic.

It was these educated men who were far more nefarious. Their education meant that much more dangerous avenues of magic were in their grasp, and it was often these men who were accused of acts of attempted or actual murder or bodily harm. It was very specific to men, for there were very few women at this time who were educated enough to be viewed capable of this. This was an important factor for the women in this book, as several cases therefore necessitated the help of learned men. Women, even royal ones, could not always summon the power for the more extreme acts of magic.

While accusations against men focused on their intellect and professions, another strand of magic tended to be more female orientated: love magic. In the fifteenth-century Munich Handbook, it is explained that evil magic ('nigromancy') could be used to 'drive a person mad, arouse passionate love, to gain favour at court', among others.[8] The ability of witches to influence a person's thoughts and feelings was believed to be a real danger, and by the end of the century the love aspect of magic was considered a much more feminine act. One contemporary witch-hunter considered that women were inherently lusty and so used magic to tempt new lovers or take their revenge against those who had scorned them.[9] As the century progressed, and the accusations in this book took place, these assumptions about gender identity and witchcraft became ever clearer.

Witchcraft became closely identified with issues in the Church as ideas solidified. Witchcraft had usually been considered under the jurisdiction of the Church, as there were not necessarily secular laws against it. By the end of the fifteenth century, however, it was strongly believed that a witch was in league with the devil, and had turned their back on Christianity. Therefore, accused witches were tried as heretics, rather than necessarily for the crime of witchcraft. Witchcraft was also a problem within the Church, for often the most educated men of the time were members of the clergy, and therefore those implicated in accusations. Usually, if the accusations of practising witchcraft were not too malicious, the Church would let the accused go free on the promise that they did not reoffend. For most small-scale, local practitioners, it was not worth the effort to fully prosecute them.

Religion and magic could also have blurred lines. The Catholic Church in the late medieval period encouraged praying to saints for intercessions, and members of the royalty or nobility would often use relics as powerful tools. A noble woman worried about a difficult birth might borrow the girdle of a female saint to wear during the birth to protect her. A sword might be inscribed with text from the Bible, or with Jesus' name, to protect the user. In the same way, objects could be infused with magical incantations to cause harm or bestow protection.[10] Both were done for similar purposes, with different intentions, for a similar outcome. While the two acts did have distinctions to the medieval mind, it still demonstrates that distinctions between magic, religion and science were not clear cut.

The most important thing to remember is that it was truly believed that there were people in the world who could use magic, and they could use this magic to cause real harm. Even if judges may be sceptical in one particular case whether the person really was a witch or not, this was not to say that they did not believe in witches at all. This is why accusations of witchcraft were so powerful; they really could be partaking in nigromancy. Kings would issue orders for the Church to say prayers for their protection if it were thought that sorcerers were at work, and the insanity of one king or the unexplained death of another found an easy answer in witchcraft.

Accusations of witchcraft always found strongest currency in an uncertain climate – the arrival of a new, foreign queen and her foreign servants; the sudden rise of a relatively obscure courtier to a position of power; the insanity or minority of a king leading to factions at court. It was almost always within these climates that political accusations of witchcraft were to be found. It was also under these circumstances that the women in this book found themselves.

At the start of the fifteenth century, the word 'witch' was not necessarily in common vocabulary. By 1487 – just four years after the last case in this book – the *Malleus Maleficarum* was published in Germany. The book, known as the 'Hammer of Witches', was a guide for secular and religious authorities dedicated to describing what witches were, how they acted, and how they looked, so that they could successfully identify and prosecute them. The *Malleus* overwhelmingly blamed women for witchcraft, and although at the time of its publication it was just one theory among many, by the mid-sixteenth century it was regarded as the authority on witchcraft.[11] This development runs alongside the women in this book. The earliest accusation was the least severe in terms of consequence and substance, but as the century progressed and people saw its success as an accusation, each case began to inform the next. Tried and tested methods developed, and each allegation had traces of the previous one in it. As ideas of witchcraft solidified in the century, so it influenced the accusations against these women. But the relationship was symbiotic. As each woman was accused, so did their case influence contemporary ideas of witchcraft. Each time, the charges became easier to bring. It is time to learn their stories.

Joan of Navarre

2

DUCHESS OF BRITTANY

JOAN OF NAVARRE was born around 1370, the sixth of seven children of Charles II ('the Bad') of Navarre and Joan of Valois. She was always destined for greatness; her lineage demanded it. Her father had been King of Navarre since 1349.

Navarre was a small independent state that lay between the huge Spanish territories of Castile and Aragon, and the French- and English-controlled lands in modern-day France. The territory had been ruled by both Aragon and France across the medieval period, but changes in the fourteenth century in the French dynasty meant that Charles' father Philip III acceded to the throne of Navarre as an independent ruler through the rights of his wife, Joan II of Navarre. Charles II owned huge swathes of land in northern France, including extensive territory in Normandy, and was related to the French Crown through both his mother and father – his mother Joan II being the only child of King Louis X, and his father Philip being first cousin to King Philip VI.

Joan of Navarre's mother, Joan of Valois, also had impressive blood flowing through her veins. The daughter of John II of France, she was also of French royalty. Her mother was Bonne of Luxembourg, giving both Joans connections to the royalty of Bohemia. Joan of Valois died at the age of 30, three years after Joan of Navarre's birth. Charles never remarried, and so Joan grew up without a mother.

Although Joan was a princess of Navarre, she most likely spent a lot of her early years in France. Her father spent most of his time in the country, using Navarre mainly as a source of money and manpower to extend his power in France. He had spent the first seventeen years of his life there (his father being Count of Évreux), meaning he probably viewed himself more as a French native than having any affiliation with his mother's kingdom of Navarre. Joan's mother died in Évreux, and this means it is likely that Joan was in the city with her mother upon her death, considering she was only 3 years old. As such, Joan almost certainly was brought up to speak French.

As a young princess, Joan would typically have expected to spend the first six or seven years of her life living with her mother and would then have begun some training in the skills that would later be required of her as a wife to another member of European nobility. This training would typically take place in the household of another noble – in this way, children (both male and female) were essentially being sent to a finishing school, where they would serve a fellow lord or lady, while simultaneously learning the skills needed to run their own household or estate. As a princess, however, it is unlikely that Joan would have moved to another household, and teaching would have taken place in her parents' own court.

Once her mother had died, however, this became more difficult. Her mother would have been expected to be the main source of learning for Joan and a great example to follow. As with so many women in this period, no matter their rank, almost nothing is known of Joan's childhood until her marriage at 16 years old. It is impossible to know whether Joan stayed with her father's court as he travelled around France, busy in war and diplomacy with the French and English, or if – as was more likely, considering the precarious political position Charles was putting himself in – Joan kept her own small household in one of the family's properties, possibly in Évreux.

In 1337, the Hundred Years War had begun between England and France. The English King Edward III claimed the throne of France through the right of his mother, Isabella of France, who was the only child remaining of Philip IV. However, the French questioned the ability of the Crown to pass through female hands, particularly when this would mean an English king taking over. Conflicts had been raging for decades between the two countries, who both attempted to capture important territories to bring them wealth, power and resources. Leaders of smaller, independent territories around the two nations, such as Navarre, therefore came in the firing line.

Charles II had attempted to increase his own power by playing one side off against the other, and this had often burnt him. After a revolution in Paris which Charles' supporters had created, Charles found himself the subject of the dauphin's ire. On 31 August 1358, the dauphin accused him of using magic against him, with his followers attempting to 'perish all the royal house'. A man who was either a physician or astrologer (or both) of Charles' was found to have paraphernalia of sorcery in his home.[1] Charles seems to have escaped without punishment, but within six years the dauphin became King Charles V of France, and so Charles of Navarre now had a powerful enemy.

Charles continued his risky game of siding alternately with the English and the French in their wars. By 1379, Charles of Navarre had come out a loser. He had lost most of his territories in France, and his own kingdom of Navarre had been invaded by the armies of Castile, who agreed to peace only after securing twenty fortresses in southern Navarre.[2] From this point onwards, Charles was forced to mostly reside in Navarre, and Joan certainly would have joined his court there. By now she was 8 years old and was possibly aware of how her father had failed due to his rashness and unwise political moves. Considering Joan's future diplomatic nature, and apparent calmness and rationality under pressure, she may well have learnt particularly well from her father's failures.

Now that she was back in Navarre, and of a suitable age, Joan would certainly have begun courtly training. As a princess, Joan was one of the lucky women of her age who was taught to read and write. She certainly was taught French, and possibly would have been instructed in the Navarro-Aragonese language of her homeland, although this may not have been considered necessary for her, particularly as it was likely she was going to marry a foreigner. As her father had had much to do with the English, and the English played a huge part in the politics of Western Europe, especially in her father's territories, it is possible that she was also taught English as a child.

Joan was taught to read and write as necessities to prepare her for the future task of running estates and possibly to intervene in politics, but much of the rest of her upbringing would have been what was tradition-ally expected of a woman in the nobility. She would have been taught how to sew, dance, play music, and would have been given extensive etiquette classes. Expected female behaviour at the time was often a contradiction. Instruction manuals such as the *Book of the Knight of La Tour-Landry* told noblewomen that they were supposed to be 'meek, easy in speech, and in answer courteous and gentle' and not answer back to men.[3] This was agreed upon by a female contemporary, Christine de Pisan, who wrote advice books for European princesses. She also stated that princesses should speak demurely and sweetly, act modestly, with good manners and courteous behaviour. She summarises why a princess should behave properly: 'A lady is more feared and respected and held in greater reverence when she is seen to be wise and chaste.'[4]

Despite this expectation – and it was certainly a realistic expectation, as those who subverted this were viewed scathingly – the reality was that men at court did not want an overtly chaste, quiet woman. Put simply, it was boring. Although they wanted a woman who held these qualities, particularly in public, as could be expected, in reality men still wanted women with whom they could have good conversations, who were witty and charming and had a sense of allure and intelli-gence. Despite writings that claimed otherwise, very few really wanted a trophy wife who would simply sit quietly in the corner and could not hold her own.

Joan would therefore have been taught how to balance these two contradictions, and whoever taught her obviously did their job well as, by all accounts of her life, she was seen as acting as the ideal female leader. She was never accused of intervening too much in politics, par-ticularly for her own gain. She did, however, intervene on behalf of the poor and needy, and it is clear that she was a deeply intelligent, deeply religious and extremely charming woman. There is not a single surviving criticism of her character, and the way that both of her future adoptive kingdoms embraced her, both personally and in her public life, shows that she must have been wonderfully congenial.

As the 1380s arrived, Charles began to look around for allies. The English now mistrusted him, the Castilians and French had taken much of his land, and he must have felt in danger of losing control of his territory altogether. A territory in a similar position to him was Brittany on the north-western coast of France. Brittany was an independent state like Navarre which owed fealty to the French Crown, but which also had strong ties across the Channel. The Dukes of Brittany held the Earldom of Richmond in England, and so it also owed allegiance to the Kings of England.[5] The conflicts of the past few decades between the two countries thus put Brittany in a difficult position.

In 1381, the Duke of Brittany, John IV, had also been bullied by the French so that he was made to swear that he would oppose the English and Navarre in their attempts to claim land in France. However, within a few years John IV was once again conducting multiple diplomatic missions between England, France, and Navarre.[6] John was very similar to Charles in his attempts at maintaining power. Charles had large estates in Normandy, which neighboured Brittany, meaning the men would have had similar interests and concerns.

It therefore made sense to make a more formal alliance between Navarre and Brittany; both territories desired protection from the territorial expansions of the French and the English. Duke John IV's second wife died in 1384, and so he was now open for another marriage. Meanwhile, Charles' daughter Joan was approaching 15 years old and the perfect age to marry. Charles did have an older daughter, Marie, but as she was about 25 years old by this point, and John did not yet have any heirs, perhaps it was decided that a younger bride would be more suitable in order to give more time to provide children.

Letters were drawn up on 13 April 1385 agreeing to the marriage, but the confirmation process was slow. It was agreed that Navarre would provide 120,000 francs for the alliance, but there were problems raising the money which slowed the process. By the summer of 1386, preparations were sufficient for Joan to begin her journey to her new husband and kingdom.[7] On 20 June, a party of John's men left Le Croisic in Brittany to collect her. Four vessels carried horses, men-at- arms, squires, crossbowmen, pages and sailors, totalling at least 156 men. Members of the duke's household were also on board, to aid Joan's comfort and give her any information she might require for her new life. This included Robert Brochereul, who had acted as one of the chief negotiators of the marriage. Brochereul had been given a generous reward of 500 Aragonese florins per year from Joan's father for his role in proceedings.

Special quarters were built for Joan on one of the boats, possibly showing that the vessels were not necessarily the most luxurious or expensive of the duke's ships – or perhaps he did not have any of a high enough standard. However, John did employ seven carpenters for twenty-four days to build Joan's quarters, suggesting he did care that his new wife was to have as comfortable a journey as possible. Her quarters were located on the deck, and it seems she was given extra privacy in her room as a frame was constructed upon which a cloth was hung. Although these preparations had been made, it evidently was not enough, as furniture and more pieces of wood were bought when the ships landed in Pamplona, Navarre.

As the round trip was to take over two months, significant food provisions were gathered for the first leg. Beef, salted pork or bacon, and dried fish were the principal meats consumed, while spices, condiments, cheeses, 60 livres of butter, 6 livres of almonds, and 12 livres of rice were also bought. Pewter utensils, plates, bowls and saucers were procured for the more esteemed members of the entourage, while sixty wooden and clay bowls were stored for the crew's use. Large quantities of candles, lanterns and coal were also taken on board to provide lighting during the night.

The entourage was to sail to San Sebastián in Navarre, then travel inland to Pamplona where it would meet dignitaries of the country, finish negotiating the particulars of the alliance, and prepare suitable gifts. Next, they were to bring Joan to Saint-Jean-Pied-de-Port, part of the northernmost territory of Navarre, then on to the port of Bayonne where the party would sail back to Brittany. Messengers were also dispatched to travel by land to send messages to both the King of Navarre and Jean IV.

The Breton party landed in San Sebastián on 30 June, then travelled down the Adour Estuary to the port of Bayonne between 10 and 12 July. There, the ships were to wait for six weeks. At the end of August, news finally reached Bayonne that Princess Joan was to arrive any day. She entered Bayonne on 25 August, and two days later a group of Navarrese delegates, including her brother Charles, inspected the ships.

On 2 September, Abbot Pierre Godiele, who was Charles II's secretary, celebrated a marriage by proxy in Bayonne Cathedral in the
presence of Charles' son and representatives of John IV. This was a
common method used by members of the nobility and royalty and
acted as a way to tie a couple closely together when one or both
members were absent, prior to being able to confirm the marriage
together in person.

By 4 September, the party was ready to set sail for the final leg of the
journey to Joan's new home in Brittany. The crew on board the ships
appear to have been very cramped, particularly as horses were brought
back on the return journey. These most likely belonged to Joan in
order to pull her carriage. But even with these conditions on board the
ship, it must be assumed that Joan was given the most space. Within a
week, the entourage had returned to Le Croisic, around two and a half
months after leaving. On 11 September 1386, at the manor of Saillé on
the outskirts of Brittany, Joan, Princess of Navarre, and John IV, Duke
of Brittany, had their wedding ceremony.

To 16-year-old Joan, Saillé – a town located in the heart of the salt
marshes of Guérande – must certainly have felt like a strange place for
her wedding. Their marriage in the local church was very simple, it
being only a small chapel. Although Joan was a princess of a relatively
small nation, she still would have expected a grander wedding than
this, particularly when the wedding was sealing an important political
alliance. Perhaps monetary constraints were an issue – after all, John's
faithful servant, Lesnerac, who had been in charge of payments for the
trip, spent around 3,400 francs. Regardless, Joan was now the third
wife of the duke, who was 47 years old, thirty-one years her senior.

If Charles had hoped that this new alliance with Brittany was to be
fruitful for him and possibly even help him reclaim some of his lost
lands, then he was sadly mistaken. Just a few months after Joan and
John's marriage, Charles II of Navarre died. By most accounts, it was a
most grisly end; Froissart, who was writing within a couple of years of
Charles' death, recounts how the 54-year-old king was shivering with
cold as he went to bed (after, Froissart enjoys telling us, he had spent
a night with his mistress). He could not get warm, and ordered his
bed heated with warm air as had been done many a time. This time,
'either by the will of God or the devil, it turned out very unfortunate,

for the flames somehow set fire to the sheets ... and the king, who was wrapped up in them, horridly burnt as far as his navel'.

Charles lived for fifteen days in agony, with nothing that could be done to save him, and he thus died 'in great pain and misery'.[8] Other, often much later, accounts say that he had been wrapped from head to toe in alcohol-soaked bandages to help alleviate some of his ailments, and a careless maid accidentally set fire to him with a candle she was holding.

His death was universally viewed as a moral story – a horrific end to a horrific man. Whether this was quite how his life ended, or if it was an embellishment by chroniclers who often took the opportunity to give moral lessons, is unknown. Considering the proximity of Froissart's writing to Charles' death, it does seem likely that this was indeed how the King of Navarre met his end.

It is not known how Joan reacted to the sudden news of her father's death so soon after her departure, especially as there is no evidence about how close or distant they may have been. Even if they were distant, however, the potential news that her father had been burnt alive in his bed could not have been pleasant, and would have left her with one less ally in a foreign land.

However, Joan turned out to be the perfect bride for John as it did not take long for her to fulfil her wifely duty and provide children. Her first was born in August 1387, a daughter or possibly even twin daughters. It is suggested, but unclear whether true, that Joan had two daughters across 1387–88, leading some to believe they were twins, but records are not sufficient to solve the mystery. Many have expressed that John must have been greatly disappointed to have a daughter but, at the age of 47, he would indeed have been acutely aware of his lack of progeny. However, when John's previous two wives had produced no children, the fact that his new bride had given birth to a live child in less than a year of marriage would have been an encouraging sign. Sadly, this daughter (or daughters) would be dead by December the following year, most likely from any number of prevalent childhood diseases, in what surely must have been a tragedy for the couple.

Nonetheless, on Christmas Eve 1389, at the Château de l'Hermine, Joan delivered a healthy baby boy, John. This was a triumph for the couple; providing the child survived, John would finally have a male heir to succeed him, and as the mother of a male heir, Joan would find her position as duchess more secure and enhanced. Many have argued that Joan's future abundance of children – particularly sons – would have given her a greater influence at court.[9] Indeed, there is evidence that Joan was not simply an ornamental bride, and if her actions in England later in life are anything to go by, she certainly wielded power at the Breton court. However, it must be remembered that across her time as duchess, Joan gave birth to nine children in ten years, and this almost constant state of pregnancy would have had a severe impact on her ability to be truly powerful. The birth of John, though, would have seemed like a Christmas miracle for the couple, and likely a sign of blessing on their union.

Château de l'Hermine was an obvious location for the ducal couple to be spending the Christmas season. John had only recently completed the castle, with it being built between 1380 and 1385 – John had chosen the location, as it was built into the ramparts of the city of Vannes who had been on John's side during the War of the Breton Succession. John, with English help, had eventually won control of Brittany from his father's cousin Joanna of Penthièvre and her husband Charles of Blois, making him duke in 1365. Since its completion, the château was John's main residence and the centre of his government. It housed stables, large kitchens, sports courts and various accounting and currency buildings.

The château was also the site of political dissent within the kingdom. Two years previously, in 1387, John had invited Olivier de Clisson, a powerful Breton lord and commander-in-chief of the French army, to the castle, ostensibly to view the newly completed building.[10] John and Clisson had a fraught relationship, particularly because Clisson had betrothed his daughter to the son of Charles de Blois and Joanna of Penthièvre, John's old enemies. When Clisson arrived at the castle at the end of June he was seized and imprisoned. John had ordered Clisson's death by being thrown into the nearby river in a sealed bag, but his weapons master did not carry out the act. Eventually, Clisson was released after paying a huge ransom. As Joan gave birth to her first child within two months of the event, one has to wonder whether she was at the château when his arrest and attempted murder was carried out, and what she made of it. One can hardly imagine she approved of such actions.

John's ruthlessness and rashness seems to have been a recurring theme in Breton politics, and one story at least gives us a suggestion that Joan may have been a calming influence on him. A few years later, in 1391, John was incensed by some French ambassadors at his court and threatened to arrest them. This obviously went against generally accepted treatment of ambassadors at the time, and could have led to a dangerous situation with the French Crown. The Chronicler of Saint Denys recounted what happened next.[11] He said that Joan's brother Pierre de Navarre was at the court and begged her to intervene and save the situation.

The story goes that Joan, who was heavily pregnant (presumably with her fifth child, Marguerite), took her son John and her young baby Marie, who had been born in February that year, into her arms. In her dishevelled nightgown and loose hair, she burst into John's chambers that night. There she flung herself to her knees and begged him to think of his actions, as it would not only be a felony against his king, but he should remember that the French Crown might protect his children after his death.

In all likelihood, this is a fabricated or exaggerated event. One cannot help but see the similarities between this description and one of Queen Philippa of England in 1347. In Froissart's *Chronicle*, he recounts that when Edward III ordered the execution of six burgesses of Calais after it had been conquered by the English, his heavily pregnant wife, Queen Philippa, threw herself at his feet, begging for his mercy on behalf of the burghers.[12] In medieval society, one of the greatest sources of power for female leaders was their ability to produce children for their husbands. It was an often-used emotive tool to show the vulnerable, emotional queen carrying a child and laying herself at the feet of her angry husband and thus placating him. In fact, many male leaders used this rhetoric purposefully to allow themselves to be seen as merciful without seeming weak – instead of being a feeble leader who does not act on the bad behaviour of others, he is instead a righteous leader who allows his wife to temper his policies. Queens were often expected to fulfil the role of tempering a king's policies, and so stories like these were acceptable rhetoric to medieval ears.

In that light, it is unlikely that the event happened in quite as dramatic a fashion as the Chronicler of Saint Denys described – but that does not mean that Joan had nothing to do with calming John down. Indeed, Joan, throughout her life, seems to have held a level head in difficult situations. John certainly seems to have been more extreme in his policies, perhaps owing to his insecurity as duke after fighting for so long for his territory. Joan almost certainly changed his mind with regards to the French ambassador, particularly as her words in the chronicle ring true.

By this time, John was in his fifties, whereas Joan was still only 21 years old with several young children. The possibility of his death would likely have been on her mind. Joan's ties to the French royal family and the desire of the French Crown to control events in Brittany would certainly mean that in the event of John's untimely death they would intervene in affairs, particularly in order to prevent English interference in the territory. There are indications that Joan was an intelligent woman, and she must surely have these thoughts in her mind when John was making his threats. She would also be aware of how unwise it would be to encourage the French Crown to send in an army to invade Brittany when it was currently enjoying great independence from its overlords.

Whether the incident happened or not, the very fact that the story was circulating shows that Joan must have held some influence in government and was being seen as an ideal duchess. She was fulfilling her role as mother and intercessor, but was not acting for power but in the interests of her children. Whether intentional or not, Joan had certainly cultivated a successful image of a female ruler in her adopted kingdom. For the next few years little more is heard of Joan, but she continued to provide John with children: three more sons, Arthur (1393), Gilles (1394) and Richard (1395), and one more daughter, Blanche (1397). In 1396, however, a potentially life-changing meeting occurred.

At the end of October 1396, the English King Richard II was due to marry Isabella of Valois, daughter of Charles VI of France, in order to bring peace between the two kingdoms. As a result, there were huge celebrations at the French royal court, followed by a formal wedding in Calais at the end of the month. Many nobles of the English court travelled across the Channel for the occasion, including numerous members of the royal family. One such man was Henry Bolingbroke, the king's cousin. Henry's father was John of Gaunt, who was himself the third son of King Edward III. Richard II generally appreciated the advice and loyalty of his uncle John, and was happy for him to take an active role in government. However, he seems to have greatly despised his cousin Henry, and this would eventually lead to his downfall.

In the meantime, however, Henry was part of the royal wedding festivities as a Prince of England, and during this stay in France he travelled to Saint-Omer in the north, along with various members of the English royal family. While there, they were met with notable French nobility, including Joan of Navarre and John of Brittany. A magnificent banquet was held, and it is tempting to suggest that Joan and Henry held conversations together. Joan and Henry were third cousins, but it is unlikely that they had had any contact before this point. Henry would later become Joan's husband, but at this point Joan was possibly already pregnant with her ninth child, and although John was in his fifties, he was displaying no sign of ill health. As such, it is unlikely that Joan was casting her eyes around the feast; yet, the swiftness of marriage arrangements between the couple after John's death do suggest that the pair may well have hit it off at this meeting in Saint-Omer.

Whether Henry and Joan continued contact after this initial meeting is unclear, but Joan missed a chance to see him again in the near future. In April 1398, Joan and John travelled across the Channel to attend the Garter Feast at Windsor Castle. John had been invested as a Knight of the Order of the Garter by Edward III between 1375 and 1376 – the only Duke of Brittany to have attained this English honour.[13] As such, he was entitled to attend the Garter Feast. It does not appear that he was a regular attendee, but certainly, for whatever reason, he and Joan made the journey this particular year.

If Joan had been hoping to see Henry again at this feast, then she was to be sorely disappointed. In January, Henry had quarrelled with the Duke of Norfolk, and Richard took this opportunity to remove his disliked cousin. Richard, with the approval of Henry's father, John of Gaunt, banished both Norfolk and Henry from the kingdom for ten years. Henry was forced to settle up his affairs, make provisions for his six children, and head for France. He spent the next eight months at the Hôtel de Clisson in Paris.[14]

The following year was to be life changing for both Joan and Henry. On 1 November 1399, John IV, Duke of Brittany, died aged 59 in

Nantes of unknown causes. Joan was now a widow with a brood of young children and, more importantly, was now regent of Brittany as her eldest son, now Duke John V, was only 10 years old. This once again shows the esteem and trust that the territory must have held Joan in, for although it was not unusual for mothers to act as regent for their sons, often a male relative would be sought to help keep affairs in order.

In the meantime, Henry's life had changed when his father, John of Gaunt, was taken ill at the start of the year. In February John died, meaning that Henry was never able to be reunited with him. It also meant that his cousin Richard II took advantage of the absence of such a powerful presence to get his revenge on Henry. He denied Henry his right to inherit his father's lands, seizing them for himself. He then extended Henry's exile from ten years to life.[15] This was a gross insult to Henry's position and legal rights, and so he organised a meeting with the exiled former Archbishop of Canterbury who had also suffered at Richard's hands. Together, Henry and the archbishop returned to England and began a military campaign. The rest, as they say, is history. Richard was unpopular in England and had alienated much of the nobility, so many swiftly put their support behind Henry. It was not long before Richard was imprisoned, and he died in January the following year. It is widely suspected that Richard died of starvation, but whether this was through his own choosing or that of his captors is unknown. Henry was declared King Henry IV of England and his coronation was at Westminster Abbey on 13 October 1399.

Henry became king just a few weeks before John IV's death, and it was not long before he and Joan made contact with each other. On 15 February the following year, Joan composed a letter to Henry.[16] It was full of pleasantries that would be above and beyond the formalities of the time. It was common for people writing letters to each other to express their love and loyalty, but the amount that Joan writes in her letter certainly suggests that this is beyond mere convention. She told Henry, 'Whenever I am able to hear a good account of you it rejoices my heart most exceedingly', and then assures him that she and her children are in good health. She asked Henry if there was anything in Brittany that she could do for him, as she would do it 'with a very good heart'. Intriguingly, she mentioned that one of her ladies, Johanna of Bavalen, was coming to see Henry, possibly to deliver this letter in person, or else this letter was to inform him of her journey. Joan explained that Johanna was going to have a 'matter' to transact. She ended the letter praying that the Holy Spirit would have Henry in His holy keeping.

Joan's reference to the Holy Spirit shows that she was a believer in the Trinity, and alongside her many references to God in her letter, demonstrates that she was a deeply religious Catholic. Her mention of Johanna's visit certainly provides a mystery, as the details of Johanna's mission have never become clear. It seems very likely, especially considering the language of the letter, that Johanna was sent to gauge Henry's thoughts and feelings of a marriage between the pair. If the mission was a political one, then Joan would have sent a male representative of her government or an ambassador. To send a female member of her court suggests that the journey was a far more personal one, and that Johanna was a woman very close to Joan whom she trusted with such a secret and sensitive mission. Joan's husband had only died four months previously, and so if she was indeed already considering marrying the handsome Englishman who was now king, it would have been politically unwise to announce these intentions so soon after his death.

If marriage was the mission, then Johanna's testing of the waters was certainly a success. On 11 May 1401, a curious payment was listed in the Issues of the Exchequer giving 1s 8d to 'a certain woman, prosecuting certain affairs for the King, concerning which, as is asserted, great profit and advantage would arise to the Lord the King'.[17] It is impossible to know the identity of this woman, or what her business was, but considering the events of the next two years it seems more than likely that this was Johanna or another female servant of Joan's entering negotiations with Henry for a marriage. In December the same year, another payment shows Henry sending messengers to Brittany.[18] This is the first concrete evidence that Henry was engaging in negotiations with Joan. By spring of 1402, rumours were spreading at court that Henry IV of England was planning on marrying Joan of Navarre, Duchess and Regent of Brittany. The proverbial cat was out of the bag.

3

OUR MOST DEAR MOTHER

HENRY AND JOAN appear to have been keen to get married as quickly as possible. In March 1402, a papal dispensation from the Avignon Pope arrived allowing Joan to marry whoever she wanted to within the fourth degree of consanguinity (being descended from the same ancestor).[1] This was necessary as Joan and Henry were third cousins through their mutual descent from Philip IV of France. By 3 April, Joan's trusty servant Antony Riczi had arrived in England, and he took part in a proxy marriage with Henry IV on her behalf.

In Joan and Henry's case, a proxy marriage was not necessary; there was no huge diplomatic alliance occurring where peace, alliances, wars or money relied on the marriage going through, such as in the case of Joan and John. By all accounts, it appears to have been largely a marriage of love (although historic strife between Brittany and France may have been a factor in trying to gather more allies for any future wars against the French) and so there was no real need to rush a marriage by proxy. But marry they did.

Joan was still tied up in Brittany trying to sort the affairs of her family and adopted kingdom. Under advice and pressure from her subjects and from the French Crown, she gave her uncle, Philip the Bold, Duke of Burgundy, the regency of Brittany. Philip was Joan's maternal uncle, and had been acting as the principal ruler of France for several years.[2]

He was powerful, held significant territories and was probably best placed to protect the interests of Brittany – certainly far more than an English king, who was suspected of wanting to dissolve Brittany's independence and merge it with the English Crown.

Finally, in the last week of 1402, Joan of Navarre was ready to travel to England to become its queen. She was allowed to bring her two youngest daughters with her, Blanche and Marguerite, who were 5 and 10 respectively, and she also brought a large train of her Breton household servants.[3] She made her way to the port of Camaret where an English squadron was waiting to meet her. Henry's personal ship was to carry Joan across the Channel. It was kitted with royal quarters which were fitted with imperial cloth of gold and a royal bed, hung with curtains of red and crimson satin. It somewhat outshone the hastily built personal quarters on the boat that had carried her from Navarre for her previous marriage.[4]

The men waiting to carry her across the Channel were also of somewhat higher status. Henry Beaufort, who was Bishop of Lincoln, and John Beaufort, Earl of Somerset, were among the party. They were both Henry IV's half-brothers, being John of Gaunt's children by his third wife, Katherine Swynford. They had, however, been debarred from succession to the English Crown as they had been born out of wedlock. Even so, both had excellent relationships with their half-siblings, and Henry IV had rewarded them sufficiently when he became king. That he trusted both of them to be among the party bringing his new wife to the country demonstrates the strength of their relationship.

There were also numerous other magnates in the party, including Thomas, Lord de Camoys, who had been directed to ensure Joan's safe conduct and was rewarded with a £100 gift upon his return.[5] Henry also entrusted the Earl of Northumberland as a prominent part of the escort. Northumberland was part of the Percy family, whose military, monetary and titular support had been instrumental in getting him the Crown. Henry owed a lot to them.

It was not until 13 January 1403 that the party was ready to travel to England.[6] The journey should have been a relatively quick one, unlike Joan's journey from Navarre to Brittany, but the weather was suitably awful for the time of year. A storm appeared, which meant that the party was stuck at sea for five days and nights. One can only imagine how uncomfortable a journey that must have been, even in the king's royal quarters, and eventually the ships had to be diverted to Falmouth in south-western Cornwall, instead of its original destination of Southampton.[7] After such a terrible journey, Joan and her train rested in Cornwall for a few days before progressing through Okehampton and Exeter and on towards Salisbury. The citizens were clearly excited for the new queen, with Joan receiving gifts of money from mayors and townspeople as she passed.

Meanwhile, Henry had been spending Christmas at Windsor Castle, having planned to meet Joan on the last stage of her journey. He had also been receiving gifts on Joan's behalf, accepting a significant amount of cloth of gold from the Abbey of Reading. From 20 to 27 January, Henry was staying at the castle at Farnham which belonged to his friend, William of Wykeham. Farnham was roughly halfway between Windsor and Southampton, perfectly positioning Henry to meet his bride as soon as possible. However, it was here that he heard of Joan's diversion and again his eagerness to meet his new wife is evident as he left Farnham without delay. He travelled to his palace at Clarendon, just east of Salisbury, with due haste.

Clarendon Palace had been extended significantly in the thirteenth century by Henry III and Eleanor of Provence, with the queen alone having a chapel, great hall, three chambers and a wardrobe across two floors. By the fourteenth century, Clarendon Palace was most likely the most spacious royal residence in England and it also boasted the largest park in medieval Britain.[8] This would certainly have meant that there was enough space for the significant entourage who would be staying for the royal wedding.

Joan arrived at Clarendon on Sunday, 4 February, and the same day the couple travelled to nearby Winchester together. By this time, the wedding guests had all arrived and it was certainly a huge event that the nobles of the realm had flocked to see. This would have been excellent for Henry's reputation as he was still new to the throne and a lavish wedding would show the wealth and power of the new regime. Of course, it would have helped that his new bride was beautiful, intelligent, kind and regal. She had been brought up knowing how to behave as a princess, duchess and now queen, and she would have given a good impression to her new subjects, without a doubt.

The wedding ceremony did not occur straight away, but the festivities began with immediate effect. On the Monday, the nuptial feast was held at Winchester Castle and luckily the menu survives in a fifteenth-century cookbook.[9] A feast it certainly was. It consisted of thirty-three dishes spread across three courses, as well as three fish courses containing another thirty-three dishes, and it must have been absolutely sumptuous. The courses were not starters–mains–desserts as is usual today, but rather a mixture of sweets and meat across all three courses.

The first course included cygnets, pheasants, '*vyaund ryalle*' (a white soup of almond milk, rice flour, milk and spices) and a '*sotelte*'. Also known as a subtlety, a *sotelte* was an elaborate sugar structure which aimed to impress. In the second course, there was more meat in the form of venison with wheat boiled in sweetened and spiced milk served with potage, as well as pork, rabbit, partridge and brawn (meat from a pig's or calf's head which is cooked and pressed in a pot with jelly). There were also some sweeter dishes of jelly, a '*leche fryez*' which could be fried sweet cottage cheese or a concoction of cream, sugar and almonds, and another sugar subtlety. The third course was yet more meat – roasted venison, woodcock, rabbit, quail, snipe, and other small birds, as well as crustaceans and sturgeon. Sweets included pears in syrup, almond cream, '*fretoure*' or pancakes, and another subtlety.

The three fish courses had all manner of fish, from roasted salmon, pike, bream and sturgeon to crab, lampreys, trout, eels and perch, to name a few. These fish courses also included sweet dishes, with more pears in syrup, almond cream, jelly, and *leche fryez*. There were three more subtleties, including one 'coronys for a sotelte' and another 'egle coronys in sotelte'. The first one obviously involved some form of figures wearing crowns (*coronys*) and the second was a crowned eagle, a Lancastrian symbol. It is difficult to imagine so much food, and although the feast would have been packed with hundreds if not thousands of people, there certainly would have been plenty to go around.

The dishes would have been laid on the tables, and people would help themselves to what they wanted. Forks were only used in the kitchen and for serving, with people eating only with knives, spoons and their fingers – even royalty. Pairs of diners might share cups, and it is likely that Henry and Joan would have had a 'loving cup', a shared drinking container traditionally used at weddings and banquets.

The seating arrangement was organised by hierarchy of title and status. Henry and Joan may have sat at a separate, elevated table with relatives such as the Beauforts and Joan's daughters, with the rest of the nobility at long tables below them.

Joan and Henry's wedding took place two days later, on Wednesday, 7 February. Henry's half-brother Henry Beaufort officiated the wedding, a somewhat intimate decision by Henry. Beaufort, while reasonably up the ranks of the Church as Bishop of Lincoln, would not be a usual choice for a royal wedding: normally they would be looking to one of the archbishops to perform the ceremony instead. This shows the close relationship between the half-brothers and the esteem that Beaufort was held in – particularly as his wealth was to prove vital to the Crown through the next few reigns. Later that month, Beaufort was made Chancellor of England, an extremely prestigious and important position in government. This meant that Beaufort was in charge of producing most of the charters and writs of government – vital for keeping the country running.

As a wedding gift for his new bride, Henry commissioned a goldsmith of London to produce a collar of gold with 'S'-shaped links, with the motto '*soveignez*' (remember) worked in it. The collar had ten amulets garnished with nine large pearls, twelve large diamonds, eight rubies and eight sapphires, while the collar was brought together with a large triangular clasp which also had a great ruby and four large pearls on it. The collar was delivered to Winchester for the wedding and cost the extravagant price of £385 6s 8d.[10] (This would be the equivalent of over £265,000 today.)[11] It is thought that this collar may be the one that Joan is pictured wearing in her tomb effigy.

It appears that Henry had a similar collar made for himself, at the cost of £333 6s 8d.[12] Although the date of payment for Joan's collar is a few years after the wedding, the similarity in cost and design to Henry's, dated to the wedding, and the fact that the collar was also delivered to Winchester, suggests that it was indeed for Joan for their wedding. There is the possibility that this collar could have been created for Henry's daughter Philippa, as payments preceding it relate to covering the costs of her wedding trousseau. However, this type of 'S'-linked livery collar was a Lancastrian symbol, and had been for decades.[13] It is unlikely that Philippa would have need for such an overtly Lancastrian symbol in her new kingdom of Denmark. Either way, Joan would have received a very similar collar to the one described here. By giving Joan this collar, Henry was officially welcoming her into the Lancastrian family.

Joan was also given gifts by Henry's sons, Humphrey (later the Duke of Gloucester) and John (later the Duke of Bedford). In typical family fashion, Henry had organised the payment of £79 to goldsmiths of London for two golden tablets to be delivered to John and Humphrey so that they could present the gifts to Joan when they were at Winchester for the wedding.[14] Tablets was the name used for several decorative items in this period, but the ones referred to here are most likely large pendants which were usually decorated with jewels that would hang from a girdle or chain. At the time of the wedding, John was 14 years old and Humphrey a year younger, and both boys were to grow close to their new stepmother, who appears to have showered them with affection – perhaps partly due to her inability to see her biological sons who were left behind in Brittany.

Every stage of the wedding celebrations oozed wealth. The cost of running the king's household alone on the day of the marriage cost a fortune. Henry's friend, William Wykeham, Bishop of Winchester, gifted Henry the substantial sum of £333 6s 8d for the expenses of his household on the wedding day.[15] For the entire week of celebrations, the household seems to have spent over £1,000.[16]

The celebrations did not end with the wedding, with the guests remaining at Winchester until Saturday, 10 February. After these final few days of celebrations, Henry and Joan – now husband and wife – began to make their way to Eltham, stopping at another of Wykeham's properties on the way. Joan formally entered London on 26 February where she was to be crowned as queen. The coronation saw public celebrations, with more feasting and a jousting tournament held in her honour. A picture of the event survives in the late fifteenth-century *Pageants of Richard Beauchamp*, commissioned by Beauchamp's daughter, Anne, Countess of Warwick. Richard took part in the joust as Joan's own champion, and is shown centrally, with Queen Joan looking on.[17]

Soon after Joan's wedding and coronation, Henry declared her extremely generous dower. Henry gave her the largest dower of any English queen up to that point, a huge 10,000 marks (around £6,666) a year.[18] At this time, the total revenue of the English Crown was just under £56,000 a year, meaning Joan was receiving roughly a ninth of the total annual income of the government. Joan's dower made her one of the wealthiest people in the land – perhaps only below the king himself. Nearly three decades later, in the 1430s, even the Dukes of Buckingham and York only had estates worth £3,500–4,000, while most barons had an income of less than £1,000.[19]

The grant was so large that in reality it proved exceedingly difficult for Joan to actually receive close to what she was promised. Within just the first year, her dower had fallen £5,000 into arrears, and the Crown continually struggled to find payments and lands to reach her promised amount.[20] Matters were made worse by the fact that one of Henry's daughters, Blanche, had been married the previous year to the eldest son of King Rupert of Germany. The terms of the marriage stated that England had to give a dower of 20,000 marks – twice Joan's annual allowance – to confirm the marriage, meaning the coffers were already crippled.[21]

It did not take long for Joan to get involved in asserting her official position as queen consort. Throughout the first few years of her marriage to Henry there are dozens of grants trying to obtain money and lands to fulfil Joan's dower. She was granted lands that had been previously granted to Richard II's wife, Anne, as well as lands and incomes in Brighton, Ipswich, Great Yarmouth, Bristol, Leeds Castle, Sherwood Forest, Stafford and the territory and castle of the Isle of Wight, as just a few examples.[22] On 10 December 1404, there is a grant for life for Joan to have a tower at the entrance of the Great Gate of the Great Hall in the Palace of Westminster for the management of her councils and businesses, the auditing of her accounts and the keeping of her charters, writings and other official business.[23] While Joan would not be seen to be over-interfering in governmental business, she was clearly not shy to assert the rights given to her by Henry in terms of her dower, and ensuring she had a proper department to carry out her official business as queen.

Joan was seen to be the ideal queen. She interceded on behalf of petitioners when people wrote to the Crown asking for a favour in the form of a position, a grant of land, or help in a legal dispute, and she gained rights and privileges for clergymen.[24] It was never claimed that Joan was unduly influencing the king. Her French connections also aided the English Crown on several occasions. In July 1407, a crucial Anglo–Breton truce was procured and Joan's son, John V, who was now ruling Brittany, acknowledged that his 'very dear' mother's desire for peace had been instrumental in organising it.[25] Meanwhile, Joan was fostering a good relationship with her new stepchildren. Their mother, Mary de Bohun, had died in 1394 when they were still young, and so, particularly to the younger John and Humphrey, Joan was the only mother they had really known. That she built a long-lasting relationship with her stepchildren was evident throughout her life, such as in a letter to John, Duke of Bedford, in 1415 where she called him her 'dearest and best-beloved son'.[26]

Henry had a somewhat fraught relationship with his eldest son and heir, the future Henry V. The young Henry was keen to have an active role in government, but as with many medieval kings, Henry IV was wary of giving too much power or responsibility to his son – particularly when his own grasp on the throne was far from certain as he had gained it through military coup. However, as Henry's reign went on, father and son began to clash more often. Ever the diplomat, Joan excelled in reconciling the two time and again, often even siding with her stepson over her husband.

Henry IV had seized the throne of England in 1399, several years prior to his marriage to Joan. What had initially been a military venture to reclaim his father's lands led to him becoming king. However, while he was popular at first, those who had placed him on the throne soon grew restless. The Percy family, who controlled vast swathes of land in the north, had wanted more independence from the Crown and lower taxes, which Henry had granted. However, they also wanted more money from the Crown, as the Scots had taken advantage of the political unrest in England to increase their raids in northern English territories. As prominent northern barons, the Percys were left to deal with the brunt of the attacks and the cost of defending the lands, which was crippling them financially. Much of the north was being left to waste. However, Henry was unable to meet their demands of more financial and military help, precisely because he had followed their demands of lower taxes. The Percys wanted to have their cake and to eat it too.

It was not long, therefore, before the Percys decided they would be kingmakers once more. In placing Henry on the throne, they had skipped over part of the chain of inheritance in the royal family. Henry was the son of John of Gaunt, the third son of Edward III. Richard II had been son of Edward III's first son, the Black Prince, who predeceased his father. There was, therefore, a son in between – Lionel of Antwerp. Lionel had only had one child, a daughter, Philippa. This would then, in theory, allow the Crown to pass to John of Gaunt and his sons. However, Philippa had married Edmund Mortimer, 3rd Earl of March, and they had two sons, Roger and Edmund. As descendants of the second son of Edward III, these sons had a strong claim to the throne themselves; however, both had given their support to Henry.

As the Percys began to dislike the rule of Henry IV, they decided they would throw their hat in with the Mortimer family. Not only did Edmund Mortimer have a claim, but his older brother Roger (who had died in 1398) had a son, another Edmund, who was therefore in line to the throne. The claim of the Mortimer males to the throne should not be underestimated. They had as strong an entitlement, if not more, to the throne as Henry – with Henry's claims perhaps only being strengthened through right of conquest.

While Joan and Henry were enjoying their honeymoon at Eltham Palace during Easter 1403, the Percys were plotting. If Joan had thought coming to England would bring her more peace than with the arguing Breton nobles, then she had been mistaken. In July, the whole Percy family took up arms against Henry, including the Earl of Northumberland, who had just a few months earlier escorted Joan to England for her marriage. By 17 July, there was open revolt against the king, and Henry sent an urgent letter to his council to come to his aid immediately.[27]

Henry could waste no time in dealing with the Percys. They were claiming that Henry had ordered Richard II starved to death and that he had committed perjury and could not pay his debts. Luckily for Henry, he was already marching north with an army, ironically intending to aid the Percys against Scottish raids.

Henry changed direction to march west towards Shrewsbury, where Henry 'Hotspur' Percy (Northumberland's son) was travelling in order to meet his uncle, Thomas Percy. The Percys gained considerable forces from the county of Cheshire, who were already hostile towards

Henry IV and renowned as experienced soldiers. Some of the archers they recruited had even served as Richard II's bodyguard. The rebels reached Shrewsbury, but the town did not open its doors to them, meaning they had no time to capture it prior to Henry's arrival. As such, both forces were camped in a stand-off on either side of the river which looped the town.

Henry appears to have attempted to resolve the Percy grievances through diplomacy, but for whatever reason the talks broke down and Henry sadly realised that battle was the only option. On the morning of 21 July, Henry drew up his plans. The importance of this battle cannot be emphasised enough. It was the first time that English archers were going to fight each other on English soil, and the Percys were powerful. Henry only had his limited forces, as any reinforcements from his council had not had time to arrive, and it was clear it was going to be a battle to the end. The outcome of the battle was either going to be victory for Henry, confirming to all that he was rightful King of England, or death.

Henry's forces were at a disadvantage, as they would have to advance within easy range of the Percy archers, and many were indeed slaughtered. However, his forces managed to push through and Henry was aided greatly by his eldest son, Henry, Prince of Wales, who had brought the forces he had been leading in Wales over to the battle. The danger of the battle was demonstrated perfectly when Prince Henry was hit in the face with an arrow during the fighting, penetrating his skull just below his left eye.[28] Miraculously, he was saved from his injury by the king's extremely skilled surgeon, although he was left with a permanent facial scar.

The chronicler of the *Brut* said that the Battle of Shrewsbury was the heaviest, unkindest and sorest that had ever taken part in England, mourning the fact that it was son against father, brother against brother, kin against kin.[29] Indeed, it is estimated that around 2,000 men died that day – at this time, there were only around 2 million people living in the whole of England.[30] In 1377, just a few decades previously, the tenth most populous town in the country, Boston, had just under 5,000 citizens.[31] This was a huge death toll.

Henry, as well as his son, nearly died. Henry Hotspur led a charge against the king, but one of King Henry's supporters had seen the charge and persuaded Henry to retreat; instead, the rebels, who were confused because Henry had ordered several of his guards to wear royal armour, hacked down his standard bearer. Believing the king dead, the rebels began to shout, 'Henry Percy King!' However, Henry Hotspur had in fact been killed during the charge – he was shot in the face when he opened his visor. Henry IV, therefore, shouted, 'Henry Percy is dead!' in response, and as soon as it became clear that King Henry was alive, and Henry Hotspur dead, the battle quickly ended.

Henry was saved by the death of Henry Percy, as his forces actually suffered the greater number of losses. Thomas Percy had been captured during the battle and was quickly executed by a traitor's death of being hanged, drawn and quartered. His head was placed on London Bridge as a warning. The Earl of Northumberland, however, managed to procure a reprieve as he had not actually reached the battle, although he still received punishment from Henry.

The rebellion must have shaken Henry and showed how thin his grip on the throne was still. The rebellion had been led by three earls – a significant fact – and both he and his son had come inches from death. How must Joan have felt waiting for news? She had only just married the man that it seems, by all accounts, she loved and was a perfect match for, and within months he could have been killed. She must also have wondered what would have happened to her as queen had the rebels been successful. Would she have been dragged into the rebellion too, imprisoned or even killed? Or would the rebels have acted favourably towards her, as they had to Richard II's queen, and sent her home to Brittany? It was hardly the honeymoon of her dreams.

Although the Battle of Shrewsbury allayed dangers for now, the rest of the year was not to be much more peaceful. In August, Bretons burnt Plymouth and in retaliation the men of Plymouth attacked Breton ships.[32] The people of England had a long-standing hatred of the Bretons, and clearly Joan's marriage to Henry had not created even a temporary alliance between the two countries. The knowledge that Joan's people had attacked the English would have vilified her in the eyes of some of the commoners.

The end of the year may well have seen tragedy for Joan and Henry. According to the *Northern Chronicle*, the couple had '*duos abortiuos*' – two stillbirths.[33] There are no other records of this stillbirth, presumably of twins, but it seems plausible. Not only was the writer close in time to the events, it lines up eerily well with Joan's first marriage where she also seems to have given birth to twins who died just past their first birthday. Joan and Henry did not have any children together – particularly strange when between them they had sixteen children from previous relationships. Joan was 35 upon their marriage and Henry 38, and so their ages were not necessarily a bar to fertility either. In these circumstances, a stillbirth makes sense. The death of these children would surely have been heartbreaking for the couple who would have been looking forward to sharing their own children together, and the reminder of Joan's earlier lost twins must have made it even more difficult to bear.

The next year the country was reasonably quiet, though there were some grievances raised in Parliament which forced Henry to make concessions, particularly to royal finances. However, Christmas 1404 may not have been a quiet affair. Henry and Joan spent it at Eltham Palace, one of Henry's favourite residences. In fact, Henry spent ten of his thirteen Christmases as king at Eltham. By this time, Eltham was certainly an impressive royal palace.[34] Improvements had been made to the palace since the reign of Edward II at the start of the previous century. It was one of the largest royal residences in England, and in the mid-fourteenth century the moat walls were altered, a new drawbridge and service buildings were built, as well as new royal lodgings on the east side. A sumptuous tiled bathroom with glazed windows was installed for the king, and the king and queen each had their own chapels.

Enclosures by Richard II, Henry IV and his successors meant that the total parkland surrounding the palace was almost 1,300 acres, so the court would have privacy at Christmas as well as plenty of recreational space. Henry had ordered a new set of timber-framed apartments for himself, and after his marriage to Joan he had work started on improving the queen's quarters. This new suite of rooms was two storeys high and 35ft wide, including a parlour and two withdrawing chambers for her and her ladies.[35] This would not be completed until 1407, but the current quarters would hardly have been poor for her. It is easy to see why Henry loved to spend Christmas there.

However, during the Christmas festivities there may well have been an attempt on Henry's life. In February 1405, the younger Edmund Mortimer and his brother Roger were abducted from Windsor Castle, where they were in Henry's custody, in an attempt to gain control of the potential claimants to the throne. Luckily for Henry, they were quickly recaptured and placed back into his hands. Constance, Countess of Gloucester, was held responsible for the abduction. She quickly accused her brother, Edward, Duke of York, who was Henry's cousin (being the eldest son of Edmund of Langley, Edward III's fourth son), of being involved in the abduction. He later admitted to knowing of the conspiracy and was imprisoned for seventeen weeks.

Constance not only accused Edward of knowing of the abduction, however; she also said that Edward had attempted to assassinate Henry at Eltham. She claimed that he had planned to either ambush Henry's entourage on the road there, or else scale the walls of the palace.[36] Whether the plan had ever truly existed is unclear, especially as there are no surviving records suggesting an attack had taken place, which means the assassination must have been aborted if it had indeed been planned. Either way, the seizure of the Mortimer heirs in February meant that seven plots had been made against Henry in the five years of his reign. Although Joan had risen to the position of Queen of England, she was still in very real danger by being associated with Henry, and could not even consider herself safe at the court's Christmas celebrations.

In November, Henry agreed to the marriage of his daughter Philippa to King Erik of the Kalmar Union, the name given to the single monarchy of Denmark, Sweden (including most of modern-day Finland), Norway and its territories (including Iceland, Greenland, the Faroe Islands and the Northern Isles). On 26 November 1405, the 11-year-old Philippa had a proxy marriage at Westminster with representatives of the nearly 20-year-old Erik. The following summer, preparations were made to send Philippa to her new home.

Ships were chartered for the journey, and a suitable wedding trousseau had to be prepared to give Philippa enough dresses and jewels to show off the might of England. This time, the English coffers escaped having to pay a dower, unlike for her sister Blanche, but Philippa had a suitably illustrious train to escort her across the sea, including several members of the upper nobility, six knights, three ladies, eight damsels, three squires, eight clerks, an usher, eight minstrels, fifteen pages and around eighty grooms or yeomen. The cost of this entourage and providing Philippa with suitable provisions still reached a significant

£4,000.[37] Once again, a royal wedding had cost the English government dearly. The coffers could not take much more lavish expenditure.

In mid July, Henry travelled to Hertford where he met Joan and three of his sons – Henry, Thomas and Humphrey – to join Philippa's escort. They all progressed to King's Lynn on the Norfolk coast, arriving there by 7 August. Here, they spent nine days in order to celebrate, say their goodbyes and finish preparations for the voyage. Philippa finally set sail in mid August, never to see her family again.[38] If Henry mourned for the departure of his daughter, Joan certainly would have been in a position to comfort him, for this year Joan said goodbye to the two daughters she had brought to England with her.

Under the terms imposed upon Joan by Brittany and France for her marriage to Henry, all of her sons had been required to stay in Brittany, as they were the most politically important of her brood. Her eldest daughter was already married and so did not come to England with her mother. However, Joan had been able to bring her two youngest daughters with her due to their age and because they had not yet been contracted to anyone. In 1406, however, those in power in Brittany decided it was time for Marguerite and Blanche, who were now 14 and 9 respectively, to return to the kingdom so that marriages could be organised, and alliances made.[39]

Joan was now separated from all of her own children. She perhaps took comfort in the love and care of her stepchildren. Henry's children were often found with him, particularly his youngest son Humphrey, and Joan and Humphrey clearly formed a strong bond. Humphrey is found time and again in residence at the same place as Joan and Henry, and it will be seen later in Joan's life that Humphrey was her constant supporter. This also provides some evidence against the accusations by some historians that Joan did not care for her birth children and was an unfeeling mother; why would she have no maternal feelings towards her own children, and yet form such a strong, loving bond with her stepchildren?

If Joan did miss her children, then it would have brought her comfort that she was not completely cut off from them. Her sons Arthur and Gilles visited England on a number of occasions, and this would have been an excellent opportunity for Joan to spend some quality time with the children she had been forced to leave behind. It does not seem that Joan ever saw her eldest daughter Marie again, who had been married when she was 7 years old, the year before John IV's death. Marie had married John I, Duke of Alençon, an area in Normandy, and by 1407 she had children of her own and so was unlikely to travel. However, it was usual for royal brides to not see their family again after marriage, as alliances usually meant that the bride was marrying a groom in distant lands. In the same vein, it is unlikely Joan ever saw Blanche and Marguerite again after they left England this year.

However, there is plenty of evidence that Joan kept up correspondence with her Breton children as a mother, and not just for diplomatic purposes. On 20 July 1418, she sent a '*papegeay*' (probably a parrot or popinjay) and three horses to her daughter-in-law, John V's wife, Joan of France, Duchess of Brittany.[40] In this record, the tenderness in which Joan was held by her stepson, now Henry V, comes across. It shows that Henry was ordering the ports to allow Joan's goods to pass through without tariff – already a favour – but she is also repeatedly referred to as '*carissimae Matri nostrae* [our most dear mother]'. This language is affectionate, as it may usually be expected for Joan to be referred to simply as the queen, suggesting a real care between the two.

Now that the last of Henry's and Joan's daughters had left England, they had to once again turn their attention to politics. A few years of relative stability was once more interrupted by the Percy clan. In 1405, the Earl of Northumberland had fled to Scotland having supported another failed rebellion against Henry, and his estates had subsequently been confiscated by Henry. At the start of 1408, Northumberland invaded England. His army met a force gathered by the High Sheriff of Yorkshire at Bramham Moor. The Yorkshire army had been hastily gathered after the surprise invasion, but still contained some noble retinues and trained men. Northumberland's force was not as large as he may have hoped because he had failed to gain widespread support. Whether this was due to fatigue of fighting in the north, or because Henry had successfully won over more of the population, or because the multitude of Percy rebellions had all failed and so they no longer commanded loyalty, is up for debate.

Northumberland was also probably hoping for aid from the rebel forces in Wales who had helped during other rebellions. However, Prince Henry had focused great efforts on containing the Welsh rebellions of the decade, gradually retaking the country by cutting off trade and supply of weapons. By 1407, many areas were starting to surrender to the English, including important lordships. The rebel leader, Owain Glyndŵr, was therefore in no position to offer aid to Northumberland as he himself was finding the tide was turning against him.

As with all the previous Percy rebellions, the Battle of Bramham war ended in victory for Henry's side. Northumberland died during the battle, and as with his brother Thomas a few years earlier, his severed head was displayed on London Bridge. The Percy family was shattered at last, and Henry could finally breathe easy that they would not be causing him trouble any time soon. Joan must have also felt far more confident that the worst of the challenges to her husband were finally over and he was safe.

Henry had been preparing forces to ride north and meet Northumberland, but his loyal followers in Yorkshire had defeated him before Henry had a chance to leave. Nonetheless, he thought it prudent to go anyway, to quell any others who might be tempted to follow in the earl's footsteps. At the end of the year, the Issue Rolls show that war was still very much on Henry's mind. Payments were made in November to Prince Henry to support his successful efforts in Wales. He was given £666 13s 4d to pay 120 men-at-arms and 360 archers for one-quarter of a year in order to defend the Abbey of Stratfleure in Cardiganshire, Wales (known today as Ceredigion).[41] After that, he was 'to ride and give battle to the rebels, as well in South as in North Wales'. Great trust was placed in Prince Henry's abilities. At the start of the following year, there are entries that show that Henry was not just an armchair general; in January, payments were made to the Keeper of the Wardrobe for making a new large cannon, and in March further payments specify that this 'certain great cannon [was] newly invented by the Lord the King himself'.[42]

The year 1409 was to bring personal tragedy to Henry. Although he had once more defended the kingdom, he could not protect his family from the forces of nature. On 22 May, his daughter Blanche died while pregnant or in childbirth at just 17 years old. Not only was it painful to lose his daughter at such a tender age, but it would have brought Henry bitter memories of the death of his first wife. Mary de Bohun and Henry had been thoroughly in love, but she had also died after giving birth to their last child, Philippa. To have his own daughter suffer the same fate – although not uncommon during this period – would hurt all the more. Joan had, in all likelihood, never met Blanche, as she left England for her marriage before Joan arrived. While she would have shared in Henry's pain, she was probably more worried about how the news may have affected his health.

Henry had long suffered with ill health, starting not long after he married Joan.[43] He had suffered acute attacks of illness from 1405 onwards, despite only being 38 years old and having a reputation for athletic prowess and energy. Henry apparently suffered from a horrendous skin disease which was described as leprosy in various sources, though this may not have had the same meaning as it does today. In June 1408, he was said to have suffered a sudden and violent seizure, losing consciousness for hours so that people were not sure if he was still living.

During that winter his health continued to decline, so much so that towards the end of January he made a will – the first royal will made in English.[44] In his will, he asked that Joan be endowed with the Duchy of Lancaster, the size and wealth of which would be plenty to sustain her in her widowhood. Henry had spent his illness at Greenwich with Joan and at various points with his sons – particularly Humphrey, but also Prince Henry who was waiting to see if he would become king. It was not until mid March that he was well enough to make the journey to his favoured palace at Eltham, which was just a few miles away. This extended illness had truly shaken the royal family, as it seemed in all likelihood that Henry would die. The news of his daughter's death just two months after he was beginning to make improvements would certainly have been a worry.

For the last few years of his life, Henry's movement was severely limited. From spring 1411 until his death two years later, he never ventured far from London, and by spring 1412 it was reported that he could no longer walk. Henry's declining health would have been compounded for Joan this year, as her son Gilles died, aged 18. He had only recently visited her in England, and it seems he died not long after his return to France. The nature of Henry's acute attacks has eluded historians and medical professionals alike, as the scant evidence does not provide enough clues. Whatever the cause, on 20 March 1413 Henry IV of England suffered a final severe attack and died within a few hours, at the age of 45.

Just prior to his death, on 4 January, Joan began to make provisions for her position after Henry was gone. She had it confirmed in the Patent Rolls of government that she was entitled to whatever dower Henry had assigned to her.[45] Her excellent relationship with her stepson, now King Henry V of England, must have reassured her that her position in the kingdom would be secure upon her second husband's death. Joan was never again to remarry. She was 43 years old, had given birth to up to eleven children and had two marriages with two men who she cared for deeply.

It has often intrigued historians that Joan decided to stay in England, rather than return to her children in Brittany, but, in reality, it is not such an unusual decision. Breton members of her household had settled into their new home, as shown a few months previously when one of her damsels, Joan Perian, was granted citizenship after marrying one of Henry's squires.[46] Female rulers often stayed in their adoptive homeland after their husband's death, probably largely due to the fact they were usually married off young and had often been living in their adoptive home for longer than their birth country. Joan clearly cherished Henry IV, and it is not so unusual that she might have wanted to stay close to him, visiting the places they had been together and keeping his memory alive.

She had also grown close to her adoptive children and so had a familial connection to the kingdom. There is also, of course, the matter of her dower lands now that Henry was dead. It had been difficult enough for her to receive the payments and lands due to her while Henry was alive, and she may have thought that by returning to Brittany she would not have enough power to assert the continued reception of these lands. After she had left Brittany, she had found it exceedingly difficult to receive her income from her dower lands there, and she was ultimately forced to give many of them up. The lands in England were far more valuable and losing them would leave her with almost nothing. England had been her home for ten years, and now that she was older and her children were not in need of her motherly influence, she may simply have wanted a quieter life in luxury retirement, rather than to uproot her home once again.

The first few years of Joan's retirement were indeed quiet. She enjoyed fine food, fine clothes and fine wine, travelling between her dower properties, particularly enjoying residing at her manor house of Havering-atte-Bower in Essex. Certainly by 1408, the manor had found its way into Joan's possession. The manor of Havering, also known as Havering Palace, had been constructed before the Norman Conquest and had remained in possession of the Crown since. It was usual for the queen consort to be given the manor, a tradition started when Henry III gifted it to his queen, Eleanor of Provence, in 1262. Eleanor began extensive building work, resulting in a great chamber, apartments for both the king and queen, two chapels, and various out-buildings.[47] There was extensive parkland surrounding the manor, and the area was sparsely populated, giving sufficient privacy and peace and quiet. It was the perfect place to retire after ten years of court intrigue, rebellions and attempted regicide.

The year of 1415 was a crucial one in English history, and ultimately for Joan's future, too. In this year, Henry V decided to renew the war with France which had been raging intermittently since 1337, giving it the epithet the Hundred Years War. The war had been started by King Edward III, who intended to push his claim to the French throne through the right of his mother, Isabella of France, former Queen of England. Intermittent fighting had taken place ever since, but when Richard II began to suffer monetary problems and the war became increasingly unpopular with the English public, he lost interest in pursuing any claims. In 1389, therefore, a peace treaty was signed between the countries, initially for three years, but in fact lasting throughout the reign of Henry IV who could not start a war with France when his hold on England was so tenuous.

By the time Henry V took over, the situation was vastly different. He had taken to the throne unchallenged and the kingdom was in a far more peaceful place now that the issue of Wales and the Percy family had mostly been dealt with. Moreover, the French King Charles VI suffered from mental illness, which resulted in deep rivalries between princes and nobles who jostled for power in the vacuum. This made France an easy target.

In August 1415, therefore, Henry sailed from England with a force of 10,500 men and laid siege to the port of Harfleur in Normandy. It took around a month for Henry to successfully capture the town, and this meant that winter was quickly approaching so the time to make battle was limited. While making raids across France on his way to English-held Calais, his forces, who were low on supplies, were confronted by a much larger French army in the county of Saint-Pol, south of Calais, in October. What followed was the infamous Battle of Agincourt. Agincourt was an unprecedented triumph for Henry and the English. Modern estimates place the number of English troops at between 6,000 and 9,000, while the French forces had anywhere between 12,000 and 36,000.[48]

A series of fortunate events and the emerging dominance of the English longbowmen led to a victory for Henry that was not expected by either side. The English seemingly lost fewer than 100 men, whereas the French lost thousands. However, one notable death on the English side was that of the Duke of York. Just a few years earlier he had plotted against the life of Henry's father, but now he was seemingly firmly on the successor's side.

One near-death experience was crucial to the future of Joan and later to a woman named Eleanor Cobham. Joan's favoured stepson, Humphrey, who had been made Duke of Gloucester the previous year, had finally stepped up to the military mark of his brothers. While his brother Henry was fighting insurrections in Wales during the reign of his father, Humphrey had been busy studying at Oxford. Now, at 25 years old, Humphrey finally decided to join the campaign of his brother.

Although Humphrey had not experienced battle before, his classical education had proved invaluable during the siege of Harfleur due to his knowledge of ancient siege warfare. Agincourt was his first pitched battle, but it was nearly his last. He had been given control of 142 lances and 406 archers, but during the fray Humphrey was himself involved in hand-to-hand combat.[49] A song composed not long after the battle recounts that Humphrey 'manfully' entered the fight and 'he wrought there wonders wide'.[50] Wonders he may have accomplished, but he was about to be caught unawares.

John I, Duke of Alençon, the husband of Joan's daughter Marie, was leading the charge – on the French side of the battle. He rallied some of the French troops and managed to break through the English ranks. During the charge, Humphrey was 'gravely wounded', seemingly pierced by a blade, and fell to the ground. Humphrey was lying flat on the floor, vulnerable to being killed, but luckily his brother, King Henry V, was by him and stood between his feet defending him until his men were able to rescue Humphrey.[51] John I, Duke of Alençon, was killed in the resulting fighting, though he has sometimes been credited as being the one who killed the Duke of York.

The outcome of the battle must have resulted in conflicting emotions for Joan. Her daughter's husband had been killed, leaving her a widow with five children at 24 years old. Within two years, the English attacks and gains in the area meant that Marie had to flee Normandy with her children, losing much of John's old lands and thus her children's inheritance.[52] On the other side of the battle, Joan had nearly lost Humphrey and, as a result, Henry had been further endangered. The problem of Joan's previous life as Duchess of Brittany, and her descent from the French royal house, meant that as Dowager Queen of England the renewed war with France was always going to give her allegiances to both sides.

The war also had a negative impact on Joan's life in England. In November 1415, the Commons presented a petition to Parliament asking for the expulsion of all Bretons in the country, including those still remaining in Joan's household. The petition called the Bretons the enemies of the realm, accusing them of exporting money and jewels from the kingdom to Henry's detriment and sending secrets back to the French.[53] Joan's status as past Duchess of Brittany was still causing suspicion around her. Although Joan herself was not targeted in any complaints, the fact that even she was forced to give up members of her household shows the extent of the hostility. This must have been painful for Joan, as many of those who were now to leave her had probably been with her since she arrived in England. Now she had lost her husband and her long-time faithful servants – the last connection to her previous kingdom.

Joan of Navarre was now in a strange position in her life. She held an esteemed position as Queen Dowager, and while the Commons hated her previous homeland, she seems to still have been viewed if not fondly, then with respect for her conduct during her time as consort. Her help in diplomatic matters, while staying distant from embroiling herself in politics, was also appreciated. She held the love of her stepchildren, who continued to call her their most dear mother, and the new king showered her with favours. As part French, and now part English, she was to be unfairly tangled up in the renewal of the Hundred Years War, with losses on both sides impacting upon her.

The war was to have a far more personal impact on Joan, however. By the end of the decade she was under house arrest, having been accused of attempting to use malicious magic to kill King Henry V.

4

IN THE MOST EVIL AND TERRIBLE MANNER IMAGINABLE

AFTER THE EVENTS of 1415, the fortunes of the English Crown began to change. During the Battle of Agincourt, notable French leaders had been captured, including Charles, Duke of Orléans, John I, Duke of Bourbon and, most importantly for Joan, her son Arthur de Richemont. These men were sent to England, and instead of being immediately ransomed for huge sums of money, the English decided to keep hold of many of these important political players in order to cripple the French position. Moreover, two brothers of the Duke of Burgundy had been killed in the fighting.

The incapacity of the French king due to his mental illness was leading to ever-increasing conflict at court, only compacted by the loss of men at Agincourt. In 1407, the Duke of Burgundy, John the Fearless, had had his rival, the previous Duke of Orléans, assassinated. In 1419, Orléans' people, the Armagnacs, decided to seek revenge. Having been alienated from the French court for some time, Burgundy was now in the process of reconciling with the king's son, Dauphin Charles.

The return of Burgundy would reduce the influence of the Armagnacs at court. Therefore, at a meeting between John the Fearless and Charles on the bridge across the Seine at Montereau, the Armagnacs had John assassinated. Such an affront could not be forgiven by the Burgundians. Believing the dauphin had planned his father's murder, John's son, now Duke Philip III 'The Good' of Burgundy, felt he had no option left but to ally with the English. Henry V's cause was now gaining allies in his planned new dominion.

In England, meanwhile, Joan was enjoying a comfortable widowhood. After the expulsion of her servants she had suffered no further affronts to her position. She had been living mostly at her manor at Havering-atte-Bower, and Henry continued to give her extensive privileges. The trust that Henry placed in Joan was evident to all, and this is shown by a mistake made in a sixteenth-century chronicle. This chronicle claimed that when Henry left for France to begin his campaign in 1415 he had left Joan as governor of the realm. In fact, the Proceedings of the Privy Council show that Henry appointed his brother, John, Duke of Bedford, to be Lieutenant of England in his absence.[1] That during the next century it could be believed that Joan would be entrusted with such an important job shows that she must have held an excellent reputation that continued long after her death.

However, it does show that during this absence from England Henry wanted his stepmother to be able to live in the utmost comfort. He did allow his 'most dear mother' to use his own royal castles of Windsor, Wallingford, Berkhamsted and Hertford without hindrance during his absence.[2] Some have questioned how far Henry cared for Joan, but instances such as this show that he must have thought of her kindly. His behaviour towards her goes beyond any formal performance of deference to his father's wife. As late as 1418, Joan was still receiving favours from Henry.[3] It is under these circumstances that the events of the following year seem even more shocking.

In August 1419, the possessions of Joan's personal confessor, Friar John Randolph, were seized. Parliament ordered Lady Joan of 'Bergevenny' (Abergavenny) to 'seize all gold, silver, things, goods and jewels of any kind' in Randolph's possession 'or committed by him to any other person to keep, and bring them before the king and council'.[4] No reason was given for the seizure of Randolph's items. Lady Joan was a Lancastrian, descended from Henry III and referred to in the seizure as the 'King's kinswoman' and so it is perhaps due to her trusted position as relative to the king that she was chosen to deal with Randolph. Moreover, her husband was one of the Barons of the Welsh Marches and his lands were close to Randolph's residence in Shrewsbury.

When the inventory of goods is studied it is clear that the objects that had been taken actually mostly belonged to Joan. The items collected were extremely sumptuous and showed the utter luxury that Joan had been living in.[5] There were rings and brooches of gold and silver studded with jewels, a basin of silver and gilt, tablets of silver and gold and ivory with religious symbols, more jewels, silver goblets, cups, forks, spoons, ladles. If there were any doubting the fact that these items belonged to Joan (other than that a friar could not afford these items), then near the end of the list is a nightcap 'for a woman, rede after the gise of Bretaigne [Brittany]'.

There were also many items that clearly made up Joan's private chapel, which would understandably be in the possession of her private confessor. These included silver and gilt chalices engraved with religious messages and the image of the Trinity, as well as the Corporal cloth used during the celebration of mass where the consecrated elements would be placed. Randolph's own items are named at the end: a feather bed and bedding, clothes and furs, a coffer with some small books, and napery – household linen, tablecloths and the like.

For a short time everything was quiet. Randolph had attempted to flee the country, obviously worried about what moves might be being made against him, but he had been captured at Guernsey and taken onwards to Normandy.[6] He was kept at the Castle of Gaillard after its capture in December that year by the English as part of the skirmishes of the Hundred Years War. By the start of February 1420, Randolph was in the Tower of London and £10 was paid to nine men who had been responsible for conducting him safely.[7]

The reason for Randolph's capture became clear in September 1419, an entire month after the seizure of his and Joan's items. It is recorded in the Parliament Rolls on 27 September that Randolph sensationally claimed that Joan had 'plotted and schemed for the death and destruction of our said lord the King in the most evil and terrible manner imaginable'.[8] Two other members of Joan's household were implicated: Roger Colles of Salisbury and Petronel Brocart. Their goods and chattels were also seized. No further mention of Roger and Petronel can be found, so their fates are unclear. As a consequence of these serious accusations, Joan was arrested and placed in the custody of Sir John Pelham. She was taken from Havering-atte-Bower to the royal manor house of Rotherhithe, south-east of the Tower of London.[9]

Rotherhithe had been built seventy years previously by Edward III, and it was probably chosen due to its proximity to government; Westminster was just a few miles away. Rotherhithe Manor was not a luxurious palace, but it still consisted of several stone buildings around a courtyard, a hall, private apartments for the king, and kitchens. It was built right up to the River Thames, and was surrounded by a moat on the other sides. It is believed to have been used as a falconry, though Henry IV did stay there during some of his period of illness.[10]

John Pelham was an excellent choice to take charge of the Queen Dowager.[11] He had served with Henry IV (then Bolingbroke) and John of Gaunt during the reign of Richard II, campaigning in Spain with John of Gaunt. He was rewarded for this service by being appointed as Constable of Pevensey Castle in East Sussex in 1394. John was a loyal servant to the Lancastrians, appearing to have accompanied Henry during his exile by Richard II, then returning with him in 1399 and attending him while he claimed the throne. At Henry's coronation, he was rewarded by being made a Knight of the Bath, an honorary knighthood reserved for major royal occasions.

He continued to serve as a member of the royal household and acted in a military role when asked, but he had been consistently trusted with the custody of important prisoners. In 1405, he had been the one entrusted with the custody of the Duke of York after his attempt to claim the Mortimer heirs, then later that year he became custodian at Pevensey Castle, taking charge of the Mortimer boys themselves. John received countless favours, gifts and promotions under Henry IV's reign, and had even been shown favour by Joan herself, who gifted him the manor of Birling in Sussex.

During Henry V's rise after his father's severe illness in 1408, and then into his own reign, John slipped from royal favour, but Henry still trusted him with important diplomatic missions and a plethora of prisoners to look after. Just a few years prior to Joan's imprisonment, John had held King James I of Scotland in his custody for nearly a year. When Henry embarked for France once again in 1417 to invade

Normandy, John was held in high enough esteem to take a place on the King's Council.

John had therefore been entrusted for decades with extremely high-profile prisoners, had been involved in many military campaigns, and was part of the council in the king's absence. If anyone were to be trusted with keeping the Queen Dowager safe, it would be him. It is important to note, however, his close friendship with Henry IV and, by extension, Joan – she had not been placed in a hostile environment, but in the custody of a man who would be likely to favour her.

Joan was now no longer an influential Queen Dowager, but instead a prisoner in custody. Parliament had confiscated all of her goods, lands, rents and other appurtenances. She now had nothing. Before exploring her time in custody, it is important to understand why exactly Joan had been accused. The roots of this are in the politics of Henry V and France.

At this time, Henry's campaigns in France had been going exceedingly well. Agincourt had been the jewel in the crown that turned the tide of battle, particularly when the incapacity of the French King and increasing splits and factions at the French court were debilitating the French side. Randolph had been arrested in August 1419, so plans were already being made against Joan, but the assassination of John the Fearless in September and the new alliance with Philip, Duke of Burgundy, meant the time was perfect for the English Crown to make its move. The French government was in chaos, the English had been making important gains in their military campaigns, many important French noblemen were prisoners in England, and now an important faction in France turned their allegiance to England. Henry needed to strike while the iron was hot.

However, the English Crown was penniless. The turbulence of the overthrow of Richard II and the extortionate costs that Henry IV had to bear to quell the continual rebellions against him by the Percys, the Welsh and other quarters had crippled the Treasury. This had been damaged even further by the costs of marrying Henry IV's daughters to foreign powers and by the burden of Joan's exceptional dower which, as seen, had been impossible to fulfil even from the start. Henry V renewing the wars with France a few years previously had just meant more expenses for war – one of the most expensive things a medieval monarch could choose to do – at a time when the Treasury simply could not afford it. Although England had been winning the war, it could not continue to fund the campaigns in France for much longer.

Henry must have been aware of the precarious position he was in. He had been using the wars with France to increase his popularity in England and stabilise the monarchy, and after victories such as Agincourt this had certainly worked. He had seen at first hand how a lack of money had encouraged the Percys to revolt against his father and created political instability. He could not back out of France now, when he was on the winning foot – it would have been politically unwise, and would have caused great unpopularity in his kingdom. However, he could not risk running out of money and upsetting the nobles who kept him in power or become unable to pay his armies.

This is where Joan plainly comes in to the picture. Joan was one of the wealthiest people in the country, probably second only to the king, and her annual income of £6,666 would be looking incredibly appetising at this point of time. If the Crown could find a way to requisition this money, it would be invaluable in keeping the country, and the war effort, running. Agnes Strickland, the great nineteenth-century authority on English royal women, records a document from the start of 1419 where Henry ordered one of his servants to 'borrow of the dower' of Joan, 'leaving her only money enough for her reasonable expenses'.[12] The document appears to have been lost since, but if this is correct then even from at least the start of the year, Henry had been attempting to find ways to acquire Joan's wealth.

It is unknown whether the idea of the accusations came from Henry himself, or someone close to him, perhaps on the council. Wherever it came from, Henry must have had knowledge of the plot and agreed to it. It was a conspiracy of the highest order; Henry was conveniently fighting in France, so could not be blamed directly in future. His brother, Bedford, who was acting as regent in his absence, signed Joan's arrest warrant. One cannot help but wonder whether his uncle, Henry Beaufort, was also involved. As Chancellor and one of the main donors of money to the Crown, not to mention his trusted position with Henry, he would have been in prime position to be involved in the plot.

The accusations against Joan were a stroke of political genius. Joan was arrested, all of her lands and incomes were confiscated and given to the Crown but, crucially, she was never placed on trial. This worked in Henry's favour twofold. By having her accused of using witchcraft to try and kill him he was able to gain her income, but by not putting her on trial he also, in a strange way, protected her. If Joan had been put on trial and found guilty of attempting to kill the king, that was a treasonable offence for which she could be executed. Even though Henry would be able to prevent her execution, she would still have the stigma for life of having committed treason, and would never have been able to recover. If she were put on trial and found innocent, however, the Crown would have to return all of her property to her, thus losing her income. This was therefore the perfect halfway point where her money could be used, but she would be able to recover from the accusations.

At first glance, witchcraft seems an intriguing accusation to be used against Joan, especially as it did not have much precedent in English politics of being used as a political manoeuvre. In fact, a century previously, a conflict with a previous Queen of England had shown that the king did not, in fact, need any excuse at all to confiscate a queen's properties. In 1324, Edward II seized all of the lands of his wife, Isabella of France, ostensibly because her French birth made her a danger during the war with France. The order claimed that because Isabella's territories included places such as Cornwall, Dorset and Devon, which were 'in the more remote parts of the realm and in lands by the seacoast' which could easily be attacked by a fleet of ships, he was regarding the safety of the realm in the seizure.[13] In reality, Edward had a strained relationship with his wife, and favoured a particular family at court. He probably wished to curb her power, or simply did not view her as a threat and so she was an easy target to increase his own personal assets.

Henry, therefore, could have easily done the same with Joan. She also had French connections and he was also at war in France, so he could have used this same tactic. However, there were very important political reasons as to why Henry would have wanted to avoid this tactic. Yes, the English were at war with France, but with the aim to gain the French Crown. If successful – as it would seem within just a few months – then Henry would become King of France as well as England. If Henry were to call Joan's loyalty into question because of her French connections, he would be stirring up hatred of the French, an unwise move if he were planning on incorporating the two kingdoms into one. The following year, he married the daughter of the French king, and if the plans for this marriage were already afoot, that would be even more reason not to want to encourage mistrust or hatred of the French royalty.

Thus, the government came to the idea of an accusation of witchcraft. In the official records in Parliament, and any other official record, the use of witchcraft by Joan and Randolph is never mentioned. It is merely stated that she tried to kill Henry in the 'most evil and terrible manner'. The mention of witchcraft only comes from the chronicles, and even then not all of them mention it. Three texts of the *Brut* simply record her arrest, with no mention of why. The *St Albans Chronicle* is ambiguous, saying that Joan was arrested for partaking in a '*maleficio*' that would cause '*lesionem*' (injury) to the king. At this time, '*maleficio*' usually referred to an evil deed or a crime, but certainly by the end of the century the word was also being used to describe magic used to cause injury and death.[14] Which meaning is alluded to here is unclear.

On the other hand, the *Chronicle of London from 1089 to 1483*, the first part of which was written in the early 1440s, raises the idea of the use of malevolent magic, stating that Randolph was incited by Joan to use sorcery and nigromancy to destroy the king. The later date could suggest that the rumours of witchcraft were added at a later date – this is striking, considering the chronicle was composed at the same time that Eleanor Cobham, our next woman, was being convicted of using sorcery to kill the king.

However, there is, in fact, another manuscript written contemporaneously to Joan's imprisonment which also mentions the charges of witchcraft. The phrasing in the two pieces is remarkably similar, suggesting that the later chronicle may simply have copied from the earlier record.[15]

The records, therefore, suggest two things. Firstly, that while it was not being officially recorded that Joan and Randolph had used witchcraft, it was perhaps being suggested in the language used, and the government must have circulated rumours of the use of sorcery which then found its way into the Commons; and secondly, that the rumours being circulated were not necessarily believed by the majority of the nation.

Chroniclers of the medieval period were notorious gossips. While they often focused mostly on the deeds of the king and various wars and battles, anything that might have been a huge scandal was almost always recorded in multiple sources. The idea, therefore, that the chroniclers would not have jumped to tell the story of the Queen of England who tried to murder the king – with witchcraft, no less – seems almost impossible to believe. Indeed, a few decades later, the downfall of Eleanor Cobham for the same witchcraft charges was recorded in every single English chronicle. To merely mention Joan's arrest in passing, as several of the chronicles do, suggests that it was not considered a significant event in the realm.

While the excuse of Joan and Randolph's use of witchcraft was certainly known, the lack of sorcery being recorded as the reason for their arrest in the chronicles makes it seem that no one really bought the official story. Perhaps Joan's reputation had been so impeccable up to this point that it was difficult to believe that she would suddenly turn on the king. This is especially true when it is considered that Joan had nothing to gain by killing Henry. She had no children with Henry IV, so she could not be plotting to put her own child on the throne, and Henry V had not passed her over when he became king. If anything, her privileges and status increased when he took to the throne. Why, then, would she want to kill the man who was keeping her in such an exalted position? Perhaps there were enough people in the know in the government who knew the real motivation behind her arrest that rumours were not spread with enthusiasm. She also still had many friends at court who would not want to smear her name.

The lack of records recounting Joan's alleged witchcraft may have come from the government itself. The government simply did not have a great need to make a big deal out it. Witchcraft was an easy excuse to use, as it did not require much evidence. It was very difficult to prove that someone had not partake in something which was inherently secretive and performed behind closed doors. As a woman, Joan also did not have a retinue of men behind her who could perform a military coup in the way the Percys did, although it would not be impossible for her to raise a military force. It would therefore be unbelievable that she was organising a military rebellion against the king, and it would also require a far wider network of proof of collaboration, thus endangering other nobles. Witchcraft was a neat and easy solution on all fronts, and just the verbal suggestion of the act was enough in this case to achieve the desired ends. The government held all the power and was declaring it true, and that was enough to take Joan's land. There was no need to convince the Commons through widespread propaganda.

Nonetheless, there was a climate of sorcery in the air. It is important to remember that while this was a time when people could be sceptical of charges of witchcraft, there was still a real fear from all levels of society of the danger of evil magic. For a king of a new dynasty that still had a shaky hold on the Crown, it would not be implausible that Henry did have some real fears for his life. On 25 September – just two days before the Parliamentary record of Joan's supposed involvement in the plot against Henry's life – Archbishop Chichele issued a letter to all of his bishops informing them that Henry himself had ordered the clergy to perform prayers 'to preserve, to protect' him from 'nefarious deeds'. This was necessary because there were necromancers who were working for his destruction.[16]

Now, the proximity to the charges against Joan and Randolph cannot be ignored. It is highly possible that this statement was released as part of the propaganda against the two. Nevertheless, it cannot be completely discounted that it was a genuine proclamation; on 8 November, a chaplain named Richard Walker was found guilty of practising sorcery in Worcester.[17] This was a time when ideas of sorcery and witchcraft were beginning to form more cohesively, and unrelated cases such as this show that it was believed by many that there were people in society truly capable of using magic – and who may wish to use that magic to harm others. It is also important to remember that Joan's father had been accused of using evil magic against the dauphin sixty years previously, and this could possibly have lent credence to the idea that Joan would also have partaken in the craft. Whether those in England would have been aware of this so many decades later cannot be known, but it certainly cannot be discredited that it may have affected the accusations against Joan.

By the start of October 1419, Joan of Navarre, Queen Dowager of England, previous Duchess of Brittany, was in custody at Rotherhithe Manor, her goods were confiscated and she had been accused of using evil magic to try and injure or kill the king. Looking at her household accounts for the first three months of her captivity, however, it would not be immediately clear that she was in such a precarious position.[18]

This further proves that the accusations were fabricated and Henry still intended Joan to be cared for.

Daily payments were being made for her kitchen, her buttery (which provided and stored alcoholic drinks), for sauces, poultry, her stables, her wardrobe, and other costs necessary for the running of a household of a noble woman. This first week of expenses amounted to £52 6s 9d, a significant amount. Joan stayed at Rotherhithe until December that year. The cost to maintain her, while greatly reduced from her income as queen, was still fairly expensive. In October, £160 was spent on maintaining her, while in November it cost £143, and the last two weeks of her time at Rotherhithe came to nearly £75.

There is a lot in the accounts that suggest Joan was given a fair amount of freedom at Rotherhithe. She was allowed at least nineteen grooms and seven pages – an extraordinary retinue for an accused treasonous witch – and daily expenditure on her stables suggests that Joan was allowed to ride in the area around Rotherhithe. While it was not unheard of for high-status prisoners not to be strictly confined to their place of imprisonment and allowed to roam the grounds surrounding it, it is still striking that Joan was allowed this privilege immediately after her confinement.

In December, Joan was moved from Rotherhithe to Leeds Castle in Kent, travelling via Dartford and Rochester. Joan was accompanied by 'damisellis', female servants, perhaps even ladies-in-waiting, for there were generous payments relating to them recorded in Joan's wardrobe accounts from 1 October 1419 to 7 March 1420. This shows that not only was Joan continuing to be provided with luxurious clothes, but so were her attendants. A cloth merchant of London was paid for 9 yards of black cloth, at a cost of 36s, to create two petticoats for Joan, and another 8 yards to make a gown. A tailor was then commissioned to make the petticoats and gown, and to make some stockings as well. Following this, Joan had even been able to provide gifts for her attendants: Margaret Crumpyngton and Isabelle Thorley were given 5 yards of coloured cloth each to make a dress; Agnes Thorley and Katerine Whatton were given 4 yards for the same purpose; John Canterbury was given 2 yards of black cloth for stockings; and Randolph Barton had obviously impressed the queen somehow, as he was given the extremely generous gift of nineteen bundles of minever, which cost the huge sum of £4 18s 6d. Minever is a white fur edged with grey that comes from the coat of the northern red squirrel and was used to trim clothes. It was held in great esteem at this time, just below ermine in value. The total cost of these rolls of cloth came to over £16. While in the context of a royal court this is not too outrageous, for this amount of money to be supplied to a supposed prisoner is strange indeed.

Other purchases and gifts during this time included more valuable fur, fine linens and 'tartarini' cloth – a rich, silk fabric imported from Asia. There were also listings for Flanders linen, the best linen in Europe at this time, and a plethora of coloured silks, silk laces, golden bands for garters or girdles, as well as plenty of payments to tailors to create gowns, petticoats and other items of dress. There were also payments to a goldsmith for a buckle and pendant of silver gilt, a silver candlestick, a girdle of gold, a gold chain with the Lamb of God and a rosary of gold.

In these first few months, there were countless other purchases for shoes, gloves, gauntlets, boots, pepper, jewellery, cinnamon, ginger, myrrh, treacle, aqua vitae (brandy that had been repeatedly distilled), a cage for her parrot or popinjay, and the repair of a harp. Plenty of expensive medicines were bought for her by her Portuguese physician, Pedro de Alcobaça, who had previously attended Henry IV. Joan seemed to still be living the life of a queen in all but name – but, granted, on a reduced budget.

Although Joan had been temporarily moved through Kent during December, during the second half of December through to March 1420 Joan resided at Pevensey Castle. This was the castle that John Pelham had been granted decades previously by John of Gaunt, and it was now to hold a royal guest under different circumstances. Pevensey was much more of a defensive fortification than a kingly retreat like Rotherhithe. Originally a Roman fort, it was rebuilt and repaired numerous times over the centuries. There was a moat, two fortified baileys, a keep, huge curtain walls, a drawbridge and gatehouse, numerous towers, a mount which may have held a catapult and some domestic buildings including a great hall and a chapel. Pevensey had been the place of residence for previous noble prisoners of John Pelham, namely the Duke of York and James I of Scotland. These were more precious prisoners who needed to be kept safe, and so it is interesting that Joan was moved there. Perhaps it was decided that more security was necessary to contain her, at the very least to keep up the pretence.

While Joan's generous allowance continued during her time at Pevensey, in March she was moved back to Leeds Castle in Kent. This was to be her place of residence for the next two years. Built on islands on a lake, it was originally a Norman military post. However, in the late thirteenth century it was bought by Eleanor of Castile, wife of Edward I, and it became a favoured royal residence. Edward enhanced the fortifications and probably created the surrounding lake and barbican, and the castle then passed through the next few medieval queens, who all resided there.[19] It was now to hold another English queen, but under very different circumstances.

Joan was also to see her expenses reduced for the next year, with no more provisions for a stable and no new purchases for her wardrobe or chamber. While in the first eleven weeks of her captivity the average weekly expenditure for her household was just over £37, from March 1420 to the following March it decreased drastically to just over £11 a week.[20] However, this reduced expenditure may be deceptive, as Joan still continued to bestow expensive gifts on her servants. Instead of maintaining her own stable, she may have used a horse and carriage owned by John Pelham to enable her to continue to ride out. This suggests she may have received money from extra sources, perhaps even from John himself. Nonetheless, the official governmental expenditure on maintaining Joan for this year came to £700.[21] In terms of the living standards of many of the nobility, this was still a significant sum that many would have enjoyed receiving – in the income tax of 1436, less than two decades later, the average income of the baronage was £865. Joan was therefore not living a destitute life in the slightest; the government, on the other hand, was gaining around £6,000 a year from Joan's lands after her living expenses had been taken out.

Although Joan's move to Leeds Castle, a far more fortified residence, and her reduced expenditure could suggest tightening security on her person, in reality Joan's life does not seem too affected by her confinement, apart from her inability to roam freely. She continued to live in comfortable circumstances, and although Leeds Castle was more fortified, it had been luxurious enough for the previous three Queens of England to live there at various times. Moreover, this year numerous important members of government visited Joan.

On 1 April, Henry Chichele, the Archbishop of Canterbury, visited Joan for dinner.[22] Chichele had become archbishop in 1414, and not only was he the highest leader in the English Church but he was a trusted member of government, having organised a peace treaty with France in 1413. More recently, in January 1419 he was present at the English siege of Rouen, the capital of Normandy, personally negotiating the surrender of the town. That the leader of the Church in England could dine with a supposed witch who attempted treason certainly dispels any possibility that the accusations against Joan had any basis in truth. It also raises the question of Chichele's involvement in Joan's imprisonment. He had, after all, issued the proclamation for the Church to pray for Henry's protection against necromancers just as Joan was being arrested for such a charge. It is highly unlikely, considering his character, that he had been involved in concocting the accusations against Joan. However, his visit and continued friendship towards her clearly shows he knew the accusations to be false and as such he was at least complicit in the deception later on.

This month, Joan continued to receive distinguished guests. On Friday 12 April Lord Thomas Camoys arrived at Leeds Castle, and stayed there until 31 January the following year, returning for a few days between 5 February and 13 February 1421. Lord Camoys had been in the party which escorted Joan to England for her marriage to Henry IV, and clearly, he must have remained a good friend of Joan to stay for such a long period of time. It is even tempting to suggest how far their relationship may have gone, considering the length of his stay. However, Lord Camoys died at the end of March 1421, not long after leaving her, and so it is impossible to know if a romantic relationship had existed between the two as Joan had no chance to remarry until she was released from her confinement.

Lord Camoys' presence certainly would have made Joan's confinement far more comfortable, and it must have been nice to have been in the presence of a friend. In fact, Lord Camoys may have been the source for extra income, solving the mystery of her liberal gifts to her servants – and, of course, any luxuries that Lord Camoys bought for himself in the form of food, clothes or goods could be used by Joan as well. This would have supplemented her reduced lifestyle and made life still feel sufficiently queenly.

Two days after Lord Camoys arrived, Joan was visited by Humphrey, Duke of Gloucester, who stayed for supper. This visit must have brought her much happiness. It seems to be the first visit by any of her stepchildren during her imprisonment, and to have come from her closest stepchild must have given her great joy. It must also have been a welcome reassurance of her position. Joan must have been aware that the accusations against her would not be taken further, as per the conditions of her confinement and perhaps through verbal reassurance. However, it must have still been a lonely and cruel place to have had her freedom taken away and her reputation besmirched, all in the name of money.

Joan had loved her stepchildren as her own, sided with Henry against his father often, and become part of the family, with England her home. To now be treated in such a way, even if she was still protected and looked after, must have been difficult. Humphrey must surely have provided further reassurance that action was not going to be taken against her, and perhaps provided hope that the situation was only temporary. If this were the case, then Joan would be disappointed to realise that her confinement was unlikely to end any time soon.

In the meantime, Henry V was making huge gains in France. This culminated on 21 May 1420 when he signed the Treaty of Troyes with King Charles VI of France. The English cause had been strengthened when the Duke of Burgundy joined their side and they had continued to capture important French territories. The fall of Rouen in January of the previous year meant that Normandy became an English territory for the first time in two centuries. Charles VI was completely incapacitated by his mental illnesses and his queen, Isabeau of Bavaria, had run out of options. She was probably also tired of fighting for a kingdom that her husband was incapable of running, and saw that it was a matter of time before the English took the rest of it by force.

As such, Isabeau and Charles met Henry in the city of Troyes in north-central France in May and the treaty was ratified. The treaty declared that the dauphin was disinherited from the Crown of France, based on his 'enormous crimes' such as ordering Burgundy's assassination. Many rumours were also circulating in the kingdom that the dauphin was illegitimate, having been born as the result of an affair between Isabeau and the Duke of Orléans. The treaty, however, did not mention this, as it would have offended the honour of both the king and queen. It stated that Henry V would marry Charles and Isabeau's daughter, Catherine of Valois, thus uniting the royal bloodlines. Henry was to be made Regent of France for the remainder of Charles' lifetime, and after his death Henry and his heirs were to inherit the French throne.

This was the singular greatest triumph of Henry's lifetime. It seemed he had finally won the war that his forebears had been fighting for nearly 100 years. He would now be king of two significant countries in Western Europe, creating a powerful empire that would be a real force on the Continent. However, he had to secure the Treaty of Troyes and marry Catherine fast. The marriage needed to be the greatest spectacle of the age; Henry had to announce to everyone in both kingdoms that he was indeed the heir to the throne and had the power and wealth to make it happen.

In this respect, Henry certainly achieved his aims. The French chronicler Enguerrand de Monstrelet described the wedding of Henry and Catherine on 2 June 1420: 'Great pomp and magnificence were displayed by him and his princes, as if he were at that moment king of all the world.'[23] Henry had firmly marked his territory, and it seemed as if a new dynasty was born.

The Treaty of Troyes had implications for Joan and her family. Her son Arthur was still imprisoned by the English, her pleas for his release prior to her own arrest having been ignored by Henry. Meanwhile, earlier in 1420, her eldest son, John V of Brittany, had been captured by Olivier, Count of Penthièvre. Olivier was the grandson of Charles of Blois and Joan of Brittany, from whom John IV had wrestled control of Brittany. The Counts of Penthièvre had never given up their claim in spirit.

John's wife, Joan of France, rallied the Breton nobles to John's cause and they responded, besieging all the castles of the family. Meanwhile, Joan turned to England. On 5 April, she petitioned Henry V requesting that he release John's brother Arthur so that he could help recover John, and on 12 April Arthur himself petitioned the king to allow him into his presence so he could plead for his release to assist his brother.[24] Arthur signed this letter 'your humble prisoner', but in another letter the following day where he requested that Henry punish Olivier, he did not sign off with the same phrase. It is reasonable to assume that he must have been suitably persuasive for Henry to allow his immediate release.

With one son free, and the treaty with France signed, Joan may have hoped that she would be shortly released – after all, her money was no longer needed to pay for the war. However, if this was her hope she had forgotten an important factor – the new Queen of England. Catherine had been granted the same dower as Joan (it would have been an insult to offer anything less), but the Crown was still not in a position to offer 10,000 marks a year to the new queen. If Joan were restored to her position, then that would be 20,000 marks – over £13,000 – that the Treasury would have to find. The war may be over, but the royal finances were still not in a position to provide this much money.

Although the treaty had been signed, parts of France still held out against English rule, and so Henry spent the rest of the year conquering, returning to England by Christmas. The year had been a quiet one for Joan. In August she received Henry Beaufort, Bishop of Winchester, for a weekend visit. One must wonder how they interacted during this stay, as Beaufort must have been privy to the plot against Joan considering his position in government, his wealthy purse funding the government, and his close relationship with Henry. Did he feel guilt at how Joan had been treated, particularly considering how well he must have known her because of his deep friendship with her husband, his half-brother Henry IV?

At the end of February 1421, Catherine of Valois was crowned queen in Westminster Abbey and the following month she fell pregnant. For this new year of Joan's confinement, her expenditure rose again, surpassing £1,000. Perhaps now that Henry was more secure in his position and had a new queen and a possible heir on the way, he felt more sympathy for Joan and wished to make her imprisonment more comfortable. The account books show that once more Joan was able to buy cloth to create new clothes. She commissioned a special gown to be made for the Easter feast, she bought dozens more yards of black cloth for gowns and capes for herself, as well as more luxurious grey squirrel fur, and fur for a collar and mantle which would probably have been of an even more expensive kind.[25]

Joan also retained her royal taste for expensive wine, spending just over £56 this year on Gascon, Rochelle, and Rhenish wines. In November, the Patent Rolls recorded an order (possibly from Henry himself) for a group of men to take food to Joan and there is a huge variety of food listed, including some sumptuous meats, 'wheat, barley, beans, peas, oats, wine, ale, oxen, cows, calves, sheep, lambs, pigs, little pigs, capons, hens, poults, geese, ducks, pheasants, partridges, coneys, salt and fresh fish and other victuals and hay, litter, coals, firewood, rushes and other necessaries'.[26] Joan's household account books also show a payment to two serjeants-at-law to plead for 'the queen's gold' – Joan was trying to get her dower returned to her.

This year, Joan received more visits from her family. Humphrey joined her for supper once again on 10 February 1421 and again on 12 June. He obviously still cared for Joan, but he was in fact one of the beneficiaries of her imprisonment. A record from August the previous year showed that one of Joan's damsels from before her imprisonment, Pernell Aldrewiche, was attempting to assert a gift from Joan. The record stated that in 1416, Pernell had been granted rents and customs from within the town of Havering-atte-Bower 'which Humphrey, duke of Gloucester, chamberlain of England, Henry, bishop of Winchester' and others 'at present held in demesne' alongside other lands of Joan, including her manor at Havering.[27] Pernell was trying to get these incomes returned to her, a matter in which she was successful.

Those who had visited her, who had been her close family members during the life of Henry IV, were in fact part of the group of vultures receiving benefits from her confinement. Bishop Beaufort himself also visited Joan again this year, dining with her on 2 July. Both of these men, while being deeply involved in the accusations against Joan and being very close to her throughout her life, could not know now how this experience would affect them in a similar, but far more menacing way just two decades later. Beaufort, at least, was learning how successful such accusations could be at achieving political ends even if, for the meantime, it was for more innocent reasons.

On 6 December 1421, Queen Catherine gave birth to a healthy baby boy, named Henry for his father and grandfather. This was a further triumph for Henry V, as a male heir only made the Treaty of Troyes even more secure. However, Henry was never to meet his only son. While the king had been in England at the start of the year for the coronation of his wife, his brother Thomas of Lancaster, Duke of Clarence, had continued to lead English forces in France. Towards the end of March, Thomas entered battle at Baugé against a joint French and Scottish army. The battle was a huge defeat for the English and Thomas was killed during the fighting. In June, Henry had to return to France to maintain his foothold. His campaign was going successfully, and he was relieving besieged loyal towns and capturing new territories.

During the siege of Meaux, north-east of Paris, between October 1421 and May 1422, however, it is believed that Henry contracted dysentery. As it became clear that Henry was dying at the age of 36, he began to set his affairs in order. He ordered that his eldest surviving brother, Bedford, act as Regent of France on behalf of his son, who was only 9 months old, and continue the war in his name to ensure that the Treaty of Troyes be fulfilled. He asked that his last surviving brother, Humphrey, act as tutor and protector of the young Henry VI.

On 13 July 1422, Queen Joan was finally granted her freedom. Henry V addressed the lords of his kingdom, recorded in Parliament, and ordered the full restoration of Joan's position and property.[28] At the end of a long official passage in French detailing her restitution was a personal, poignant entry of Henry's own words in English. The words are an excellent insight into this now-sentimental king and stepson nearing the end of his life.

The charges of witchcraft and treason were not specifically mentioned in Henry's speech, and instead he said that Joan's dower had been confiscated 'for suche causes as ye knowe'. Poignantly, he said that Joan should be fully returned her dower and freedom 'lest hir shuld be a charge unto oure conscience'.

Henry died just over a month later, on 31 August, still in France, and so at the time of this record he was probably well into his illness, and almost certainly aware of his impending death. How many have regretted past actions upon their deathbeds? Henry clearly felt immense guilt at how he had treated Joan the last few years and wanted one of his final actions to be her full restitution.

Henry's language in his speech makes it completely clear that Joan was to be fully restored to her previous exalted position as Queen Dowager, and no questions or further moves were to be made against her. Her goods and dower were to be received as 'she did here afore' and he also returned 'hir Beddes [beds], and al other thing Mevables [moveable], that we had of hir', such as her jewels and chapel items taken from Randolph three years previously. To underline that he wanted Joan released with immediate effect, Henry also ordered that there should be payments made to procure horses for two carriages and she should then be allowed to travel to any other place in his realm that she wanted, whenever she wanted. He was restoring Joan's complete autonomy.

Henry also declared that Joan could have five or six gowns made for her, of whatever material and colour she might desire 'such as she useth to were'. Although Joan had been ordering fairly luxurious clothes during her confinement, she was not able to afford the highest quality material, or the most expensive colours reserved for royalty. That Henry was giving her carte blanche to create the most expensive gowns that she would like, befitting of a Queen Dowager, again underlined that her position as previous Queen of England was to be emphasised and reinstated, never again to be questioned. He also continued to call her his 'Moder Quene Johanne' in his address, showing that he still viewed her as a family member and that others should as well. It reminded the kingdom that Joan was a senior lady in the royal family and should hold authority and respect.

Henry's refusal to address the charges in his declaration come in part from a selfish position. By not mentioning the charges of witchcraft and treason, he was in effect playing it down. This would certainly have been an attempt to minimise the impact of the accusations for the rest of her life, as bringing them up again would remind everybody of what she supposedly did. However, it is also an inability to admit that the charges were fabricated in the first place. If Henry mentioned the charges and merely said that Joan had been pardoned and forgiven, she would still have the stigma for life that she had, in fact, committed these horrible acts. But, the Crown could not admit that the accusations, and thus her imprisonment, had been false. Not only would it be impossible for the government to admit to such a conspiracy, it would also mean that Joan would have the right to claim a reimbursement for the revenue she lost while her lands and goods were confiscated. By restoring her position and wealth to its previous level and skipping over the charges altogether, her innocence was implied, and it thus saved the Crown from any embarrassment or inconvenience.

Joan wasted no time in leaving her place of confinement. It cost the government over £100 to obtain horses for her, and it is no wonder that she would want to leave the place she had been forced to stay for two years, even if it had been in relative comfort. She did indeed find her position returned to how it had been before, and she never again seems to have suffered any negative consequences from the charges. She did struggle to regain her dower, but this was largely because the government had given away or sold much of it and so it was difficult to recover.[29]

Some have accused Joan of greediness in her determination to assert her dower rights, but this is almost certainly untrue. While it is entirely possible that Joan may have had a greedy streak, and she certainly did enjoy purchasing the finer things in life, her dower was her legal right as a wife and widow. The rights of the widow had been enshrined in law and were even considered important enough for the barons to put into Magna Carta two centuries previously. Why, therefore, should Joan not enforce her dower rights? Especially now that she had been imprisoned and denied her rights for three years on false charges. One has to wonder if the same accusations of greed would come if Joan had been a male member of the royal family recovering his wealth and power after such an experience.

Although Joan had been returned to her rightful position, she was now 52 years old and had been a widow for nearly ten years. She had been imprisoned for the last three, and it seems she was, in all likelihood, exhausted. Joan became an elusive figure in the records, and it seems for the most part she was simply enjoying a quiet widowhood, without any drama, at her manor houses.

During her imprisonment, her Breton children had not forgotten about her, despite the political upheaval going on in their own lives.[30] Joan's arrest was a delicate diplomatic problem. Brittany had sent the Bishop of Nantes on a mission to try and negotiate her release but he had obviously been unsuccessful. The year after her release there were more hints at international tension due to Joan's treatment. Despite everything, Joan had still decided to stay in England and this was obviously a sore point for her relations in Brittany. On 18 April 1423,

Joan was mentioned in a treaty between the Duke of Burgundy and Duke of Brittany.

In the treaty, John V, Duke of Brittany, as well as his brothers and sisters, 'see the pardon of their mother, who for such a long time has been far away from her children and they so want to see her, that there is nothing which could bring them comfort nor rejoicing until she can come here to see and visit them, and to be here in innocence and liberty'.[31] This is certainly very emotive language, and does suggest that perhaps there was upset and bad feelings among her children that she had abandoned them for the English family.

However, this could potentially have been a political move because they wanted Joan in their custody, so the English could not imprison her again and use her as leverage. The previous day, John V had also signed a treaty with John, Duke of Bedford, where the men said they 'will live in good and true love, fraternity and union with one another and we will love, cherish and get along together as brothers, relatives and good friends'.

However Joan's children felt, diplomatic relations had not been damaged. The Bretons, Burgundians and English entered into a triple alliance that month in Amiens, and to seal the alliance a double marriage was arranged. Bedford was to marry Burgundy's younger sister, Anne, while Joan's son Arthur was to marry Burgundy's older sister, Margaret. All parties also agreed to recognise the infant Henry VI as King of France because, just two months after Henry V's death, Charles of France had died. Henry's relatives were keeping their oath to ensure that his son would carry the crown.

This alliance was crucial to the English foothold in France for the rest of the decade, although Arthur reneged on the alliance the following year. In the meantime, however, England was functioning successfully with a child king. Bedford had been made Regent of France, and whenever he was in England he was to be the most senior decision maker. During his absence, however, Humphrey of Gloucester was to act as 'protector and defender of the realm and chief councillor of the king', working alongside a council. For this, he was to receive 8,000 marks a year, a very sizeable income.[32]

In 1425, perhaps at Joan's instigation, Humphrey attempted an important assertion of his powers as regent which caused chaos among the council. Although Joan had been released three years previously, Friar Randolph was still languishing in the Tower of London. It is unclear why Randolph was not released when Joan was. Perhaps Henry had forgotten about him and no one else cared or thought of him. Perhaps the government was wary of releasing him in case he exposed their lies. Either way, Randolph had now been in the Tower for five or six years. It would seem likely, therefore, that Joan did remember him, and now that her own freedom was secured she wanted to free her poor confessor.

As Humphrey had a very close relationship with her, it doubtless would have taken little persuasion on Joan's behalf to get him to release Randolph for her. In fact, it is quite possible that Humphrey had a relationship with Randolph himself, whether professional or amiable. Humphrey owned a set of astrological charts, currently held in a fifteenth-century manuscript at the British Library, which were created for him by Randolph.[33] He therefore had his own reasons for wanting to free Randolph. However, this had the unintended consequences of a political disaster.

Humphrey, under his authority as Protector of England, ordered the Lieutenant of the Tower of London, Richard Woodville, to bring Randolph to him.[34] However, as soon as Bishop Beaufort heard of this, he immediately tried to prevent it, arguing that only the king had the authority to release such a prisoner. The two already had simmering tensions between them, and this encounter only escalated matters.

Not long after, Beaufort started to gather archers in Southwark, causing Humphrey to fear for an uprising. He then requested the mayor and aldermen of London to be on their guard, and they duly patrolled the streets. When Beaufort's men tried to gain entry to the city they found their way barred, and this led to a conflict. Unfortunately for Beaufort, Humphrey was held in the highest esteem by Londoners, and as soon as word spread that Beaufort was in arms against him, the streets were filled by men willing to support Humphrey. London was in revolt.

The situation was so volatile that it took great effort, not only from the mayor but from the Archbishop of Canterbury, to calm everybody down. In fact, it had been such a risk to national security that Bedford had to be urgently recalled from France to restore law and order. At Parliament the following February, the main focus was the hostility between Beaufort and Humphrey, and who was to blame for the events in London. Humphrey drew up a damning indictment against Beaufort.

Humphrey claimed that Beaufort had told Richard Woodville to refuse him entry to the Tower against his rights as Protector of the Realm. Even worse, he said that Beaufort had attempted to gain control of the body of King Henry VI in an attempt to gain control of the government. He even claimed that Beaufort had the aim of killing Humphrey. Despite this, Parliament ended with Beaufort declaring his loyalty to all three King Henrys, and with Humphrey and Beaufort shaking hands and supposedly reconciling.

It was clear, however, that both men could not remain in power. One would have to fall. As such, on 13 March 1426 Beaufort was forced to resign his position as Chancellor, which he had held since he was appointed by Henry IV back in 1403.[35] Even years after his imprisonment for using treasonable witchcraft, Randolph was causing problems.

Randolph never was freed from the Tower of London. In 1429, he got into a 'debate and strife within the Tower ward; and there this person smote this friar Randolph, and slew him; and thus he made his end of the world'.[36] The last of the evidence of Joan's crimes had gone.

Joan herself was leading an ever quieter life. The same year that Randolph died, she gifted her lavish private chapel to Humphrey's new wife, Eleanor Cobham. Joan was clearly a deeply religious woman, as the amount of items in her chapel and her many references to the Trinity and God in her letters show. To be eschewing such expensive pieces in what was probably one of her most cherished collections shows that she was looking for a simpler life. From 1430 onwards, Joan seriously reduced her income, living on around 500 marks a year in 1433.[37]

Joan had spent a lot of time during the 1420s in the palace at King's Langley, Hertfordshire. In 1424 or 1425, Humphrey and his first wife, Jacqueline, had visited Joan here with a large escort of forty-two horses. Joan also spent time making pilgrimages, travelling in 1427 to the Cell of Walsingham, the Priory of Norwich, the Abbey of Peterborough and finishing with a devotion at the Abbey of St Albans, returning to the palace at Langley afterwards. That Christmas, Humphrey spent the festive period at St Albans and, considering the proximity of Joan's residence at Langley, it is possible they spent their time together.[38]

Despite everything that had happened, Joan appears to have remained friends with Beaufort. In 1428, she was again at Langley when Beaufort visited the Abbey of St Albans, ending the day by dining with her 'attended by a great escort'. Although he had to resign his position as Chancellor, Beaufort was still one of the most powerful men in the country and he did not shy away from showing this.[39]

On 25 March 1431, Joan suffered a personal tragedy when the palace of Langley suffered a terrible fire. Supposedly, a drowsy minstrel did not take proper care of a lit candle, and several rooms were devastated by the fire. All of the gold, silver plate, utensils, jewels and furniture in the rooms were destroyed, but Joan escaped unharmed.[40] Although the palace was not totally ruined, as subsequent repair work attests, it appears that she returned largely to her old manor house at Havering.

The following year, however, Joan had the joy of meeting her grandson Gilles for the first time. The 12-year-old Gilles was a son of John V of Brittany, and from 1432 to 1434 he stayed at the English court.[41] Gilles was only two years older than King Henry VI. Their similarity in age and the fact that they were cousins through Joan and Henry IV's marriage meant that the two boys became great friends. During this stay in England, Joan must surely have seen Gilles on numerous occasions.

Although Joan had been accused of attempting to kill his father, all Henry VI had ever known of Joan was as a free woman, Queen Dowager and his grandmother. Although he was a child for most of the remainder of her life, as he grew up, he clearly displayed a fondness for her, which probably increased as he became close friends with Gilles. She received expensive New Year's gifts from Henry, and although she chose to live on a reduced pension, she was still free to receive as much of her dower as she wished.

Joan's life was, however, slowing down. Away from the eyes of the court, she lived comfortably but simply, continuing to visit religious institutions and having friends and family to visit. The Christmas of 1436 she was back at Langley, it clearly being repaired enough to spend the holiday there. By summer, she had returned to her manor house of Havering. There, on either 2, 9 or 10 July (accounts differ) 1437, Queen Joan passed away at the age of 67.[42]

Henry VI honoured his esteemed grandmother by having her buried with full honours next to her husband, Henry IV, in St Thomas Becket's Chapel behind the High Altar in Canterbury Cathedral. Her funeral was held on 11 August and Henry ensured that there was a plethora of illustrious mourners present. The principal mourners were Humphrey and his wife, Eleanor, and it must indeed have been a sad day for Humphrey. Present as well were three earls, two lords, a duchess, three countesses, the Archbishop of Canterbury, two bishops, two priors and three abbots.[43] Interestingly, Beaufort and Henry were not listed as attending in the minutes of the Privy Council, though that does not necessarily mean that they were not there. A surviving order from Henry to a peer or peeress to attend the funeral shows language desiring Joan be properly honoured.

Joan of Navarre had come a long way from her birth as the princess of a small kingdom, experiencing all the rises and falls that life had to offer. Her royal lineage always meant that she was going to go on to great things, but Joan certainly took every opportunity she could, and fulfilled her expectations well. She had first become Duchess of Brittany, where she completed her wifely duty by giving birth to nine children, most of whom survived well into adulthood. She carried out her expected duties of duchess to the letter, not becoming too involved in politics and yet carrying out intercessions and acting on behalf of the people when necessary.

After her husband's death, she shocked many in France, England and beyond with her announcement of intention to marry the King of England. What was by all accounts a love match between a beautiful, intelligent, spiritual woman and an athletic, handsome and powerful man came with great personal consequence to Joan. She was forced to give up all but two of her children, which must have caused significant internal conflict, and move once more to a foreign land. As always, however, Joan took the challenges in her stride, and the strength of her personality is shown by the way the English people took her into their hearts and even came to admire her, at a time when the Breton people of her previous kingdom were universally despised in England. She became deeply loved by her new family, again a testament to her kindness, charm and character, and continued to act as a diplomat between her new and old kingdom, probably preventing war on many an occasion.

Joan suffered the greatest insult that such an incredible woman could when her stepsons and their government turned on her for their own financial gain. Although there is no evidence she ever did partake in any forms of witchcraft, especially considering her deep religious convictions, the accusation has reverberated through the centuries. In fact, the accusations against Joan were just the start, and three more royal women would suffer the consequences that century. Now that the government had seen the successful use of such a tactic, it was only a matter of time before it would be applied again.

However, Joan was lucky to escape unharmed from the accusations, aside from losing several years' income, and she returned to her position as the most senior royal woman in the land, alongside the king's mother, Catherine of Valois. She spent the rest of her life in retirement, performing pilgrimages and meeting family members, and took up what was, for her, a much simpler and quiet lifestyle. This great queen has often been overlooked by the history books, only mentioned as an aside. She deserves to take her place back.

Eleanor
Cobham

5

A VERY NOBLE LADY

AROUND THE YEAR 1400, a baby girl was born to Reginald Cobham, 3rd Baron Sterborough, 3rd Lord Cobham, and his wife, Eleanor Culpeper. This little girl – named Eleanor, after her mother – was expected to have a pleasant but insignificant life. As part of the baronage, her father was of reasonable social standing but was quite far down the rungs of nobility and would have lived a comfortable, but not too luxurious life. Eleanor could expect to grow up with some form of education, before being married to a knight or baron of similar status to her, then hopefully fulfil her duty as a wife and provide children for her husband, while also helping to run their reasonable estate. What Reginald and Eleanor could not have expected was that this little girl would experience one of the greatest turns of the wheel of fortune her contemporaries had witnessed, coming tantalisingly close to being queen of the realm, but ultimately ending in lonely imprisonment with scarcely a friend in the world.

As with many women of her age, the exact date of birth of Eleanor Cobham is unknown due to a lack of records, and frustratingly little of her life before the age of 22 is known. It is possible that she was born in Sterborough Castle, Surrey, transformed from a manor house in 1341 by her great grandfather, Reginald de Cobham, 1st Baron Cobham and 1st Lord Cobham of Sterborough. Sterborough Castle was not an insignificant fortification, consisting of four towers and a gate which was surrounded on all sides by a moat. Built on a half-acre artificial island just south of the River Eden, the castle was accessible by a central bridge on the southern side. The exterior was built from Ashlar sandstone, giving it a light and classical look, and was in the quadrangular style, with a central enclosed courtyard.

Although Eleanor's parents were not part of the highest echelons of society, they boasted fairly notable ancestors.[1] Her father Reginald was descended from Roger Mortimer, 1st Earl of March. In the 1320s, Mortimer had a relationship with Edward II's queen, Isabella of France. Together, they overthrew the unpopular Edward II. For three years, from 1327 to 1330, Mortimer was essentially joint ruler of England with Isabella before being overthrown himself by the young Edward III, who claimed his rightful position. Reginald's grandfather, the 1st Baron Cobham, had been a loyal and thusly rewarded servant of the Crown, having acted as a guardian of Prince Edward, the Black Prince, at the Battle of Crécy, as well as Admiral of the Fleet for the West. In 1352, he had been made a prestigious Knight of the Garter and the following year he was made Captain of Calais, a trusted position considering Calais had only been in English hands for five years. Reginald was connected to various noble and ruling families of England, including Sutton, Dudley, Beauchamp, Despencer and Mortimer. Eleanor's mother, Eleanor Culpeper, was also of reasonable social standing. She was the daughter of a knight, Thomas Culpeper, and Eleanor Green, an heiress.

This ancestry meant that Eleanor Cobham was a respectable lady who might expect to become a member of the household of a royal woman or member of the upper nobility, before being married and gaining a household of her own. Eleanor's upbringing was likely to be typical of a woman of her class. She would not have had an exemplary education like Joan of Navarre did, but she does seem to have been taught to read in English, and she may even have learnt to write. Her education would have only been to a level that she would then be capable of running a knightly household and estate once married. The rest of her upbringing would have been focused on feminine values to help attract and keep her a husband, such as singing, dancing, music and needlework.

No known physical description of Eleanor exists, and only one contemporary picture of her survives. This is an illuminated miniature from 1431 of Eleanor with her future husband, Humphrey, Duke of Gloucester, from the *Liber Benefactorum* of St Albans by Thomas

Walsingham.[2] Eleanor and Humphrey were benefactors of the Abbey of St Albans, shown in Humphrey's hand in the picture, but little of Eleanor's real physical attributes can be garnered from the picture, it being a typically stylised miniature of the time. Eleanor is shown with a high forehead, the popular style, but her hair is hidden under a covering, so the colour is left a mystery. She is shown as slim and tall, but whether this mirrored her real stature cannot be known for certain. She is wearing a sumptuous red dress with a golden belt, a black head covering with a golden circlet, and a thick golden necklace, representing the wealth of her station as Duchess of Gloucester.

While there is no surviving physical description of Eleanor, it is reasonable to assume that she was an attractive woman. Jehan de Waurin, a Burgundian chronicler and contemporary of Eleanor, describes her as 'a very noble lady of great descent ... also she was beautiful and marvellously kind [pleasant]'.[3] As she was later to attract the attention of a prince, it is likely that she was at least fairly attractive, and probably had sufficient wit and charm to go with it.

Around 1422, and certainly by 1424, Eleanor Cobham entered the household of Jacqueline of Hainault as a lady-in-waiting. She was around 22 years old and it does not seem that she had yet married, given the continued use of her maiden name. While the youngest marriages tended to be by members of royalty and the upper ranks of the nobility, in order to secure alliances and land, it is somewhat notable that Eleanor had not yet married by this age. Serving as a lady-in-waiting would have been a respectable position for an unmarried young woman of her class and hopefully a way to broaden her social circle to attract an eligible husband.

Jacqueline of Hainault was herself a young woman of a similar age to Eleanor, having been born in 1401 in The Hague in modern-day Netherlands.[4] The only legitimate heir of William II, Duke of Bavaria, Jacqueline had been betrothed since the age of 22 months to John, Duke of Touraine, the fourth son of Charles VI of France. The couple had married in 1415 when Jacqueline was 14, and shortly after the wedding John's only surviving older brother died, leaving him heir to the throne of France. Jacqueline was now future queen consort, with a bright future ahead of her. Two years later, however, John died from a suspected poisoning, leaving Jacqueline a widow at 16. Just two months after this her father died, and Jacqueline came into her inheritance as sovereign Countess of Hainault, Holland and Zeeland. As a young, vulnerable woman, however, her inheritance was contested by her uncle, John III. Jacqueline was in desperate need of a husband to help her assert her territorial rights. She was therefore swiftly betrothed to John IV, Duke of Brabant, less than four months after her first husband's death.

The marriage between Jacqueline and John was rocky from the start.[5] The papal dispensation required for their marriage due to their consanguinity (they were within the forbidden closeness of blood relations) was revoked, and John had racked up considerable financial problems. In 1419, John of Brabant made a peace treaty with Jacqueline's uncle, John III of Bavaria, giving him full custody over Holland and Zeeland for the next twelve years in return for monetary compensation which Brabant used to pay his significant debts. Jacqueline was furious that her rightful inheritance had been alienated by her husband and began working with her allies to gain a formal separation.

By early 1421, Jacqueline issued a statement of her intent to obtain an annulment from John, and in early March of that year she fled to England to ask Henry V for help. Henry V, having just the previous year finally won rights to inherit the French Crown, was riding on a high. Theoretically, he was in an excellent position to aid Jacqueline in her quest to win back her lands. He gave Jacqueline a glamorous reception and made her an honoured guest of the court. When Henry VI was born at the end of the year, Jacqueline was honoured as one of his godparents.

At some point after her arrival, Jacqueline was set up with her own small household of servants to look after her, and it is possible that Eleanor was chosen from the outset to serve her in some capacity. Perhaps Eleanor had been serving in the household of another woman who volunteered her services for the displaced duchess. Eleanor's mother died in 1422, the year it is believed Eleanor entered Jacqueline's household. As such, it is possible that Eleanor was placed in Jacqueline's household as a favour to the now-widowed Reginald, as a way to provide for his daughter now that her mother was gone and she remained unmarried.

If Eleanor did join the duchess' household in 1422, then it would have been in a flurry of activity and an uncertain time for her.

This August saw the death of Henry V, leaving the infant Henry VI, only 9 months old, as the new king. Not long after Henry's death, Jacqueline obtained her long-desired annulment from the Duke of Brabant and in 1423 she swiftly married Humphrey, Duke of Gloucester.[6] After the death of his brother, Humphrey had become Lord Protector to the child Henry VI and he was now one of the most powerful princes in Europe. The whole fiasco of their marriage was a huge scandal; the annulment was obtained from Benedict XIII, the 'Antipope', based in Avignon during the Great Schism. Benedict's authority was only recognised in a handful of kingdoms, and England was not one of them – England instead submitted to the authority of Pope Martin V. John of Brabant also submitted to Pope Martin V, and thus refused to accept the legitimacy of this annulment. For many, Humphrey and Jacqueline's marriage was bigamous and illegal.[7] Eleanor therefore joined a household that was under great change – and that might not last. Her position must not have felt very secure.

Despite the scandal of Jacqueline's annulment and new marriage, by October 1423 it was suspected that she was pregnant with Humphrey's child and it was therefore in everyone's best interests to have her annulment from John confirmed. Throughout 1424, Humphrey wrote numerous letters to Pope Martin V asking him to confirm the annulment and sanction his marriage to Jacqueline, but Martin remained indecisive, not wanting to support one side over the other.[8]

In the autumn of 1424, Jacqueline joined Humphrey in his Duchy of Gloucester, and it is likely that Eleanor followed as part of her entourage. Here, Jacqueline suffered a miscarriage. Eleanor would have seen at first hand the consequences of such a tragedy, both personal and political. Jacqueline was still young and had plenty more chances to provide an heir. However, giving birth to a live, healthy and especially male child at this point would have tied Humphrey to her. It probably would also have encouraged Pope Martin to finally give his blessing to the marriage, and thus given the couple more of a chance to reclaim her lands on the Continent.

Despite the couple's personal tragedy, plans were afoot to take back Jacqueline's lands by force, and by November they had landed in Calais.[9] It is unclear whether Eleanor followed the couple. Jacqueline must have been certain that with the Lord Protector of England on her side she would swiftly reclaim her lands. While the expedition was initially successful, with Humphrey being immediately recognised as Count of Hainault upon his entry to Mons in December, fate was to deal another blow to Jacqueline.

In January 1425, her uncle John III died after being poisoned. While this should have helped solidify her claim as rightful heir to her father's lands, in reality, it ended her hopes of reclaiming her inheritance. John of Brabant swiftly made Philip the Good, Duke of Burgundy, the new regent of Holland and Zeeland to replace John III. Philip was Jacqueline's cousin, but he was also a crucial ally of England in their French wars. Philip now had a stake in the conflict between Jacqueline and John and by taking John's side, he would now have new lands and wealth at his disposal. Humphrey had returned to England, sending a paltry force of 500 men to aid Jacqueline, but she was captured by Philip. She managed to escape to Gouda where she stayed with leaders of the Hook faction who supported her claim.

Humphrey swiftly lost interest in pursuing the claims of his wife. Now that Philip had taken an interest in Jacqueline's lands, it was too dangerous for England to antagonise him. Humphrey's older brother, John, Duke of Bedford, was acting Regent of England after the death of Henry V, but he was mostly involved in the war in France, leaving Humphrey behind to run things in his absence. However, in matters of the country, Bedford had the final say, and Bedford had entered an alliance with Philip of Burgundy which was crucial in maintaining the English foothold in France now that Henry V was dead. Humphrey and Philip had clashed over Jacqueline's lands, both wanting to claim them for their own, and even organised a duel to settle their differences. Bedford and the nobles of Paris managed to cancel the duel, but now it was time for Bedford to put an end to his brother's plans.[10] Bedford and the Council of England reprimanded Humphrey for his behaviour, fearing for the alliance with Philip. Humphrey saw the sense in what they were saying, and left his wife to her own devices in Holland. It was around this time that his affair with Eleanor began.

Whether Eleanor travelled with the couple or not, it is widely believed that she became Humphrey's mistress not long after his return to England. To have had access to Humphrey, she must have remained part of his household in some capacity, or else have taken up another position at court now that her mistress was abandoned abroad. Humphrey's household would have been a glamorous place for Eleanor. While his brother Bedford was in France, Humphrey was the most powerful man in England, although kept in check by rivals at court, and he certainly enjoyed this position. He jostled for power at court, enjoyed putting on a show, but he was a complex man who also enjoyed intellectual pursuits and the arts. He was widely read and scholarly, he revelled in the chivalric pleasures of his day, and he was a capable commander. He had been successful during his brother Henry's campaigns in France, and his classical studies helped him in battle through his knowledge of ancient siege warfare. Throughout his life he was a patron to poets, architects, religious institutions and libraries, showing a well-rounded character who enjoyed all aspects of medieval life. Contemporary illustrations of him show him with brown hair, a prominent nose and a broad face.[11] His brother, Henry V, stood over 6ft tall, and so it is likely that Humphrey also held an impressive stature.

While Humphrey and Eleanor's relationship began in 1425, it is not clear if Eleanor was his only mistress at this time. Humphrey fathered two illegitimate children, Arthur and Antigone, but the identity of their mother(s) has never been confirmed. The birth dates of both children have been commonly placed between 1425 and 1428, leading many to suggest that the children were Eleanor's. However, it is unlikely that these children were hers. If they had been offspring of the couple, Humphrey would have had the children legitimised after his marriage to Eleanor – as John of Gaunt did with his children by Katherine Swynford thirty years previously. The couple remained childless throughout their marriage, with no contemporary reference to them having children together.

Moreover, Eleanor later claimed to have solicited a witch to make her fertile in order to have a child by Humphrey, which she would not have needed to do if she had given birth to two children so soon after their relationship began. If the children were indeed born between 1425 and 1428, therefore, Eleanor certainly was not the only woman in Humphrey's sights. Whoever the other mistress (or mistresses) were, Eleanor was the woman who captured Humphrey's heart. The future Pope Pius II wrote that Humphrey held 'outstanding love' for

Eleanor and it wouldn't be long before the couple could confirm this love to each other.[12]

In 1428, with Jacqueline of Hainault firmly defeated by Philip of Burgundy, and abandoned by Humphrey and the English, Pope Martin finally made his decision on the annulment. He ruled that Jacqueline and John's marriage had always been valid, 'and declare nul and illegal all other marriages that she [Jacqueline] might have contracted during the life of the Duke'.[13] This pronouncement firmly decided that Humphrey and Jacqueline's marriage was illegal and thus it was as if the marriage had never happened. By the time of Martin's pronouncement, John had been dead for a year, and if Humphrey had wished he could now legally marry Jacqueline.

However, Humphrey had long forgotten Jacqueline and her no longer tempting inheritance and was by now deeply in love with Eleanor. Eleanor was beautiful, charming, kind, interested in learning and hassle free. Humphrey wasted no time after the pronouncement of his freedom from Jacqueline in marrying Eleanor, being wed the same year. Because she was of far lower birth than Humphrey, the marriage to Eleanor brought no material benefits, and despite the precedent of John of Gaunt and Katherine Swynford a few decades previously, his decision to marry a baron's daughter would still have caused a stir. It is precisely for this reason, however, that it was clearly a love match, and after the problems caused by his attempt at a political marriage, Humphrey probably welcomed a chance to marry a woman he cared for.

Eleanor and Humphrey's marriage would have provided gossip at court, particularly considering her previous position as a mistress, although no comments on its reception at court feature in surviving contemporary records. One protest does survive from a group of London women, however. During the Parliament of 1428, these women brought letters addressed to Humphrey, both archbishops, and other lords, protesting Eleanor's status as an '*adulteram*'.[14] While the knowledge that Eleanor and Humphrey had been having an extramarital affair would certainly have met with disapproval from some members of the public, Eleanor was not the true target of the women's ire; most of the content of the letters were protesting the abandonment of Jacqueline of Hainault.

Although the political elite of England were relieved that Humphrey had abandoned the disastrous marriage, and the pope had declared the marriage null and void, many ordinary people in the realm viewed the poor treatment of Jacqueline as shocking and unchivalrous. She had been abandoned abroad, captured, made to give up her inheritance in all but name and, to many, it would have seemed that Humphrey had abandoned his rightful wife in favour of a mistress. Jacqueline had come to England as an honoured guest, and had been left used and forgotten. The fact that the letters were not addressed solely to Humphrey, but to other members of the ruling classes, and presented to Parliament, highlight that the real issue was not his marriage to Eleanor. Despite this protest, Jacqueline was still left to fight for herself without English help.

For Eleanor, however, life could hardly get better. At the age of around 28 – very late for a woman in her position – she had finally married, and to a Prince of England. With the king just 6 years old, and Humphrey's older brothers either dead or abroad, she was married to the most influential man in the land. While to the outside world, Humphrey was the bolshy, rash soldier who had married a foreign bride and tried to collect her inheritance, his new home with Eleanor was to be an outlet for his softer, intellectual side. They gathered their own court around them filled with poets, humanists, scholars and artists. Humphrey grew his famous library to hold hundreds of manuscripts, 280 of which he later donated to Oxford University, of which he was a patron.

Eleanor shared in Humphrey's zeal for learning and reading, although her inferior education as a woman and member of a lower class meant that she could not partake at the same level as Humphrey. While Humphrey corresponded with leading Italian humanists and read Latin, Eleanor had to make do with reading in English. To a lady of her new-found rank, however, this was of little obstacle, and the couple commissioned men to make translations of texts so that Eleanor could read them.

One such example is the only known book of Eleanor's to survive. This was a semi-medical, semi-astrological work which had been translated from Arabic. The book had been dedicated to Eleanor by Roger Bolingbroke, an Oxford scholar who would later have a far more menacing part in Eleanor's life. Humphrey was interested in medicine, having procured numerous medical books, and either Eleanor's interest in medicine was something she already held or she now cultivated it under her husband's influence. Indeed, Eleanor gave her husband a medical treatise that had been translated into Latin in 1198 called the '*Antidotarium*'. Despite their difference in rank and upbringing, Eleanor and Humphrey obviously shared a deep relationship on many levels. Their marriage was one of love, respect and shared interests.

John, Duke of Bedford, kneeling before St George, from the Bedford Book of Hours. (© British Library Board. All Rights Reserved/Bridgeman Images)

The marriage of Henry V of England and Catherine of Valois in 1420, from the *Chronique de Charles VII*. The marriage was a triumph for Henry as it secured his claim as King of France. (© British Library Board. All Rights Reserved/Bridgeman Images)

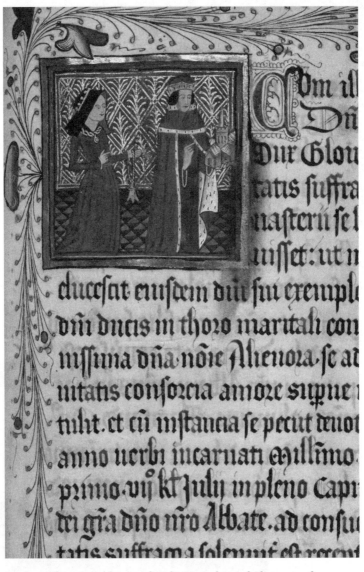

Duchess Eleanor Cobham and Duke Humphrey of Gloucester, from the *Liber Benefactorum* of St Albans. This is the only surviving image of Eleanor. (© British Library Board. All Rights Reserved/Bridgeman Images)

Opposite: The burial vault of Humphrey, Duke of Gloucester, in St Albans Abbey, rediscovered in the eighteenth century. (© the Cathedral and Abbey Church of St Alban)

Margaret of Anjou and Henry VI of England receiving a copy of the *Talbot Shrewsbury Book of Romances* from the author. (© British Library Board. All Rights Reserved/Bridgeman Images)

Edward IV of England, his wife, Elizabeth Woodville, and their son, Edward V, are seen to the right. Centre is Richard, Duke of Gloucester (the future Richard III), while kneeling is Anthony Woodville (Elizabeth's brother) in his armorial tabard, and the printer William Caxton. Anthony and Caxton are presenting the royal family with the first printed book in English, *Dictes and Sayings of the Philosophers*. (© Lambeth Palace Library, London, UK/Bridgeman Images)

A circular zodiacal lunar scheme taken from the *Guild Book of the Barber-Surgeons of the City of York* of the fifteenth century. Doctors were usually expected to consult astrological charts such as this before treating a patient. (© British Library Board. All Rights Reserved/ Bridgeman Images)

A portrait of Elizabeth Woodville dating to the late sixteenth century. Most portraits of Elizabeth Woodville from within a century of her death derive from a lost original believed to be painted during her life. (Royal Collection Trust/© Her Majesty Queen Elizabeth II, 2019)

A nineteenth-century etching of the tomb effigies of Joan of Navarre and Henry IV of England in Canterbury Cathedral. The effigies were commissioned by Joan and are believed to be accurate depictions of the couple at their deaths. (© The Trustees of the British Museum)

Leeds Castle, Kent, where both Joan of Navarre and Eleanor Cobham were held during their time as accused witches. (© Sarah Medway, provided courtesy of Leeds Castle)

6

FROM MISTRESS
TO PRINCESS

ALTHOUGH ELEANOR AND Humphrey's married life had started
with a protest by London women, the evidence suggests that personally, and in court circles, the marriage was well received. In 1429,
Queen Joan, who was now Eleanor's stepmother-in-law, showed her
approval of the match by giving Eleanor an extremely generous gift
which comprised of all the furnishings of her personal chapel.[1] Having
a personal chapel was a privilege of the higher classes in England and
was a chance to demonstrate one's piety. However, it also gave the
opportunity to demonstrate one's wealth, and as a Queen of England,
Joan's chapel was certainly one of the most impressive in the country. For Eleanor to be given such a generous gift not only reinforced
that Joan must have greatly approved of Humphrey's choice of wife,
but that she was trying to help secure Eleanor's new status at court.
It would have been an embarrassment to be one of the highest ladies
in the land and not have a suitably furnished private chapel for prayer.
As Eleanor was previously in no position to have many objects of her
own, and certainly not any form of chapel, her much lower status than
that of her husband would have been very apparent at court. Joan was
kindly giving Eleanor a secure basis on which to build her power and
reputation and adjust to life as the wife of a prince.

During the first few years of their marriage, the couple were mostly based in London, as Humphrey needed to be close to government. It was not long, however, until Eleanor and Humphrey decided to build up their own home in which to spend their lives together. In 1427, the year before their marriage, Humphrey had been gifted the manor of East Greenwich, and it was here that the couple chose to make their personal refuge.[2] With the manor came great swathes of land, and in January 1436 the couple were granted a licence to impark this land.[3] This meant that the 200 acres they were granted, which covered pasture, woodland, heath and gorse, was being made into private land to be used at their leisure only. As well as gaining permission to impark the land by their manor house, the order gave them a licence to crenellate – to enclose their manor with a stone wall – and also permission to erect a new stone tower in the park.

These were extraordinary grants, which demonstrated Humphrey's powerful position and allowed Humphrey and Eleanor to heavily fortify their manor house, as well as erect a castle on the grounds. There was certainly an excellent defensive aspect to the location of their new residence, with its proximity to the Thames and to the city, but it also provided excellent connections to the ports of the south. Humphrey was entering the height of his political power, and by building castles and fortifications, as well as a luxurious home for his wife and himself, he was putting this power on display for all to see. His enemies at court in London would indeed be casting a wary eye over towards Greenwich.

Eleanor and Humphrey set about vast works on the land in Greenwich to bring their vision to life. Evidence of what their residence looked like while they were there is difficult to piece together, particularly as it was significantly changed by Queen Margaret later in the century. Various excavations have given an insight into its extent, and records from the second half of the century and into the Tudor period show that their home was one of the finest in fifteenth-century England.[4]

Major work started shortly after, and soon construction also began on the castle tower out in the park, on top of a hill. The Royal Observatory that is on the site today was built upon the castle's surviving foundations. It consisted of a single large tower, and the basement walls which still stand today are over 1m thick, suggesting that the tower was of significant size. At 65m above sea level, the castle would have afforded excellent views across the surrounding land – as it does today – and was probably intended as a viewing platform for hunts that took place in the park. However, it is impossible to ignore the defensive significance of this fortification, and it certainly would have made Eleanor and Humphrey feel more secure.

Down by the river, work started on Eleanor and Humphrey's personal home, known as La Pleasaunce in their time. Sections excavated in 1970 suggest that it was at least two storeys high and was made of bricks arranged in English bond. Again, the use of bricks highlights the desire of the couple to impress society, demonstrate their political power and strengthen their position as forerunners of fashion at court. Manor houses and even palaces had always been made of timber and hitherto only Henry V's palace at Sheen, which had been built in 1413, had used brick in its structure. Choosing to build their palace out of brick showed that Eleanor and Humphrey intended the building and their position in society to last.

In terms of structure, the palace was impressive indeed. The building followed a courtyard plan, with a garden to the south and in close proximity to the river, affording pretty views and easy accessibility. It would have housed a chapel, which could possibly be where Eleanor chose to place the furnishings given to her by Joan. There was a gallery overlooking the garden and a great hall for gatherings and meals. This would have been supplied by a great larder and a kitchen complex which would have been staffed by a great number of servants and chefs in order to provide a sumptuous dining experience for the couple and their guests.

La Pleasaunce would have had a parlour for entertaining and would have been filled with bedrooms for guests. It also had a dovecote near a double gate which was close to the house. Evidence also suggests they may have had a bathroom in the palace which would have been supplied with running water and their own bathtub. In 1351, Edward III had paid for taps with a hot and cold water supply to his bathtub at Westminster Palace, and so it is quite possible that Eleanor and Humphrey's palace also contained this luxury.[5] In a grant from 1434, Humphrey and Eleanor were given permission to make an underground watercourse from his well in Greenwich to his park.[6] As well as supplying drinking water to the household, this may well have supplied water to the bathroom. It seems that there may also have been a second manor house as part of the complex, perhaps used as a guest residence.

The palace at Greenwich was certainly an impressive residence. With the castle on a hill, 200 acres of parkland, a large main residence and the possibility of a second mansion house, La Pleasaunce was unquestionably a kingly estate. The term 'the pleasaunce' or 'placentia' was used from the late fourteenth century onwards to denote a relatively intimate building detached from the main building ranges, intended to be used by a lord's favoured circle.[7] When looking at how Eleanor and Humphrey used their palace at Greenwich, it is easy to see how it took on this name. While the complex itself was definitely not small and intimate, the circle that they cultivated there most certainly was.

Records following Humphrey's movements are scarce, and so whether La Pleasaunce became the couple's main residence is difficult to know. However, those that do survive show that he visited it quite regularly and accounts from others suggest that the palace was well used by the couple and their circle.[8] Despite the obvious defensive aspects of the palace complex and the desire to impress, the evidence suggests that Eleanor and Humphrey always intended it to be used as an intellectual and leisurely retreat away from the difficult demands of courtly and political life. Henry IV had often resided at Greenwich, almost certainly accompanied by his queen, Joan, and his son, Humphrey. Perhaps the memories of these trips with his father and beloved stepmother are what inspired Humphrey to choose Greenwich as the location for his Pleasaunce.

Humphrey and Eleanor used La Pleasaunce as the basis for their intellectual court.[9] Both were dedicated to supporting the arts and intellectual pursuits, and it is clear that they intended to use La Pleasaunce as an intimate meeting place – and possibly providing support for the idea of a second manor house to cater for this intellectual court. Humphrey corresponded with Italian humanists and some came to visit and work for him, including Pietro del Monte, Tito Livio Frulovisi and Antonio Beccaria. All three men were well-known scholars. Monte was in England on behalf of the pope in order to raise money for the Church. Frulovisi most famously composed a biography of Henry V of England, but Humphrey also commissioned him to write a poem celebrating his own martial adventures. Beccaria became Humphrey's personal secretary from 1439 onwards, and he acted as a translator for him. One example is a copy of theological treatises, originally written in Greek, but translated by Beccaria into Latin at Humphrey's request.[10]

The couple's circle also included poets, such as John Lydgate, and scholars such as the Abbot of St Albans, John Whetamstede. Lydgate was one of the most prolific poets of his age, believed to have written around 150,000 lines of verse. Whetamstede, meanwhile, seems to have been a lifelong friend of Humphrey's. The two men appear to have studied at Oxford University together in the early 1400s, and their friendship lasted until Humphrey's death.[11] Whetamstede stayed mostly at the Abbey of St Albans, but Humphrey became a great patron of the establishment. Whetamstede had an interest in astronomy, astrology and foretelling the future, owning several manuscripts on the subjects. He also gifted books on the subject to Humphrey and his brother, Bedford.[12] Humphrey had an extraordinary number of connections with the leading intellectuals of his time, and he brought Eleanor into this world.

Eleanor and Humphrey presided over intellectual gatherings at La Pleasaunce with various members of their court, and it is clear that ideas were circulated and learning encouraged. In 1442, Humphrey commissioned a translation of *De re rustica*, and the author mentions in the prologue that Humphrey, his 'blessed lord', had gathered a group of humanists around him and had personally instructed the author on the art of poetry.[13] Between 1431 and 1438, while the couple were building up La Pleasaunce, Humphrey commissioned Lydgate to compose a huge poem, *The Fall of Princes*. Lydgate recounted how Humphrey actually closely supervised its writing and praised him for his love of learning.[14] It is possible that both of these pieces of writing had links to La Pleasaunce in some form.

With good transport links and proximity to the capital and the court, combined with the beauty of the vast enclosed park and the privacy it afforded, it is easy to see how Eleanor and Humphrey created an intellectual and cultural haven to which they could retreat. Indeed, Christmas 1428 – the couple's first together as husband and wife – was spent at Greenwich. Perhaps they were surveying the recently granted manor and its surroundings to assess its suitability as a base for their married life.

The next few years were spent consolidating their personal and political lives. In July 1431, Eleanor was received into the fraternity of St Albans Abbey.[15] This was a symbol of esteem and honour of religion, showing that the monks of the abbey considered Eleanor – along with Humphrey, who was already a member – a friend to the Church, and their abbey in particular. The *Book of Benefactors of the Abbey* records, 'that most serene Lady Eleanora ... touched by love for the heavenly realm, and urgently and piously asked to be admitted'. It also records that she gave a generous 10 marks to the monastery, and insisted that her parents, Reginald and Eleanor, as well as her brother were received into the fraternity.[16]

When Eleanor was welcomed into the fraternity, she also gifted them cloths of precious material, including altar cloths and vestments. One of the pieces was a tissue cloth of gold covered in images and interwoven pearls, and another was a tissue cloth of gold with red crimson velvet and a gold fringe. Other pieces were decorated with Humphrey's badges of suns, leopards, roses, ostrich feathers and Bohun swans.[17] These were highly sumptuous pieces that would have cost a significant amount of money and demonstrated Eleanor's wealth as Duchess of Gloucester.

The records of Eleanor's reception into the fraternity offer an interesting insight into her life from a positive source unaffected by the later accusations against her. Most records of Eleanor's character are in the wake of later accusations of her use of witchcraft and so are skewed against her. Of course, Eleanor and Humphrey had both been incredibly generous financially to the Abbey of St Albans, and the abbey would therefore want to describe them in a positive light, but the fact that Eleanor insisted on her family members also joining the fraternity suggests that she did indeed hold the abbey in high esteem.

In fact, Eleanor may have had a closer connection to the abbey than it just being a favoured place of her husband; apparently at one time she was suffering from extreme toothache, and she prayed at the shrine of St Alban at the cathedral and was miraculously cured. As thanks, she and Humphrey sent a tooth made of gold to be hung at the shrine.[18] This suggests that Eleanor was perhaps a quietly religious person; while there are no suggestions that she was overly pious, she clearly held an affinity for St Albans Abbey, sharing in her husband's fondness for it, and perhaps Joan's gift of her chapel was well used by Eleanor and not merely a status symbol. She was clearly well regarded by the abbey, and there is nothing to suggest that this is just because she gave them money and was married to another of their benefactors – the Church obviously considered her a kind and intelligent lady.

While the couple were busy making plans for their home at Greenwich, Humphrey continued to expand his power base and influence at court. Humphrey's greatest rival was his uncle, Cardinal Beaufort. Beaufort was a son of John of Gaunt, Humphrey's grandfather, and Gaunt's mistress, Katherine Swynford. Born in the 1370s, Beaufort had been legitimised after his parents' marriage, but was barred from inheriting the throne. He therefore took to religious life, but after his half-brother Henry IV took the throne in 1399 he was made Lord Chancellor of England. Through the reigns of Henry IV and Henry V he continued to hold great political power, and upon the death of Henry V, Beaufort formed part of the regency government of Henry VI alongside Humphrey and Bedford. After Beaufort and Humphrey's clash over the attempted release of Friar Randolph, Beaufort had been forced to resign from his position as Chancellor, and the two men continued to jostle for power at court. Although tensions had eased somewhat after this event, hostilities had continued to rumble beneath the surface, and both men continued to seize any opportunity to injure the other.

In 1432, Humphrey caught Beaufort secretly transporting treasure to Calais without a licence to export gold.[19] Licences were required for importing and exporting goods, so that the Crown – or those they had gifted with customs revenues as patronage – could profit financially from trade at ports. By transporting this gold in secret, Beaufort was pocketing the money that he was avoiding paying in fees. Humphrey had the ship seized and used this scandal as an excuse to dismiss all of Beaufort's supporters from office, thus eliminating some of Beaufort's power base, and creating the opportunity to reward his own loyal followers.[20] As Beaufort was no longer a threat, Humphrey spent the next few years on a high. His power was largely unchallenged at court and he was able to focus on his private life with Eleanor while continuing to cultivate a good relationship with his nephew, Henry VI, to ensure the survival of his power when Henry came into his majority.

In 1432, it seems Eleanor was given the robes of the Ladies of the Garter, a prestigious honour.[21] The Order of the Garter had been created the previous century by Edward III as an attempt to revive the legendary King Arthur's Round Table. The order was focused on chivalric love, and women were a central part of this – in fact, it was a woman, the Countess of Salisbury, who was supposedly the inspiration for the creation of the order. Under Richard II, however, women took a far more official role. He gave many distinguished women robes and hoods ornamented with garters that matched the quality and expense of the male members of the order. The women were also given the same rights as the men to wear a garter with the motto of the order.

However, after Richard II's reign, hardly any women were given the honour of membership. Queen Joan had been given the robes of the order in 1405 after she married Henry IV, but relatively few other women received the robes during his reign or that of his son. During the childhood of Henry VI, the only new woman to join the Ladies of the Garter was Humphrey's first wife, Jacqueline, who received her robes in 1423. It was necessary to extend her this honour as not only had her mother been a Lady of the Garter, her position as duchess and guest of the court afforded her this respect. However, after Jacqueline received her robes no woman was given them for the Feast of St George until 1432.

In May 1432, the Countess of Warwick and the Countess of Suffolk received their robes.[22] Just prior to this, at the end of March, it is believed Eleanor had been given hers. Eleanor's receipt of the garter robes was the first public recognition of her position as Duchess of Gloucester and the wife of one of the princes of the realm. It is interesting that it took so many years after their marriage for Eleanor to receive her robes, when Jacqueline had been given hers so soon after her arrival in England. This may have been as a slight on Eleanor's previous social position, and the view of her as a social upstart and unworthy of such a prestigious honour; after all, Jacqueline had held the position of duchess in her own right, was related to royalty and had the rights of a sovereign ruler (even if these rights were not quite enforced at that time). That Eleanor probably received the robes at the same time that

Humphrey successfully removed his rival, Beaufort, from power is perhaps no coincidence – it reflects Humphrey's power at this time and would have been a public confirmation that Eleanor was his lawful wife and should be treated with the respect she deserved.

Eleanor's receipt of the robes was also a slight on the authority of Humphrey's brother, Bedford. Bedford's wife, Anne of Burgundy, who died in 1432, had never been given the honour of receiving the robes of the garter. Meanwhile, Bedford's second wife, Jacquetta of Luxembourg, received her robes a year or two after her marriage to Bedford, either in 1434 or 1435.[23] Humphrey's wife being given the honour when his older brother's wives were not is certainly interesting, and it was perhaps an attempt by Humphrey to affirm his power in England while his brother was busy in France. That Jacquetta perhaps received her robes for the St George's Feast of 1434, the first one that Bedford was present for after his return to England the previous year, was possibly Bedford's attempt to reassert his power in England and emphasise his position above that of his younger brother.

Fate seemed to be on Humphrey's side, as the year of 1435 saw his power climb to even greater heights. In September, his last surviving brother, the Duke of Bedford, died, leaving Humphrey as Henry VI's heir presumptive. As was his legitimate right, Humphrey claimed regency of Henry VI as his most senior relative, but the Royal Council were wary of Humphrey's already vast power and were loath to give him almost unrestricted power and so this was blocked. Nonetheless, while gaining the regency would have given him greater official powers, in reality Humphrey now became the most powerful man in the country. Henry was still only 13 years old, and although he was becoming more involved in political decisions he still very much deferred to the guidance of his counsellors – particularly Humphrey. Moreover, Henry was not particularly interested in politics, and as his later mental health instabilities and personality characteristics were to show, he was not at all capable of ruling in any case. It was obvious that his uncle, who was now 45 years old and extremely experienced in the machinations of government, the court and politics, would take control.

Humphrey took this opportunity to confirm the position of his beloved wife, Eleanor. After Humphrey consolidated his power and secured his position following Bedford's death, he turned his attention to ensuring that Eleanor would be looked after in the event of his death. Thus, two months later in November he gave Eleanor a jointure in his whole estate, which would more than provide for her after he was gone; if Humphrey were to predecease Eleanor, and they did not have any children, she was given the privilege of enjoying all of his properties for life, which would make her one of the richest people in the country.[24] She would be able to enjoy the profits after Humphrey's death until her own, and this was a legal right that could only be taken away from her under extreme circumstances such as treason.

Humphrey's grant demonstrates just how deeply he loved Eleanor. It was customary for widows in England to receive a third of the lands and monetary income of their husbands after their death. True, Humphrey did not have a legitimate heir to give his estates to, and all of his brothers were dead. However, he could have gifted vast swathes to religious institutions, or to Oxford University, of which he was so fond. He was securing Eleanor's future when he was no longer there to protect her.

Humphrey also ensured that Eleanor's father was looked after. In 1436, Reginald Cobham was given the custody of Charles d'Orléans.[25] Orléans had been captured by the English at the Battle of Agincourt in 1415 and had been a prisoner ever since. Orléans was still considered an important political prisoner by the English, so for Reginald to be entrusted with his custody showed that Humphrey thought highly enough of him – or at least his daughter – to give him this responsibility. Orléans was kept by Reginald in Eleanor's birth home of Sterborough Castle for two years, until he was given over to Sir John Stourton.

Eleanor herself was enjoying the privileges afford to her as Duchess of Gloucester. She was living a luxurious life, leading a cultural court most likely based at La Pleasaunce, cultivating a good reputation with the Abbey of St Albans, and was loved by the citizens of the realm. All of Humphrey's popularity was reflected on her as his wife – she had no hint of scandal, and it was clear the couple loved each other dearly, and so those who loved Humphrey had no reason not to cherish Eleanor.

It is clear that people of the realm also considered Eleanor as someone who held influence at court. From 1435 onwards, Eleanor is found named in several requests for intercession. If a person wished to receive a pardon or favour for themselves, a friend or family member, they would write to someone who held power at court in the hope they would intercede on their behalf. In Letters Patent from 1435 to 1436, Eleanor is named alongside Humphrey in requests for pardons.[26] In 1437, Eleanor was written to by Katherine Hiperon, wife of a glover from York, who requested that Eleanor intercede with the Chancellor to enable her husband John to proceed in the Chancery against those who had falsely indicted him.[27]

That Katherine chose to write to Eleanor, and Eleanor alone, showed that, at least among the common folk of the kingdom, it was believed that Eleanor was one of the most powerful people in the country and someone who could get things done. Whether this was the reality or not is up for debate but considering Eleanor's position as wife to the heir of the kingdom and a close friend and relation of the king, it is likely that she did hold the influence necessary to procure favours for people.

Certainly, Eleanor and Humphrey were doing well to maintain power by cultivating a good relationship with the young King Henry VI. Now that Humphrey had curbed the power of Beaufort once more, Henry continued to rely on Humphrey's advice in running the kingdom, and as Henry remained in his minority until 1437 when he turned 16, Humphrey continued to be one of the most powerful men in the land through his position as Protector of England. When looking at Henry's New Year gifts of 1436–37, his favour to the young couple is evident; he gave them the finest and most expensive gifts of all those he presented that year.[28] Humphrey received a tablet of gold hung from three chains with an image of the Virgin Mary which was embellished with six gems, 'count(er)faitz in mane(r) of diamond', six sapphires and over 150 pearls. The tablet had previously belonged to Henry himself and was therefore a symbol of his affection for his uncle.

Eleanor received an equally illustrious gift, a brooch made of gold in the shape of a man, garnished with a variety of gems including a 'gret diamond', rubies and pearls. This gift for Eleanor had been bought from a goldsmith especially for her to the cost of £40, an extraordinary amount – at this time, £40 was the annual income for many prosperous members of the gentry.

Eleanor and Humphrey spent the holiday at their palace in Greenwich, but probably saw Henry at some time over the festive period. Queen Joan was also included in the festivities, although she spent the holiday at Langley. Joan was given a gold tablet garnished with pearls with a large sapphire in the middle. The record notes that this tablet had previously been given to King Henry by Eleanor. This is not a slight on Eleanor's gift – re-gifting was common at court, particularly when the king received so many fine gifts – but it does show that Eleanor herself held great wealth to be able to give such a fine gift to the king, especially one deemed good enough to pass on to a former Queen of England. It also shows that Eleanor, Humphrey, Joan and Henry all moved in the same circles and were the highest people on the list of gifts. They were all highly regarded by Henry, and the respect shown to them is reflected in the gifts they received. It also shows another interaction between Joan and Eleanor – which may potentially have influenced later proceedings against Eleanor.

Humphrey, as well as holding immense power at court, was continuing to garner the favour of commoners and nobles alike. In 1436, Philip of Burgundy reneged on his alliance with the English and attacked Calais. Humphrey was appointed garrison commander and he won a huge victory. When he returned to England, his victory had done much to restore English morale and pride in both their own position and the fight for the French throne. He was congratulated personally by Parliament the following March, and his already popular status among the commoners of the kingdom was confirmed. Going into 1437, therefore, not only was Humphrey one of the most powerful men in the land, he was one of the most revered. Unlike his grandfather, John of Gaunt, who was hated and mistrusted for his power, Humphrey had courted favour from all levels of society and was trusted in his position as Protector of the Kingdom.

Humphrey's position as virtual ruler of the kingdom was clear to see throughout 1437. His name crops up time and again in official records, and a special room was set apart in Westminster Hall for himself and his council.[29] Although Henry came into his majority this year, he clearly still relied on Humphrey for advice, particularly as Henry was ill equipped for ruling, being shy, pious and adverse to bloodshed. However, Henry also relied heavily on the council of Cardinal Beaufort who, to Humphrey's dismay, had started to regain favour at court. Beaufort was largely indispensable at court, having regularly lent money to the Crown during times of need, and Henry would have been mindful of not wanting to alienate a powerful family member.[30]

Nonetheless, Humphrey felt secure enough in his position not to worry about the idle threat of Beaufort, whom he had continually rebuffed and had outgrown in power. Beaufort had never managed to truly damage his position and so he must have thought that he was untouchable. This was, with the benefit of hindsight, dangerous; while many at court favoured Humphrey, particularly after his huge victory in France the previous year, there was still a significant faction under Beaufort who would want to take any opportunity to undermine him. Moreover, Humphrey's old-fashioned policies, shaped by the great victories of the English during the reigns of his brother and father, were becoming increasingly unpopular with those in power, who were starting to consider making peace with France.

This struggle for power between Humphrey and Beaufort and the shifting sands of fortune for Humphrey became increasingly evident at the end of the 1430s. In 1439, Beaufort – once again in the good graces of the court – had spent several months negotiating with French envoys to try and conclude peace, finally drawing the Hundred Years War to an end. However, English demands were far too steep and eventually negotiations were broken off. As a result, Beaufort suggested the release of that long-term captive, the Duke of Orléans, as a way to placate the French. For Humphrey, who had been witness to the great English victories of Agincourt and the Treaty of Troyes, giving up a man who had long been viewed as a vital prisoner was unthinkable.

Reviving the charges and complaints against Beaufort that he had submitted after their clash over Friar Randolph in 1426, Humphrey published a document in 1440 which he put on record in the Patent Rolls of government which strongly argued against the release of Orléans.[31] The purpose of the document was twofold: firstly, an attempt to prevent the release of Orléans – who, in reality, by this point was of little interest to the French – but secondly to try and remove Beaufort from power once again. He vehemently attacked Beaufort for his ambition, poor advice to Henry VI and overall contemptible behaviour. Humphrey accused Beaufort of defrauding money from the king, ruining the kingdom for his own benefit and alienating good men from court.

This document, for Humphrey, although he did not know it at the time, was very much an example of winning the battle but losing the war. Henry sided with Beaufort and agreed to release Orléans (which, in the end, did nothing to help the situation in France) but the charges levied against Beaufort, while not acted upon by the council, were enough to reduce Beaufort's influence at court, causing him once again to lose his position of power and authority. While Humphrey had not been successful in persuading Henry of his point of view, the next entry in the Patent Rolls demonstrated that Humphrey still held great popularity with the Commons of England and reflected their opinions.

The Crown now published a document justifying the release of Orléans, listing Henry's numerous reasons for agreeing to the release.[32] This is quite a significant document – it was not often that medieval kings were required to justify a political decision to the public unless they were asking Parliament for money, and this suggests that there must have been great public outcry at Orléans' release. Part of this outcry will have been because many people of the realm would have held similar idealised views of past English victories as Humphrey, and would not want to make concessions to France – especially considering Humphrey's recent spectacular victory. However, it cannot be ignored that Humphrey's very public attack of the decision must have inspired the Commons and demonstrates just how much political influence he held.

Humphrey had again been temporarily successful in removing Beaufort from court but, in reality, he had just signed his own downfall. With Beaufort gone, William de la Pole, the Earl of Suffolk, began to fill his place and swiftly gained influence over Henry VI and the court. William simply took the place of Beaufort as Humphrey's antagonist, and – as will be seen – most likely conspired with Beaufort to orchestrate Humphrey's demise. It would be Eleanor who would initially take the greatest blow of this feud.

In the meantime, however, Eleanor remained high in Henry VI's esteem. For the New Year of 1440, Eleanor received a gift from Henry of a garter of gold, barred with bars of gold, inscribed with the motto of the Order of the Garter – '*hony soit qui mal y pense* [shame on him who thinks ill of it]' – in gold letters, and garnished with 'a flower of Diamonds on the Buckle, and two great Pearls and a Ruby on the Pendant and two great Pearls with twenty-six Pearls on the said Garter'.[33] This was clearly an extremely sumptuous gift that would have cost a fortune and demonstrates that Eleanor must have been one of the closest and most liked people surrounding King Henry.

On 28 June 1441, Eleanor rode through the city of London with a train of lords and magnates in '*splendidissimo apparatu* [the most splendid attire]'.[34] Some of the greatest and most powerful men in the land were following this illustrious duchess. Eleanor was currently the most powerful woman in the realm, as Henry VI was unmarried and his mother and Queen Joan had both died. She was the wife of the heir to the kingdom, at a time when the young king seemed unwilling to take full control of the government. She was beautiful, clever and charming, she had a devoted husband, as much wealth as she could desire and the common people of the kingdom adored both her and her husband. She had reached the pinnacle of her life and seemed untouchable. By the end of the year, however, everything had been taken from her and she was a broken woman who would never recover. Such was the turning of the wheel of fortune.

7

THE DUCHESS AND
THE WITCH OF EYE

AT THE END of June 1441, Eleanor Cobham, Duchess of Gloucester, had entered London in a parade most fitting her status as highest lady of the land. Later, writers would criticise this display of power so close to her downfall, using it as evidence of Eleanor's haughty pride that meant she deserved her comeuppance.[1] However, Eleanor was one of the most powerful people in the land and she deserved such a retinue to follow her into the capital.

It is possible that Eleanor had arrived in the capital to watch the Marching Watch, a midsummer highlight in medieval towns, particularly London. The Marching Watch was a glorified spectacle where soldiers, police patrols and city constables would march through the main streets. The earliest watches dated to the thirteenth century in order to 'watch' for midsummer fires, but by Eleanor's time it was a special event where watchmen would look out for trouble and particularly look after the houses of the rich, looking out for thieves and other troublemakers.[2] The Marching Watch was particularly important to Londoners as a demonstration to the monarch that they were capable of maintaining law and order – the worry being that if order was not kept, the king would suspend the liberties of the growing mercantile class of London.

That Eleanor had gone to London to watch this popular spectacle is suggested by an anonymous chronicle of Henry VI, which claims that Eleanor was at supper at the King's Head in Cheap when she learnt of the indictment against her.[3] Charles Lethbridge Kingsford, in his annotation of the chronicle, goes on to state that she was arrested at this supper on 25 June, but this information is false, as Eleanor was not arrested and had not in fact entered London at this point. However, it is still possible that the information was half-correct, and Eleanor was indeed dining at the King's Head just prior to the devastating events she was to be thrust into.

The King's Head, previously known as the Crown Seld, was a stone gallery that had been built by Edward III for 'the Kings of England and other great Estates, therein to behold the shows of the City'.[4] Some historians have used the idea that Eleanor viewed the Marching Watch from this platform as evidence of contemporary assertions that she was too full of pride and was overstepping her position.[5] However, as the highest lady in the land and wife to the heir of the kingdom, she was perfectly within her rights to use the Seld to view the procession – she may even have been invited there by Henry himself which, considering his fondness for her, was more than likely.

If Eleanor did indeed enjoy this spectacle from the royal comforts of the King's Head, it was probably the last great event she enjoyed. On 10 July, an order had been issued to the Constable of the Tower of London to receive a prisoner on behalf of the king, a man named Master Thomas Suthwelle [Southwell].[6] This appears to have gone unnoticed by Eleanor and Humphrey, despite the fact it is likely that Thomas was Eleanor's personal physician.[7] Thomas was a learned, religious man. He had studied at Oxford University during 1406–07 and again in 1418–19, finally graduating in medicine in 1423, and by 1428 he had been awarded some prominent positions. From 1428 to 1440 he was Rector of St Stephen's Walbrook Church in London, but more importantly in 1428 he had become a Canon of St George's Chapel at Windsor Castle. A canon was a part-time position given as a reward by the monarch to their most trusted servants, showing the trust already placed in Thomas.

Thomas served in this position until July 1431, at which point he had obviously ingratiated himself further with the royal family; this same month he moved from Windsor Castle to St Stephen's Chapel in the Palace of Westminster.[8] The chapel had been completed around 1297 and the finished product was two storeys, the Upper Chapel reserved solely for the royal family, while the Lower Chapel was open to use by the royal household and courtiers. The previous century, in 1382, King Richard II married his bride, Anne of Bohemia, in the chapel. To be a canon in these royal chapels was an honour, and it is clear he was trusted by royalty. The combination of his proximity to Eleanor through the royal chapel and his qualification in medicine suggests that the idea that he was Eleanor's personal physician is not too far-fetched. Thomas was still in this position as canon at Westminster when the prisoner warrant was issued – quite remarkable, considering his status.

On a Sunday not long after Thomas' internment at the Tower of London, almost certainly on 23 July, another man named Master Roger Bolingbroke was put on display upon a scaffold in London, at St Paul's Cross.[9] St Paul's Cross was an open-air pulpit in the grounds of Old St Paul's Cathedral and an important meeting place in the city. It was where important messages could be dispersed among the Commons – often including the public display of criminals. It was for this reason that Roger was put on display.

Roger was placed high on a stage, sitting on a painted chair that had four swords standing on its four corners, with an image of copper hanging from each sword. He was surrounded by instruments of '*nigra-mancie*' – today known as necromancy – including images of silver, wax and other metals. He was holding a sword in his right hand and a sceptre in his left and had been given a paper crown to wear. Here, he recounted all that 'he had doon and wrought by the devyll and his powere'.[10] Present were the Archbishop of Canterbury, Cardinal Beaufort, the Bishops of London, Salisbury and Winchester, as well as temporal lords including Huntingdon, Northumberland, Stafford, lords of the King's Council, the mayor and aldermen of London and commons of the city. This was clearly an impressive list of men, all of whom held great power across the country and particularly in government. This was intended to be a spectacle for the entire land to see and was obviously going to be a significant event.

No formal charges of any crimes had yet been brought against Roger, but this event was clearly indicating his guilt; that is certainly how the commons who were present would have seen it. In medieval and Tudor England, criminals were often put on display in front of crowds with objects that represented their crimes – this was to send a clear message to the largely illiterate masses showing the crime the person had been guilty of committing.[11] This would only happen after the person had been found guilty, however – therefore, those present at the event would have understood that Roger was undeniably guilty of using evil sorcery.

As with Thomas, Roger was no inconsequential man, and these two events make it easy to see that a high-profile attack was stirring. It appears Roger may have been a member of Humphrey's household and Eleanor's personal clerk.[12] He was an Oxford priest and scholar, and by the late 1430s he was acting as principal of St Andrew Hall, Oxford. In the later official indictment against him, he is described as being a gentleman of London and a clerk. Roger was certainly renowned for his scholarly abilities – indeed, the chronicler William Worcester proclaimed that Roger was 'the most famous in the whole world in astronomy and the art of necromancy'.[13] This reputation was now to work against him, as it made him an easy scapegoat for accusations.

Once news had reached Eleanor of what had happened to Roger, either later that day or during the next day, she realised that something big was about to happen and wisely fled to sanctuary in Westminster Abbey.[14] At this time, sanctuary could be claimed by criminals or the persecuted in order to protect them from temporal law – churches were considered holy, consecrated places and no force was to be used in them (though in practice this was not always respected). As such, someone claiming sanctuary could not be forcibly removed by the government to be tried for their crimes. Usually sanctuary was only to be claimed for forty days, until a settlement could be reached, but large sanctuaries such as Westminster Abbey had the facilities to house claimants indefinitely.

Eleanor was wise indeed to flee for sanctuary, and this may well have saved her life, but it could not protect her completely. After Roger's display at St Paul's Cross, he had been examined before the King's Council where he admitted using nigromancy – conjuring spirits of the dead in order to prophecy – under orders from Eleanor. He said that Eleanor wanted to have her fortune cast in order to know 'if sho shulde comme to eny hier degree and astate then that sho wasse in'.[15] This essentially meant that Roger had claimed that Eleanor had asked him to prophesy the future to see if she would obtain any higher estate (position) than she currently had. As mentioned, Eleanor was currently the highest lady in the land and the only possible higher position was for her to become queen. Eleanor could only become queen if Henry VI died and her husband Humphrey became king. The implications of this were tentatively treasonous, as it was inquiring into the illness or possible death of the monarch. While not specifically treasonous, the worry would be that those involved may be encouraged to fulfil the prophecy themselves – of which, as it will be seen, they were indeed accused.

Roger was not the only witness against Eleanor's alleged crimes, however. Thomas Southwell, who was by now in the Tower of London, was accused of celebrating a heretical mass in order to aid Roger in conspiring for the death of the king. Considering his intimate access to Eleanor and the king, he would have been in a position to follow her orders and to potentially endanger him. Clearly, he was an important witness to the case.

Another man, John Home, was charged as an accessory to Roger and Thomas' acts. John was also a canon – of Hereford (since 1433) and St Asaph, Wales – and he had a very personal connection to both Eleanor and Humphrey, having acted as a secretary for them both. He was tied even closer to Eleanor as he was her personal chaplain.[16] It is interesting here to note the similarities with Joan's case in charging both women's personal chaplains. These would have been the men who were in charge of the women's spiritual lives and thus in a good position to know their misdeeds, particularly spiritual ones such as witchcraft. Finally, a woman was brought in to the accusations. This was a lady called Margery Jourdemaine, named in various chronicles as 'The Witch of Eye Next Westminster', and she was also charged with conspiring to bring about the king's death through sorcery.[17]

Two days after Roger's display, on 25 July, Eleanor was brought before the bishops of the King's Council.[18] Unfortunately for Eleanor, all of the accusations brought by her supposed co-conspirators involved witchcraft and heresy – acts which came under ecclesiastical law. In medieval law, there were two forms of crimes and courts: temporal and ecclesiastical. While temporal law was organised by the government and dealt with ordinary crimes such as theft, murder and debts, ecclesiastical law dealt with religious and spiritual matters. This could include slander, marriage annulments (or enforcements), moral crimes such as adultery and, as in this case, witchcraft. Performing witchcraft was not necessarily a crime under temporal law. Generally, if the witchcraft was not harmful, local authorities would turn a blind eye to practitioners. However, harmful forms of witchcraft would be investigated by the Church as it was tied to heresy due to its un-Christian nature and links with the devil. Eleanor could therefore be tried by the Church for her sorcery, even if she was safe from temporal law in sanctuary.

The Archbishop of Canterbury, Henry Chichele, decided that Eleanor was to be tried for her alleged crimes. He recommended that for her security she should be detained at Leeds Castle. Henry VI agreed to this and declared that she was to be kept there until the end of September, to reappear before the archbishop on 1 October. This did not change Eleanor's status under sanctuary, as the privileges of it were still to extend to her during her time there. Henry ordered that no one was to 'attempt anything against Eleanor or take her person or goods during the said cause, but that she abide peaceably'.[19]

Eleanor must surely have been aware that Leeds Castle had been home to Queen Joan during her own imprisonment for heinous witchcraft. If Joan had not spoken about it to Eleanor herself, then it is to be remembered that Eleanor was 20 years old when Joan was sent to the castle. She must have heard news of it at the time, particularly as she may have already been serving at court during Joan's imprisonment. This must have been a sore reminder for Eleanor. She would have known very well that she was not going to come out of these accusations as well as Joan did.

In October, Eleanor duly returned to London. Archbishop Chichele excused himself from proceedings, which was a remarkable turn of events. As the highest member of the Church in England, the archbishop was the best person to oversee the trial against her. In all likelihood, Joan's case two decades previously impacted heavily on this decision. He had clearly known back then that the charges against Joan were fabricated, shown by his visits to her, but he had turned a blind eye knowing she was never in danger. Now, however, it was clear that Eleanor was in real danger for her life, as were numerous other potentially innocent people.

Chichele was nearly 80 years old and by now would hardly want to be a part of such a vicious attack. There is every indication that he was good friends with Eleanor and Humphrey, and so morally he probably also found it impossible to prosecute the woman whom he knew to be friendly, religious and charming. One would have thought that as their friend, he would want to stay close to proceedings to try and protect Eleanor. However, he may well have realised that the powers working against Eleanor were too strong for him to protect her, and so with sadness stepped away.

The trusted bishops of the King's Council were thus chosen to deal with such a significant matter and this included the Archbishop of York as well as Cardinal Beaufort. Eleanor was examined in St Stephen's Chapel in Westminster Palace under eighteen charges of felony and treason, and she shrewdly denied all the charges. The location of her questioning is certainly telling of the enormity of the event. She was still in a holy place protected by sanctuary, but she had been moved from her original place of refuge to the king's own chapel – and one which she would have used plenty of times herself. Of course, Thomas Southwell was also canon of the chapel, and one wonders whether this played any bearing in the choice of location. Largely, though, the chapel was the ideal place as it exuded royal authority and would have allowed Henry and those at court to keep a close eye on proceedings.

Eleanor would have been very aware that all eyes were on her, and the power of the location must have been frightening. Despite her initial denial of the charges, the following day Roger was brought in to testify as a witness and after his evidence Eleanor confessed to five of the charges. Some historians have criticised Eleanor for indulging any of the accusations at all, but in fact at every turn she chose the wisest possible course of action.[20] Denying the accusations altogether, when such overwhelming evidence was being produced against her – particularly numerous eyewitnesses who were prepared to prove her guilt – would surely have done little to save her. However, when looking at how Eleanor spun the charges, she almost certainly saved herself again.

The figures that had been put on display at St Paul's alongside Roger were being used as evidence of Eleanor engaging in and encouraging the use of image magic in order to procure the death of King Henry VI. Eleanor instead argued that the figures were not at all intended to kill the king, but that she and Margery had used them in rituals of love magic. This love magic, Eleanor said, was first used in order to induce Humphrey to fall in love with and marry her and secondly in order to help her bear his child.[21] This is also significant evidence that Humphrey's two illegitimate children were not Eleanor's – if she had already had his children prior to their marriage, she would have no need for potions.

This claim was not so far-fetched, and in fact it is perhaps possible that Eleanor did indeed solicit the services of Margery, certainly at least to help with her fertility problems. Margery's husband and his family were prosperous Middlesex yeomen, so while she was of a respectable family, she was certainly not close to significant status – even Eleanor's original position as daughter of a knight was far higher than Margery's.

However, Margery somehow became involved in circles of sorcery and educated men. In the early 1430s, Margery had been accused of using witchcraft; on 9 May 1432, a record in the Proceedings of the Privy Council states that Margery, a male clerk and a friar, 'who had been committed to Windsor Castle for sorcery … should be discharged on finding security for their good behaviour, and that the former [Margery] should likewise be released on her husband's security'.[22] Here, ten years previously, then, Margery is found involved with clerks and men of religion under practices of witchcraft – remarkably similar to these later accusations.

The nature of the sorcery Margery had been involved in during the early 1430s is unknown, but with many cases of witchcraft those found guilty were released, often without penalty, on the proviso of never again engaging in the art – and those who did would find much harsher penalties waiting. It has been posited by many, considering Margery's obviously prolific reputation (judging by her common name in the chronicles) and using Eleanor's confession, that Margery was a sorceress often called upon by noblewomen at court.[23] Evidence for this does not exist, but this is not an unlikely scenario given the situation with Eleanor.

If Margery was indeed a known witch used by women at court, it would explain why she was included in the charges – why else would Humphrey and Eleanor's enemies need to bring in a lower-class woman when they had several educated and reliable men to testify against Eleanor? It would lend credibility to the public that Eleanor had indeed indulged in the charges levied against her. As mentioned, it is possible that Eleanor had in fact used Margery to try and conceive a child with Humphrey. Eleanor may well have been desperate to have a child by Humphrey, thus providing him with his much-needed heir and securing her marriage to him. She may well have been affected by how easily Jaqueline had been tossed aside after she failed to provide Humphrey with an heir and she may have been conscious of the fact that by being the one to give him a legitimate child, her position would be secure – Humphrey would not want to annul a marriage that would then de-legitimise his heir. If these were thoughts that went through Eleanor's mind (and it is almost certain that they did), and Margery was indeed a witch known by ladies at court, then she may well have solicited Margery for the services that she claimed. Of course, if she had used Margery for this purpose, she had not committed a crime under either ecclesiastical or temporal law.

Whether Eleanor had used Margery for love magic or not was ultimately inconsequential – it was certainly a very clever way to defend herself against the extremely serious charge of treason. In the meantime, a temporal commission had been created to deal with the charges against the three men, Margery and Eleanor.[24] Many high-status lords of the land and the King's Council were brought in to preside over such a prominent case. Notably, William de la Pole, the Earl of Suffolk, was appointed as its head. It is certainly striking that at every point of these events, Humphrey's two great enemies, Beaufort and Suffolk, were present. While their high positions in the land gave them the right to be involved in such notorious proceedings, their constant insertion at the highest levels shows how they were orchestrating events.

The commission indicted Roger, Thomas, John and Margery for treason, and Eleanor was charged as an accessory. However, Eleanor shrewdly refused to submit to the authority of the commission as she was still under sanctuary regardless of the questioning by the bishops. Despite Suffolk's best efforts, it was not possible to extract

Eleanor from sanctuary. With such a high-profile case, they could not be seen to be breaking the sacred promise of sanctuary, especially against a woman.

The results of the commission were as expected. All were found guilty, and severe punishments in line with such a horrid crime were imposed. Roger and Thomas were both sentenced to a traitor's death – hanged, drawn and quartered – while Margery was sentenced to being burnt at the stake.[25] Margery's punishment was different because by engaging in sorcery again – even if just using the love magic that Eleanor had admitted to – she was considered a relapsed heretic by the Church. She had broken her abjuration of the art in 1432. This called for a heretic's death by burning. Thus, on 27 October, Margery was burnt at Smithfield.

Roger suffered his traitor's death on 18 November but on the scaffold he professed his innocence, claiming that he had never engaged in any of the accused acts.[26] His head was put on London Bridge and his body parts scattered to Hertford, Oxford, York and Cambridge. Thomas escaped the gruesome execution by dying – supposedly of sorrow – in the Tower before he could be put to death.[27] Intriguingly, John Home was given a pardon and thus escaped execution. This certainly seems to indicate that the accusations were fabricated – why else would they pardon one of the traitors?

Considering the fate of her alleged accomplices, the situation was clearly dire for Eleanor. She could only hope that her residence in sanctuary and her position as wife of the heir would save her from a traitor's death. It must have been a terrifying wait for her. Astonishingly, there are no records of what Humphrey was doing at this time. One would assume that he would be doing everything in his power to protect his beloved wife, on whom he had so clearly doted over the past fifteen years. But no record survives of him appealing to king and council, no chronicle mentions him at all, let alone records him working and pleading to save Eleanor. It is as if he had all but vanished.

Perhaps he was so overcome with shock and grief that he did not know what to do. Perhaps he could see how cleverly Beaufort and Suffolk had planned everything, the overwhelming evidence being presented against Eleanor, the sheer weight of power against the two of them, and felt helpless. Perhaps he worried that if he defended his wife, he would be dragged into these serious accusations. But surely he cannot have left her all alone? Surely he must have appealed to Henry, even in private, and tried to persuade him that his wife, Henry's beloved aunt, would never try to harm him, let alone kill him? But all we have are questions. The man himself remains silent.

8

ALLE WOMEN MAY
BEWARE BY ME

AT THE BEGINNING of November 1441, Eleanor Cobham, Duchess of Gloucester, was completely alone. She was in sanctuary with not a friend in the world, being held under suspicion of attempting to kill the king through witchcraft, her husband having seemingly vanished and all of her servants and followers denied to her. While Joan of Navarre had recovered spectacularly from her accusations, Eleanor would have been acutely aware that this was an entirely different situation and she would not have a fairy-tale ending. It was now a matter of just how bad the punishment was going to be. Had she heard of Margery's burning a few days previously?

She did not have long to wait. Now that the punishment for her accomplices had all been decided, Humphrey's enemies turned to Eleanor. The decision of what to do with her was remarkably tricky – Eleanor had at least made things difficult for them. Although they had tried to convict her as an accessory, she was unable to be tried because of her protection in sanctuary and because there was no precedent for how to try a woman of her rank. She had been found guilty of using witchcraft by the bishops of the King's Council but, as previously seen, this was not an offence worthy of death, especially when she had only confessed to using love magic. If anything, she should have been let off with a warning (and perhaps a hefty fine befitting her rank) and then released. Of course, this would not do for Humphrey's enemies; they needed her completely destroyed.

On Thursday 9 November, Eleanor was brought before the bishops to learn her fate.[1] The punishments were indeed humiliating. Eleanor was to perform a penance across three separate days through London. The next Monday, 13 November, she was to go from Temple Bar, through Fleet Street to St Pauls Cathedral. On Wednesday she was to go from the Swan Pier in Thames Street to Christchurch, and finally on the Friday she was to go from Queen Hithe to St Michaels. Each time she was to carry a taper of wax in her hands to make an offering, and she was to go 'with a meke & demur covntenaunce', walking on her own feet without wearing a hood. This punishment was clearly intended to be as humiliating as possible and was without precedent. The three penances were on busy market days and went through some of the most bustling and populous areas of London. Clearly, they wanted as many people as possible to see Eleanor performing her penance. To walk on foot and hoodless was stripping her of her status as a duchess – no woman of her rank would ever have to do either of those things. It would have been the most humiliating thing possible for a woman of any rank, let alone for the highest lady in the land.

This choice of punishment is striking. Usually women who were forced to perform penances of offering tapers to churches while dressed only in a chemise were adulteresses or fornicators, and those of high rank who had been given this punishment were always allowed to avoid performing it by paying a fine to the Church instead.[2] Eleanor was not offered this option. It would be unthinkable for a member of royalty to perform such a cruel penance and this shows how severe Humphrey's enemies were to her – and how Henry must have been convinced by whispers in his ear of her guilt.

The reasons Eleanor was made to perform this penance in London were twofold. Firstly, London by this point was the centre of the kingdom; court and the Crown were based there, merchants from the kingdom and abroad were plentiful, and news could travel easily to all corners of the realm. News would rapidly spread of Eleanor's downfall. But perhaps more important is the fact that one of Humphrey's biggest support bases was the London burgher class.[3] They had consistently sided with Humphrey in politics, were wealthy and influential and, being so close to the centre of government, were one of the most important sections of society to have as supporters. By parading Eleanor through the streets as a disgraced woman, Beaufort and Suffolk were hoping that Humphrey's power in London would crumble as they turned away from him in association.

Eleanor's punishment was not yet complete, however. In fact, perhaps the cruellest punishment had been given to her a few days previously, on 6 November. Eleanor was told that she was to be forcibly divorced from her beloved husband, Humphrey. The senior bishops, cardinals and clergy of the commission 'deuorsed and departed the Duke of Gloucestre and Dame Alianore Cobham, as for matrimony made before between theym two', but it is not entirely clear why this divorce (or perhaps more accurately, annulment) was procured.[4] The most likely explanation lies in Eleanor's claim that she had used Margery, the 'Witch of Eye', for love magic.

Eleanor had supposedly said that she had used Margery to 'enforsed the seide Duke of Gloucestre forto love her so moche that he wedded her'.[5] Usually, the medieval Church aimed to keep people married no matter what – they were far more likely to enforce a marriage under question than to break it up. However, one of the most important recognised reasons for declaring a marriage invalid was lack of consent.[6] In medieval society, it was not unusual for one or both parties to be pressured into an unwilling marriage by parents who wanted to forge connections, alliances or build wealth. Many were not disinclined to use the threat of force to 'encourage' the couple to 'consent'. If it was revealed after the marriage that either party had been coerced into it unwillingly, the Church would sometimes annul the marriage so that it was as if the couple had never been married.

However, lack of consent was not just achieved through the threat of violence or being disowned. In Eleanor and Humphrey's case, it is very likely that the Church decided to interpret Eleanor's alleged use of love magic as lack of consent on Humphrey's behalf. If he was under the influence of a spell that was making him love Eleanor, then he was not 'in his right mind', so to speak, when he married her. Eleanor was now no longer legally Humphrey's wife, no longer a duchess. She had lost everything.

Unfortunately for Eleanor, Humphrey's enemies were not yet done with her. She could not be allowed to go free, as that would allow the couple time to scheme to get the marriage revalidated and to build up their power. Moreover, Henry VI does seem to have been genuinely convinced that Eleanor and her alleged accomplices had indeed plotted against his life. In the midst of the trials in October 1441, there was a payment of £20 issued by the king to 'Doctors, notaries and clerics working against the superstitious craft of necromancy, spell casting and diviners'.[7] This was a significant amount of money at the time and would be the equivalent of around £17,000 today.[8]

It would have been infeasible that Eleanor should escape the charges of treason because of legal technicalities and her flight to sanctuary. As a result, Eleanor – now stripped of her status – was placed under the guardianship of Sir Thomas Stanley for life. This life imprisonment does not have any source; there does not appear to be any official proclamation, no official sentencing by a common law court, just a letter of warrant from the king and subsequent records of her imprisonment.

A contemporary poem claimed that Henry VI had saved Eleanor's life.[9] This may well be based in truth. Beaufort and Suffolk may well have pushed for Eleanor's death, but Henry surely could not bear to kill his aunt whom he had loved all these years, even if he did truly believe that she had plotted against him. If it was clear that Henry did not want to see Eleanor lose her life, then this may well have inspired Beaufort to look two decades prior to the accusations against Joan of Navarre. Beaufort was almost certainly involved in her imprisonment, and he would have remembered how successful it had been. Perpetual captivity would work excellently here. Eleanor would be firmly away from court and, more importantly, from Humphrey. They could not find a way to gain forgiveness from Henry, to petition the pope for the confirmation of their marriage, or re-establish themselves, if Eleanor was locked away. It would also firmly remind the country of her guilt.

Henry's Letter of Warrant concerning Eleanor's imprisonment is dated 19 January 1442.[10] This means that after Eleanor's penance in mid November, there must have been a significant period of time where it was debated what to do with her – as well as a break for Christmas celebrations at court. Henry wrote to his chancellor, the Bishop of Bath, and detailed that he has 'ordeined oure trusty and welbeloved knight Sir Thomas Stanley, countrollour of oure householde, to have the keping of Alianore Cobham late called Duchesse of Gloucestr'. Eleanor's imprisonment was to be supervised by one of Henry's most trusted men. Stanley was to take her to reside in Cheshire, nice and far from the court and the centre of London.

Clearly there was great worry for the safety of Eleanor's person during the journey, with very real fears that there could be a rescue attempt made for her. Henry ordered his chancellor to send writs and commissions to all of the sheriffs of the counties that she would pass through, so that they and 'other personnes of the same shire, as many as shal be thought necessary, to be awayting and assisting unto the conducting of hir'. He also made a note that they should carry her forward, not letting any sickness suffered by her to prevent the journey. This is an intriguing addition and suggests perhaps that Eleanor had been ill in the interim – or that perhaps she had been using sickness as an excuse to delay her exile in the hopes that she may be pardoned. Eleanor's transport was high priority, and Henry was not going to let anything impede it.

Thomas Stanley had come from a respected lineage, his grandfather having been Lord Lieutenant of Ireland, and on numerous occasions from 1427 he had represented Lancashire in the House of Commons. He rose up the trusted ranks of government and in 1431 he too was made Lord Lieutenant of Ireland, a post he served in until 1436.[11] Not long after he returned, his father, Sir John Stanley, died and Thomas became King of Mann. Suzerainty of the Isle of Man had been in his family since 1405 and it granted them not insignificant power.[12]

In 1437, Thomas was made Constable of Chester Castle, the place he was now, five years later, to take Eleanor.[13] Chester Castle was a significant fortification which had previously held Richard II and so would have been viewed as a safe place to house Eleanor. Transporting her came at no mean cost, though. On 31 January 1442, Henry paid five of his men for keeping her in their custody from 25 November (just after her penance) until 22 January. For this they were given 10s a day, totalling £40. On 16 February, there was another payment to one of Henry's servants, Ralph Lee, giving him the huge sum of £100 for the costs and expenses which he had incurred for taking Eleanor to Chester.[14]

In a writ from a few years later, the amount Eleanor was allotted for her confinement becomes known: 100 marks a year.[15] This amount has been called a 'beggarly sum' compared to Queen Joan's budget of 1,000 marks a year during her imprisonment.[16] However, the difference in situation needs to be remembered. Joan had never been charged with anything, let alone been convicted, and her imprisonment was merely one of convenience. It is also important to note that Joan was a crowned queen, and so in a far more prestigious position. Eleanor, on the other hand, was of lower status, particularly now she had been stripped of her title as duchess and was being presented as having committed treason using witchcraft beyond a doubt. Humphrey's enemies at court wanted him gone, and by association wanted his wife gone too, whereas Henry V was still concerned that Joan had a comfortable living arrangement and was treated as her station deserved.

When all of this is considered, the allowance of 100 marks (nearly £67) a year is not too poor. Indeed, it was significantly less than Eleanor had been enjoying as duchess, but it is to be remembered that the annual income for many prosperous gentry at the time was around £40. In this context, 100 marks a year was certainly not to be sniffed at. For Eleanor, however, the prison walls of Chester Castle and 100 marks a year with a handful of servants would have been a far cry from her and Humphrey's palace at Greenwich, surrounded by courtiers, poets and musicians and filled with lavish wealth, gold and jewels.

Eleanor arrived at Chester Castle on 10 February 1442.[17] This was to be her home for the next year and a half. Her time there was hardly exciting, and one wonders whether she ever received news of her husband. Humphrey had all but disappeared from records during the trial and punishment of his wife, but he quietly returned to court a few months after Eleanor settled in at Chester, re-joining the King's Council at the end of August 1442.[18] However, he was a broken man and never again played a significant part in proceedings. Perhaps reminded of his own mortality by the experience, he turned his attention to building a tomb for himself at St Albans Abbey, his long-term ally. It was situated in the Saint's Chapel, on the south side of the shrine to St Alban, and so was in a very prestigious location, befitting both his status and his friendship with the abbey. His coffin was to be placed in an underground burial chamber and presumably a monument would be placed above ground to mark the spot.

Today there stands a chantry screen connected to Humphrey.[19] It is often believed to have been commissioned by Humphrey himself, as his coat of arms – those of England and France quartered in a border argent – decorates it, as well as other of his symbols. The screen is a triple open arch, with one side covered in seventeen figures of kings and the other side now empty but perhaps originally also holding kingly figures. The cost of building the tomb itself, to be his final resting place, came to the extraordinary total of £434 6s 8d.[20] It does not say how long it took to build Humphrey's tomb, but it was certainly completed within the next five years.

Although Humphrey had returned to court, he spent most of his time in semi-retirement between La Pleasaunce and the monastery at St Albans. Clearly he had no inclination to try and claw his way back into Henry's favour, and Henry was probably unreceptive to Humphrey through suspicion cast by his wife's murderous deeds. St Albans was an obvious choice of refuge, having been his staunch allies for so long, but something can perhaps be read into Humphrey's state of mind by his time spent at La Pleasaunce.

Indeed, he had spent a great amount time and money on his palace at Greenwich, and it would have been a beautiful place to spend his retirement. Its proximity to court so that he could be kept afoot of any potential plots against him was also important. One cannot help but wonder, however, whether it was mainly to feel closer to his lost duchess. La Pleasaunce was their home, their creation, where they held their gatherings of intellect and art, and lived like a king and queen. Perhaps, now that he had lost Eleanor, he wanted to be in the place he most associated with her, to feel her presence.

It does seem that the accusations against Eleanor and her subsequent downfall were the only things that could truly break Humphrey. He had always been rasher than his other siblings, as shown by his marriage to Jacqueline, his attempt to duel the Duke of Burgundy, his attempt to free Friar Randolph from the Tower of London and his continual squabbles with Beaufort. But no matter what Humphrey did, he always bounced back. He had won the approval of the Church, the admiration of scholars and the affection of the Commons. He had, on many occasions, been a war hero and helped the English in their battle to claim French territories, and he had helped to keep the country afloat during the minority of Henry VI. All of this, coupled with his power as a prince of the realm and heir to the kingdom, meant that even his more serious mistakes were never too dangerous to his position. However, the destruction of his beloved wife had broken his spirit.

Eleanor may well have been the only woman Humphrey had ever loved. Their marriage had been a success for thirteen years, and as far as can be seen he appears to have been faithful to her throughout their marriage. There are no reports of other mistresses, no other women named once they were married, his only discretions during their relationship being when he was not truly hers – when he was still married to Jaqueline and fathered his illegitimate children. They built their home at Greenwich, travelled the land, lived in luxury and shared intellectual pursuits and enjoyed the arts. Surely he must have been mourning the loss of his life partner. What was the point of fighting at court, ousting Beaufort and regaining a relationship with Henry if Eleanor was not there to enjoy the fruits of his labour with him? True, getting close to Henry again could have led to the opportunity to beg for Eleanor's pardon and release, but Humphrey must have realised what a grasp Beaufort and Suffolk now held on Henry, how his reputation had been forever tarnished in Henry's eyes, and he may simply have lost any fighting spirit to try.

So Eleanor continued to languish in imprisonment. On 26 October 1443, orders were made to move her from Chester Castle to Kenilworth Castle in Warwickshire.[21] Kenilworth was certainly an interesting place to which to move Eleanor. It was a significant fortification, with huge water defences, but in the late fourteenth century John of Gaunt had spent huge amounts of money turning it into a palace.[22] In more recent times, it had continued to be an important royal palace fortress, with both Henry IV and Henry V using it extensively.[23] Between 1456 and 1461, Henry VI and Queen Margaret of Anjou would use Kenilworth as their principal military base.[24] Across the period of at least a century, then, Kenilworth was deemed worthy of being the home to kings – and a luxurious one at that. Eleanor's imprisonment had certainly become much more comfortable by being moved to Kenilworth.

The reason for Eleanor's move is not mentioned in the royal writs. Perhaps two years after her punishment, Henry's heart was softening slightly and he wanted to improve the conditions of her confinement. If this were so, it is still clear that he was not considering her release any time soon; the writ once again makes clear that those who were to accompany her needed to be armed and vigilant for anyone who might wish to disrupt the move. Attempts at her rescue were clearly still a top concern.

These concerns were not without basis. Although Humphrey and his supporters had not made any indication they were planning a rescue, public support for Eleanor obviously still existed. The *Brut* chronicle recounts the unfortunate story of an unnamed Kentish woman at the end of May that year.[25] This woman, so the chronicle tells, had met with Henry VI at Black Heath in Kent, and 'spake to hym boldly, and reviled hym ungoodly and unwisely for Dame Alianore Cobham', saying that Henry should have Eleanor 'hoom ageyn to hir husbond, the Duke of Gloucestre'. It is surely of no coincidence that this woman spoke to him in Blackheath, which was right next to Eleanor and Gloucester's palace at Greenwich. If anywhere in the country was going to still support the couple, it was going to be those who had lived alongside them in their home at La Pleasaunce.

Unfortunately for this woman, Henry was incensed. Was it because someone had dared speak to the king so directly? Or had she struck a nerve? Either way, Henry reacted with great cruelty. The woman was arrested and sent to Westminster before the Justices of the Kings Bench – one of the two highest courts in the land. It is not clear what she was charged with, but the punishment was severe. She was made to stand in a cart with a '*paupire*' on her head (possibly a kind of false crown, like the one Roger was made to wear at St Paul's Cross) and pulled through London. Finally the judge declared that the woman was to have rocks piled on top of her body until she was killed.[26] This is clearly a most extreme punishment for some words said, even to a king. Perhaps Henry took offence at being spoken to so plainly by what is assumed to be a common woman. Perhaps he felt guilt at how his aunt and uncle, once so close to him, had suffered and so he struck out. Perhaps he was worried that any leniency towards someone speaking in Eleanor's favour would encourage escape attempts and rebellion and wanted to quash it. Whatever the reason, the woman lost her life and Eleanor was moved from her place of imprisonment four months later.

Henry used royal funds to pay for horses, food, transport and accommodation for the journey.[27] Thomas Stanley was rewarded for his time looking after Eleanor; a writ from 14 October 1443, just prior to Eleanor's move, gives Thomas lands, pasture and meadows in the Forest of Macclesfield, Chester, including related monetary income such as fines.[28]

Eleanor arrived at Kenilworth on 5 December, where she was given into the custody of Ralph, Lord de Sudeley, who was constable of the castle. Eleanor had twelve servants in her retinue, which included one priest, three gentlemen, one maid, five valets and two boys. Ralph was given 6s 8d per day for the responsibility of looking after Eleanor, while the gentlemen received 8d, the maid and valets 6d and the boys 4d. The writ gives a total payment for £33 6s 8d, presumably to cover the costs Ralph had incurred since Eleanor had entered his custody.[29]

Ralph was an obvious choice to be entrusted with Eleanor's keeping. At the time he received Eleanor, he was around 50 years old and had close ties to the Henry and the Crown. Alice, the wife of his older brother William's, had been appointed Henry VI's governess in 1424.[30] Ralph himself is thought to have served with Henry V in France. The most important indication of Ralph's position of trust is that the previous year, 1443, he had been appointed Lord High Treasurer of England. Ralph served in this position until 1446, and he also held the position of Lord Chamberlain – the most senior officer in the royal household – from 1441 to 1447. Just like Thomas Stanley, Ralph was one of Henry's closest and most trusted men. He could be relied upon to hold Eleanor securely.

Eleanor remained at Kenilworth for at least two more years and, again, mention of her all but disappears. For Humphrey, life at court was getting worse and worse. Although he was spending an increasing amount of time at La Pleasaunce or St Albans, he had still continued to appear at court meetings, even if his contribution had all but vanished. Beaufort retired from the King's Council in 1443, safe in the knowledge that Humphrey's power and support had been decimated and those who remained on the council were all under his influence. His co-conspirator Suffolk had become increasingly present at council meetings in 1441, suspiciously close to Eleanor and Humphrey's downfall, and as time went on he gained more and more influence over Henry, both at court and in private.[31]

The depth of the impact on Humphrey of the accusations against Eleanor can be seen as time goes on. He was unsuccessful in redeeming himself in Henry's eyes, particularly when Suffolk was whispering in Henry's ears. By the end of 1445, Humphrey had been denied access to the court and was removed from the Privy Council.[32] These were both crushing blows. The Privy Councillors were the closest men to the king, helping him rule, and Humphrey had been one of the main men running the land for over twenty years. To be removed from the council was a most public sign that Humphrey held no influence on politics any longer, and he was truly cut off from Henry's affections. As son, brother and uncle to successive Kings of England, it was unthinkable that Humphrey would not have power and influence over the running of the country, but that was precisely the position he found himself in. To be denied access to the court altogether – a privilege that even lower members of the nobility were allowed, let alone a prince of the realm – was the final insult to this once revered man.

It is perhaps not surprising that 1445 was the year when Humphrey was finally cut off from the monarchy. Suffolk had been flattering his way into the king's heart for several years, and the majority of those on the King's Council would have been supporters of Beaufort and Suffolk. Those who still held loyalty towards Humphrey would have been powerless to make any public show of this for fear of losing their own position.

Perhaps even more importantly, however, was the arrival of Margaret of Anjou in this year. With the fall of Humphrey, those at court suddenly became acutely aware of Henry's lack of a bride. Now that the only heir to the throne had been ostracised, it was more important than ever to ensure that Henry produced a male heir in case of his untimely death. Humphrey had made a suggestion of an alliance with the Count of Armagnac, who would have been likely to support continued efforts against the French.[33] This was in line with his policy of conquering territory in French regions, which he had followed since accompanying his brother into Agincourt.

However, Humphrey's enemies could never allow a bride whom Humphrey supported; knowing how malleable Henry was to their own will, it was widely known that any wife of his would have great influence over him.[34] If the bride had been chosen by Humphrey, the wife might then be encouraged to bring about a reconciliation. As such, Suffolk and his supporters decided to push for a marriage alliance with René, Duke of Lorraine and titular King of Sicily and Jerusalem, through marriage to his daughter, Margaret of Anjou. René's sister was Queen of France, and his brother was one of the French king's chief advisors, and so this alliance would implicitly bring France and England closer together, tying off the war. This was clearly in direct opposition to Humphrey's aims, and the aims of the kingdom for the past few decades.

Unsurprisingly, this proposed alliance was extremely unpopular among the commons of England, and Humphrey's opposition to the match must surely still have encouraged some of this dissent. Despite the downfall of Eleanor and Humphrey, their reputation among the commons was not as easy to destroy as their relationship with the king. Humphrey, in particular, having been left out of the accusations, would have still held great fondness and admiration among the masses. If Humphrey's position was partly responsible for public opposition, then again it is not surprising that he was pushed out of court by the end of the year. He still held too much influence.

Although attempts were made to produce the Armagnac alliance, France had invaded Gascony, on Armagnac's borders, and so Count John was hesitant to dive headfirst into an English alliance before he had protection. Due to the delays, Suffolk was able to push the marriage to Margaret, and ultimately he was successful. Once again, Humphrey had been dealt a huge blow. Had his marriage suggestion panned out, his fate could have been vastly different. Not only did Margaret turn out to be a great enemy of Humphrey's, but if Henry had been pleased with his Armagnac bride then it surely would have ingratiated Humphrey.

The arrival of Margaret in England shows a vulnerable side to Humphrey and gives an insight into his state of mind at this point in his life. Suffolk had been victorious in his choice, and he was among the party chosen to accompany Margaret to England for her marriage. However, Humphrey decided not to be left out of proceedings and, uncharacteristically, showed public acceptance of the match by being the most prominent lord to escort Margaret to London after her marriage at Titchfield Abbey. This was a far cry from the Humphrey who had protested in Parliament at the release of the Duke of Orléans. Events had obviously shaken his confidence and although he was prepared to offer his own match, he no longer had the strength – and realised he no longer had the power – to protest a marriage that had already become certain. It was best to try and seem supportive.

While escorting Margaret, however, he brought a guard of honour which consisted of 500 men who were dressed in his livery.[35] Although on the surface this wouldn't seem out of the ordinary, as it was a suitably elaborate train for the new Queen of England, it clearly shows that Humphrey was feeling insecure about his position. He had been consistently battered and beaten for the past four years, and even the arrival of this new queen was a defeat for him. This show of his followers, wearing his colours, was probably serving the dual purpose of showing that there was still support for him in the country and, on some level, to serve as security for his protection on the journey. The guard was a huge statement of his presence. He must have been feeling vulnerable.

Humphrey had good reason to feel vulnerable. Margaret, after realising the dire situation of conflicts at court and the weak nature of her new husband, turned to Suffolk as an ally. She had determined that she was going to be the strong leader that the country needed and Suffolk, as the man who brought her this new kingdom and one of the king's favourites, was an obvious choice. Margaret was to Suffolk what an Armagnac bride could have been to Humphrey. Margaret probably quickly noticed the power Humphrey had over the commons, and no doubt Suffolk filled in any gaps. He may well have slipped in Humphrey's opposition to Margaret and Henry's match. Margaret realised that Humphrey was the main opposition to her influence over the king – even if he was still in Henry's bad books – and instead of uniting with him to rule the country with experience, she followed Suffolk's lead and decided to remove him from her path altogether so that the power could be hers alone.

Polydore Vergil, writing in the sixteenth century, claims that it was Margaret who caused Humphrey to be removed from the court, and when timings are considered this is not so far-fetched.[36] Polydore was writing from a position where Margaret of Anjou had been vilified for her part in the Wars of the Roses and so perhaps had motive for blaming her. However, it has to be recognised that Margaret married Henry in April 1445, and within eight months Humphrey had been removed from court, despite having held onto his position for four years after the downfall of his wife. Margaret must have been a persuasive force in his removal.

The clearest example that Humphrey had been completely vilified in his nephew's eyes comes from the notes of the French Embassy who were sent to meet Henry VI in England in July 1445. In the king's chamber, Suffolk expressed loudly to the French delegation – in front of various lords and earls – that he did not listen to Humphrey and that he was the person that Henry loved most in the world after Margaret. Once the delegation entered the presence of the king, Suffolk continued to speak boldly and plainly about Humphrey's new position on the rung of power. He claimed that there had been a report that Humphrey was a hindrance to Henry, but that he gave the report no credence as 'he did not have the power'.[37] Suffolk had clearly won the war with Humphrey. Here he was, speaking in front of the king, earls, lords, foreign representatives of a rival nation, announcing that he was the favourite of the king and Humphrey was nothing. There could be few things more humiliating for this prince.

After 1445, Humphrey could do nothing more but retire to St Albans and Greenwich. His wife was gone, locked away with no contact, he had lost the love that Henry once held for him, he had lost his power and influence, and he could no longer rule the country. It was a far cry from ten years previously, when he was the most powerful man in all but name after the death of his brother, Bedford. He gave up the fight at long last, realising he was defeated. Sadly for Humphrey, his enemies were not yet done with him.

Eleanor, meanwhile, was still at Kenilworth, but in July 1446 the Records of the Privy Council show that Henry made orders under his seal for her to be handed back into the custody of Thomas Stanley and to be sent to his castle on the Isle of Man.[38] Again, the reason is unknown, but as the Isle of Man was very isolated and under the rule of one of his most trusted men, it is possible that Margaret, now that Humphrey was removed from the King's Council, was aware of the proximity of his wife and wanted her as far away as possible while still being secure.

By 1447, Humphrey, Duke of Gloucester, was not a dangerous man. While the commons still held out in their love and support for the man they had been behind for decades, his power base at court had been utterly destroyed and the king viewed him as a traitor after years of whispers in his ears from Beaufort, Suffolk and now Queen Margaret. Despite this, those at court still could not let Humphrey rest and they wanted to get rid of him once and for all. This year, a Parliament was called, initially at Cambridge, then moving to Bury St Edmunds where Suffolk had a strong power base. The *English Chronicle* says that it was called with the sole purpose of killing Humphrey and this does not seem to be too much dramatic licence on behalf of the chronicler.[39]

Humphrey's old friend, John Whetamstede, recounted that Henry was made to believe that Humphrey 'was the great enemy of the King, that he was constantly trying to steal the Crown, and was secretly trying to procure his murder, and so to usurp the government of the kingdom'.[40] This does not seem to be merely a conspiracy written by Humphrey's friend and resident of the abbey that he greatly patronised; many other chronicles recount the same charges.[41] Convincing Henry of these charges would not be difficult, particularly when Eleanor was a prime example of the couple's nefarious deeds and propensity to want Henry dead.

That the Parliament was called at Bury St Edmunds also lends credence to this idea, as it was far enough away from Humphrey's power base in London to leave him more isolated and vulnerable. A series of notes written in the late fifteenth century, possibly by a monk of Ely, recounted that Henry was protected day and night on his way to the Parliament, and that 60,000 men were stationed around the town.[42] The amount of men must surely have been exaggerated, particularly as all chroniclers seem to be agreed that Humphrey had no idea that there were moves being made against him – he surely would have noticed an army of this size. However, the display of protecting Henry day and night and having what must have been a significant regiment of men surrounding the town would certainly have sown seeds that there was a move being made against the king. Certainly Henry himself would have believed the threat was real if his closest advisor was procuring such great protection.

Humphrey approached Bury St Edmunds around mid February. Some contemporaries report that Humphrey went to Parliament in order to petition Henry with regard to Eleanor.[43] This would not be impossible. Perhaps now that he had been completely removed from court for two years and was living quietly, he hoped that Henry would have pity on him and Eleanor and allow them to retire together. It is difficult to see why Henry would agree to this, particularly when he now seemingly hated his uncle, but perhaps Humphrey believed he could persuade him somehow. Perhaps it was a desperate attempt to cling to his lost love and lost life. However, Humphrey may not have had this intention at all, knowing how Henry had turned on him, and it may have just been the invention of chroniclers setting the scene of a man pleading for his beloved wife in order to bring greater contrast to the horrific betrayal that was to happen to him instead.

As Humphrey approached the town, he was met by officers of the king's household who told him that Henry did not want him to visit the court, but to go straight to his lodgings. This he duly did, where he ate dinner, and then he was met by various members of the upper nobility, including the Duke of Buckingham, the Earl of Salisbury and Viscount Beaumont. The men then arrested him, seemingly on charges of treason. His servants were all dismissed. Humphrey was kept in custody for a few days, but he appears to have slipped into a coma, and on 23 February 1447, Duke Humphrey of Gloucester died.[44]

Humphrey's death clearly panicked his enemies, as they were terrified that they would be accused of murdering him in their custody, so the next day his body was put on display for everybody to see that there were no marks on his body. This was unsuccessful, however, as countless accounts still record that Humphrey was murdered – and even the ones that do not say it outright, recount the rumours floating around that he was murdered.

The move against Humphrey were clearly intended to be a hugely orchestrated event on a par with the accusations against Eleanor, for it was not only Humphrey who was arrested. Forty-two members of Humphrey's household were arrested alongside him. These were all men, and included a significant number of Welshmen. Henry Ellis explains this by the fact that Humphrey, at the time of his death, owned significant lands, castles and lordships in the Welsh Marches.[45] Included in those arrested was Humphrey's illegitimate son, Arthur. They were accused of plotting at Greenwich to kill Henry in order to make Humphrey king and rescue Eleanor from prison.[46]

The arrests and the death of Humphrey turned out to be a colossal disaster for Suffolk and his supporters at court. Humphrey was still the apple of the nation's eye and his suspected murder was never forgiven by the public – even late into the Tudor reign of the next century, stories were being written about 'Good Duke Humphrey' and his tragic murder and the plots against him and his wife. The decision to continue to prosecute his servants also seems to have garnered great hatred from the public.

All of Humphrey's servants were eventually pardoned, but it is unclear how long they were imprisoned for. The pardons for those accused of being the main conspirators (including his son Arthur) are dated to July, September and October of 1447, but the National Archives date them to 1449 as this was the first Parliament after the accusations and the pardons were approved by Parliament.[47] Therefore, they are clearly backdated to cover the period from the accusations. This suggests that the men could have been imprisoned up until this time – or else that Henry had pardoned them previously, and the first Parliament was being used merely to put the pardons on official record. If they had been imprisoned for the past two years, however, it would have been a miserable time. It also raises the question of why it took so long to pardon them when the true target of their ire, Humphrey, had died. Perhaps Humphrey's enemies decided the war was won and there was no point punishing his servants, but because they had done such a good job convincing Henry of Humphrey's guilt, he was not so ready to sign a pardon for treason.

If the chronicles are to be believed, the pardons for the main conspirators came conveniently late. *The New Chronicle of England and France* recounts that five men, including Arthur, were sent to London and sentenced to be hanged, drawn and quartered – the typical traitor's death.[48] The men had already been hanged, and while still alive were cut down and prepared to be quartered when Suffolk arrived and presented the king's pardon so that they were saved.

It was not unusual, in this period and later, for pardons to arrive at the last minute like this, in dramatic fashion. But, as mentioned, this apparently backfired greatly for Suffolk. The chronicle tells us that when the pardons were delivered there was 'great rejoicing of the multitude of the people there being present' which, considering they were in London, means they were probably still great supporters of Humphrey and, by extension, these condemned servants and his illegitimate son. More menacingly for Suffolk, however, the chronicle continues 'but for this the grudge and murmour of [the] people ceasid nat agayne the marquys of Suffolke, for the deth of the good duke of Glouceter, of whose murdre he was specially susspected'.[49]

To the end, then, Humphrey still found great support and allies in the people of the kingdom he had loved and ruled for decades. Nonetheless, the charges against his wife Eleanor had been overwhelmingly successful in bringing about his destruction, and he died alone and under the threat of charges of treason. He was duly interred in the abbey he had so loved and patronised and which continued to support him even after his death, in the tomb that he had specially designed. Candles were to be lit daily on the altar above his tomb and every year on the anniversary of his death thirteen poor men were to carry torches around his tomb, with money given out to the abbot, the monks and two local anchoresses.[50] Thus ended this noble Prince of England.

When Eleanor learnt of Humphrey's death cannot be known. How must it have affected her, six years after she had last laid eyes on her beloved husband, to know that she now would never be reunited with him? Her grief must also have been tinged with the knowledge that she was probably never going to be rescued from prison. Humphrey had been her only hope. She was still living on the remote Isle of Man and it cannot have been the most comfortable of abodes. Although Thomas Stanley was king of the isle, there is no evidence that he resided there during this time, so it is unclear how well looked after or luxurious Peel Castle would have been for Eleanor.

Peel Castle sits on St Patrick's Isle, a small mass of land just off the mainland of the Isle of Man, and was built in the eleventh century by the Vikings. By Eleanor's time, there was an armoury and barracks as well as a cathedral on the site. In the late 1440s, however, the Isle of Man was subject to Scottish raids, as was much of England north of Carlisle, and it was probably due to this that once again Eleanor was moved to another place of imprisonment, this time to Beaumaris Castle in north Wales. This was to be her last abode.

Beaumaris, situated in Anglesey, was another property where Stanley held authority, as he was a joint justiciar of north Wales – alongside Suffolk.[51] It was this joint authority that probably encouraged the choice of location. It was firmly in Welsh territory, so Eleanor was still extremely isolated, but English control had tightened in northern Wales which probably made it seem more secure than the Isle of Man. It is still intriguing that she was moved to Wales, however, when the list of Humphrey's servants arrested for treason showed a significant number of Welshmen; support for Eleanor may still have been strong in the country, so it seems a bit of a risky location to take her.

In 1449, Beaumaris was urgently reinforced, having never been fully completed during the previous century.[52] It is possible that these repairs were brought about specifically because of Eleanor's move to the castle. The Crown and court still seemed to be terrified at the idea of Eleanor being freed. This seems strange considering Eleanor's power lay solely in her marriage to Humphrey, who was now dead. At most, if she were freed, she could attempt to claim her dower rights as Humphrey had declared them in the 1430s, but there were many ways to escape this. Her marriage had been annulled by the Church, and having been found guilty of treason her lands would be forfeit anyway. Moreover, in the fateful Bury Parliament that led to Humphrey's death, king and Parliament passed an act, 'considering the gret mis-governaunce of Alianore, that was the wife of his Oncle late duc of Gloucestre', that Eleanor should be excluded from having any dower claim on his lands or possessions, including anything that Humphrey and Eleanor had owned jointly.[53]

As it was, Henry declared that as Humphrey had died intestate (a claim very unlikely – what seems more likely is that his enemies did not like the terms of his will and wanted to claim the spoils for themselves), the Archbishop of Canterbury, Thomas Stanley, and others should dispose of his goods and chattels.[54] As expected, most of Humphrey's property was seized by the Crown, Suffolk and his allies. Henry seems to have donated some of Humphrey's possessions to

Royal Witches

Eton and Cambridge Colleges. One such example is a loving cup, a shared drinking container traditionally used at weddings and banquets. This cup, held at Christ's College, Cambridge, after Margaret Beaufort, mother of Henry VII, donated it in the early 1500s, bears the arms of Humphrey quartered with Eleanor's arms.[55] This could even have been the cup they used at their own wedding, now plundered by those who hated them.

Eleanor was transferred into the custody of William Bulkeley, who was acting on behalf of the constable of Beaumaris Castle, William Beauchamp, on 10 March 1449, and once again her keepers were given 100 marks a year to look after her.[56] At least her conditions had remained steady throughout her captivity. Once again, however, the cost of transferring her was far higher than her usual care, showing the protection given to her during the journey; the cost of the move came to £150 8s 7d.

Beaumaris was to be her home for the next three years and no more is heard of Eleanor after this move. She was forgotten by chroniclers, none of whom even record her death on 7 July 1452. She was buried at Beaumaris, with her guardian William Beauchamp bearing the cost of the burial. She was not given the privilege of being buried next to Humphrey, or even somewhere close to her childhood home of Sterborough, if that had been her wish. Thus ended the lives of Eleanor and Humphrey of Gloucester. They had both reached the greatest heights, but ultimately both ended their lives in sorrow and destruction.

After Humphrey's death, the couple's long-cherished home of La Pleasaunce had been snatched up by Queen Margaret. She wasted no time in making her own changes to the home, as shown by the accounts of Robert Ketelwel, Clerk of the Works to Queen Margaret, from 1447 to 1454.[57] She enlarged it, and added a pier so that boats could access it, even at low tide. Eventually, the palace became the main home of the Tudors, with various monarchs being born there, including Henry VIII, Mary I and Elizabeth I. By that time, however, it had been extended and refurbished so many times that any traces of Eleanor and Humphrey's marital home and intellectual court had probably long disappeared.

Within a few decades of her trial and death, a poem was written down by a citizen of London named Richard Hill, called 'The Lament of the Duchess of Gloucester'.[58] Although Hill was the first to write the poem down, it is believed that it had been circulating since not long after her penance. The poem was certainly known among literary circles and in all likelihood it had spread through the commons of London, if not the country. The poem is written from the point of view of Eleanor, who wails at her fate.

Eleanor described how she had been 'browght up of nowght' when a prince (Humphrey) chose to marry her. Although she had become most magnified of all women, she performed a 'gret offence' which, in law she should have been killed for. However, Henry VI had pity on her and saved her. Now that she had completed her penance, she said, 'Ffarewelle, London, and have good day' and she left behind all of her gowns of gold, velvet, and damask. Now, 'under mens kepyng I must abide'. The poem, although it does criticise Eleanor for her pride and wrongdoing, does have an undertone of sympathy for her. It is significant that it does not mention what crimes Eleanor had supposedly committed. If the poem was intended to capitalise on her and Gloucester's pain, it would surely have taken glee in describing her witchcraft and treason. There is, however, one clear message in the poem: every single stanza ends with the line 'Alle women may be ware by me'.

Eleanor's case, particularly in the wake of the accusations against Joan, meant that royal women now needed to beware. For the second time this century, men at court had been successful in using a woman in the royal family for their own ends. While Joan was simply used to gain money, the accusations and punishment against Eleanor Cobham were nefarious and cruel. Her life, and that of her husband, had been utterly devastated. Eleanor Cobham died without a friend in the world, having never been reunited with the man who had loved her for so many years. Future women at court certainly needed to be on their guard.

Jacquetta of Luxembourg & Elizabeth Woodville

9

LIVELY, BEAUTIFUL
AND GRACIOUS

THE EYES OF the whole country were on Eleanor Cobham as the accusations were thrown against her and she and her husband experienced one of the greatest falls the century had seen so far. One pair of eyes that would certainly have been watching particularly closely were those of Jacquetta of Luxembourg. For a time, Jacquetta had been Eleanor's sister-in-law, and once Eleanor fell Jacquetta was the only female member of the English royal family remaining. These events most certainly had an impact on Jacquetta, even if she had never been close to Eleanor, and it is unlikely she ever forgot what happened to Humphrey and Eleanor – indeed, later in life she was acutely aware of the dangers posed to her own family as a result.

Jacquetta was not a native Englishwoman. Born between 1415 and 1416, she was the eldest daughter of Peter of Luxembourg, Count of Brienne and future Count of Saint-Pol, and his wife Marguerite of Baux. Through her father, she was descended from John II, Duke of Brittany, meaning that she was loosely related to Joan of Navarre (he was Jacquetta's fifth great-grandfather and Joan's third great-grandfather, making them fourth cousins twice removed). Jacquetta was born just as Henry V of England was winning his glorious victory at Agincourt, and so from her birth her destiny was affected by the Kingdom of England.

Her family, as part of the royal family of Luxembourg, were vassals of the larger state of Burgundy. As such, when the house of Burgundy joined the English cause at the signing of the Treaty of Troyes, the territory of Luxembourg also pledged its allegiance to Henry V. From then on, Luxembourg's destiny was intertwined with England's. Jacquetta's uncle, Louis of Luxembourg, was trusted by John, Duke of Bedford, to act as his chancellor in France for ten years from 1424/25 until 1435.[1] Her other uncle, John of Luxembourg, provided continued military support for the English throughout the 1420s and remained loyal to the English even when Philip of Burgundy betrayed them in 1435. He stayed loyal to the English until his death in 1441.

Throughout her childhood, however, Jacquetta was not greatly affected by the politics her family were a part of. Her father was count of the territory of Brienne in northern France and also owned the commune of Conversano in south-eastern Italy. However, it was Brienne where Peter based himself, his family being from the France and Luxembourg area. It is almost certainly here where Jacquetta was born and spent a significant proportion of her childhood. Brienne was located in fertile lands and its castle being placed on one of the main trade routes in the Champagne region also helped contribute to the wealth of the county.[2] Jacquetta would have spent a lot of time at this chateau, but her family travelled between various castles and chateaux in the English-held territories of Northern France.

Due to her high birth and her family's connections in France and England, it is almost certain that Jacquetta would have been taught how to speak, read and possibly write both languages. Despite her noble birth, like Joan and Eleanor, almost nothing is known of Jacquetta's childhood. However, she probably had a similar childhood to Joan, being of a roughly equal rank and also living in the territory of northern France. Jacquetta had her mother throughout her childhood and so would have been instructed in how to be a good countess from her mother's own experience. As eldest daughter of the couple, it was likely that Jacquetta was going to make a most advantageous marriage when she was older and so Peter and Marguerite would have ensured she received the greatest education that could be afforded to a woman of Jacquetta's time.

The first tantalising suggestion of Jacquetta's connection to significant political events comes from the infamous capture and trial of Joan of Arc. Joan had been instrumental in turning the tide of the Hundred Years War back in favour of France. Although arguments have been made about the extent of her contribution, it cannot be denied that Joan held incredible symbolic power and hope for those who championed the cause of the disinherited dauphin, Charles. Joan's success was not never-ending, however, and on 23 May 1430 she was captured by troops of Burgundy and Jacquetta's uncle, John of Luxembourg, north of Compiègne.[3]

Joan of Arc was now under the keeping of John, and he knew just how important a prisoner she was. Joan was imprisoned in his home, Beaurevoir Castle in northern France. At the time of Joan's arrival, Jacquetta's brother Louis was residing there in the care of his uncle. Louis was around 12 years old and would be staying with John to be trained in chivalry, warfare and leadership. It has been suggested that Jacquetta may also have been at Beaurevoir Castle, and this is not impossible.[4] Although Jacquetta would be less likely to be at her uncle's, when looking at those who were in charge of looking after Joan of Arc, it could certainly be a possibility.

Joan had been placed in the custody of three women: John's wife, Jeanne de Béthune; Jeanne's daughter from her first marriage, Jeanne de Bar; and John's aunt Jeanne of Luxembourg, who was Countess of Saint-Pol and Ligny. With three female relatives of Jacquetta's residing at Beaurevoir Castle – one of whom was the senior matriarch of her family – she could well have been sent there for courtly training, as she would now be around 13 years old.

If Jacquetta was indeed at Beaurevoir, then Joan's stay there must have been highly influential on the young girl. Her female relatives treated Joan exceedingly well, with Joan remembering their kind treatment fondly during her trial.[5] Although all three women begged John not to give up Joan, he eventually sold her to the English for 10,000 livres. This led to her trial and burning at the stake. If Jacquetta had witnessed the imprisonment of this incredibly high-status prisoner and thus followed her trial and execution, she would have learnt valuable lessons about how dangerous being a powerful woman in politics could be.

Whether Jacquetta was at Beaurevoir Castle or not, her fate changed forever on 13 November 1432. On this day, Anne of Burgundy, the sister of the Duke of Burgundy and wife to John, Duke of Bedford, died of the plague at the Hôtel de Bourbon in Paris.[6] Anne's marriage to Bedford had been instrumental in sealing the alliance between Burgundy and England, but beyond that, Bedford had been deeply in love with Anne and her death hit him hard. However, although Bedford mourned his wife, it did not take long for his eyes to stray, and Jacquetta caught his attention.

To marry Jacquetta was an understandable political move on Bedford's behalf. Her uncles had proven exceedingly loyal to the English cause across the past decade and had even delivered the thorn in their side, Joan of Arc, on a silver platter. The English cause was also starting to flounder, with limited numbers of troops being sent from England due to the monetary problems that were crippling the kingdom, and with the death of Anne, Bedford knew that his relationship with Burgundy would start to deteriorate. Anne had been the main peacekeeper between the two and her importance in maintaining the Anglo–Burgundian alliance cannot be overstated.

It made sense, therefore, for Bedford to turn to the Luxembourg family, who could provide him with further military support and strengthen the trading ties that already existed between the two territories. Moreover, Jacquetta's fourth cousin twice removed was Sigismund of Luxembourg, the Holy Roman Emperor. In terms of European medieval royalty, this was a close connection, for it was forbidden to marry within four degrees of consanguinity. As Holy Roman Emperor, Sigismund was one of the most powerful men in Western Europe, and if John could in any way bring Sigismund closer to the English cause it could turn the tide in the Hundred Years War.

Negotiations began in secret, but clearly Peter jumped at the chance to have his daughter married to a prince of England, the man who was heir to a throne which was currently occupied by a 10-year-old boy. On 20 April 1433, at the Cathedral of Thérouanne, just five months after the death of Anne of Burgundy, the 43-year-old Bedford and 17-year-old Jacquetta were married. Thérouanne was the episcopal seat of Jacquetta's uncle, Louis, who also performed the ceremony, and so it was safe territory in which the two could marry.

Safe territory was necessary because the marriage was a gross insult to Philip of Burgundy on two fronts. Not only had his brother-in-law remarried far too soon after the death of his sister – the usual mourning period lasting a year – but Peter had not asked his permission for the marriage. As a vassal, Peter was required to ask his overlord, the duke, before he married off any of his children. Peter did not do so because he knew that Burgundy would never agree to this marriage.

The account of the chronicler Monstrelet of the wedding gives the first known description of the 17-year-old Jacquetta. Although he recounts the ire of Burgundy, he is generous in his assessment of Jacquetta, calling her '*frisque, belle, et gracieuse* [lively, beautiful, and gracious]'.[7] As Monstrelet did not necessarily have the goal of flattering Bedford in his chronicle – particularly as he was writing under the service of Burgundy – it is reasonable to assume that this was an accurate description of Jacquetta.

It is particularly helpful to have such an early description of Jacquetta, as she is unique among the women in this book in that her appearance remains a total mystery. No manuscript images or portraits of her survive, no real description of her looks, hair or eye colour, or other features survive. Her place of burial has been lost to history, with no tomb monument to give suggestions as to her appearance. Her granddaughter, Elizabeth of York, was described as having blonde hair, and it has been suggested that Jacquetta's daughter, Elizabeth Woodville, may have had blonde hair to pass this on to her daughter, so perhaps Jacquetta was fair herself. In reality, this is one of the best surviving descriptions of Jacquetta. Monstrelet also recounts that Bedford gifted the cathedral two bells of great value so that the event would be forever remembered.

It has been suggested that the ageing Bedford had become besotted with Jacquetta, as the haste of their marriage was so unwise and he gained nothing politically, receiving no territory, title or dowry from the marriage.[8] This is, indeed, possibly true. Jacquetta was clearly beautiful and personable and was the type of woman who would easily appeal to a man of the time. As mentioned, however, there were still some political advantages for Bedford. He may well have underestimated how gross an insult the marriage would be for Burgundy, perhaps thinking their alliance was strong enough to weather the storm. At 43 years old and childless, Bedford would also have been conscious of his lack of male heir and his increasing weariness with his difficult life, and was probably keen to find a young bride to provide children for him.

Whatever Bedford's reasons may be (in likelihood, a combination of all of the above), Jacquetta had certainly made the excellent marriage her parents would have envisioned for her at her birth. She had married the heir to the English throne, a man who was single-handedly controlling huge swathes of France and thus one of the most powerful men in Western Europe. Although he was around twenty-five years her senior, he was a cultured, amenable, intelligent man and was therefore a good option for her. As the daughter of a count, Jacquetta was already of high social standing, but she was now Duchess of Bedford, the highest woman in English-controlled France. When she was to return to England, she would be second only to Catherine, the mother of the king. She therefore would displace Eleanor, who was currently the second woman in England through her marriage to Humphrey, and Joan who, as Queen Dowager but not Queen Mother, would be moved down to the fourth most important woman in the royal family. For the first two months of their marriage, however, Jacquetta and Bedford remained in France. Celebrations of the marriage lasted just a few days, for Bedford had to immediately travel to Calais.

Just a few weeks previously, Calais had been in revolt. Bedford had quietened the rebels by promising the resident soldiers their long-overdue wages. As he now returned to the town, however, he arrested 120 of them, ordered the execution of four and the banishment of 110. At Calais, he was met by his brother Humphrey and his uncle Bishop Beaufort to discuss the state of French affairs. The three men for once managed to come to reasonable agreements, with Humphrey helping Bedford to persuade Beaufort to once again lend money to the English Crown. Beaufort agreed to give 5,000 marks to help pay those who were holding castles and forts in France on behalf of the English.[9]

Once matters had been sorted in Calais, Bedford and Jacquetta moved for a short time to Paris, back to Bedford's home of the Hôtel de Bourbon, where Anne had died just a few months previously. This was quite the marital home for Jacquetta to arrive at. Located on the right bank of the Seine next to the royal palace of the Louvre, it had only been built the previous century. The hôtel was originally intended as a huge townhouse to place courtiers who had visited from far and wide to see the Kings of France in residence at the Louvre. It was a significant building, with a chapel and a great hall that even in 1724 were being described as the largest and most sumptuous in Paris.[10] The hôtel had been Bedford's main residence in France, and so it was filled with his possessions.

Like his brother Humphrey, Bedford was an avid reader and had a library that could rival Humphrey's. Bedford's library was filled with religious texts and it also held thirteen volumes of stories about King Arthur, popular reading at this time.[11] It seems fairly certain that Jacquetta enjoyed Bedford's library greatly. In his will, he left the entire library to his young wife, and it seems she kept it, or at least parts of it, after his death. That Jacquetta read at least some of the books in this library must be certain: a collected work of Christine de Pisan held in the British Library bears her signature across several pages.[12] The book itself is quite a relic, having been the original manuscript given to the Queen of France, Isabeau of Bavaria, by the writer herself.

In the 1420s, however, Bedford purchased the Louvre Library after becoming Regent of France upon his brother's death. Jacquetta may have read the book during her marriage to Bedford and perhaps took the lessons written inside to heart – Christine's advice was, after all, for princesses and queens. She certainly must have enjoyed it, though, as her signature and her motto '*sur tous autres*' (above all others) appearing several times throughout suggests more than just a signature of ownership on a book that sits unopened on a shelf.

If Jacquetta had hoped to spend time in the lavish palace in Paris, then she was mistaken. Her new groom was far too busy. Bedford and Jacquetta's marriage had seriously damaged the Anglo–Burgundian alliance which was already on rocky ground, and at the end of May Beaufort attempted to broker peace between the two.[13] He organised for Bedford and Burgundy to meet at Saint-Omer, and while both turned up to the meeting, they never actually ended up seeing each other. Neither wanted to appear of lower status by visiting the other, Bedford claiming he was of highest status as regent, while Burgundy claimed authority because Saint-Omer was in his territory. Beaufort tried his best to act as intermediary but both men refused to back down from their pride. Eventually, the pair left the town having never met, and were never to meet again.

After the disaster of Saint-Omer, Bedford knew that he needed to renew vigour in England for the French cause. The English would be in dire need of troops and money now that they had all but lost the support of the Burgundians. As such, he sent out writs to summon a Parliament at Westminster to commence on 8 July 1433, and on 24 June he and Jacquetta made the crossing to England.[14]

This was likely to have been Jacquetta's first visit to the country and she certainly got quite the welcome. Bedford had not been in England for six years, and he and his new wife received a state entrance to the capital worthy of the heir to the throne and virtual ruler of the kingdom. Pageants were thrown in their honour and Parliament itself seemed overjoyed at Bedford's achievements in France.

In November, the commons came before Henry VI and presented a petition that Bedford should retire from his duties in France and stay in England as his presence had been beneficial. This was most likely true, as he had been able to mediate the in-fighting between Humphrey and Beaufort.[15] Astonishingly, this request was agreed upon by both Beaufort and Humphrey, even though it would have curbed their power.

This must have been an appealing option to Jacquetta. She and Bedford had been welcomed to England as their status befitted, and Parliament had rewarded them generously. Bedford already had a significant income and vast lands but the couple now made their home at Penshurst Place in Kent. The manor house had been rebuilt 100 years prior to their arrival and the couple soon set about making improvements. Bedford built a second hall on the western corner of the house and filled it with his symbols, showing he intended to make his mark on the property and reside there for some time.[16]

In the Parliament of this year, Jacquetta was officially welcomed into the English royal family, with Henry agreeing to a petition to grant denization to Jacquetta and her heirs.[17] This meant that although Jacquetta was foreign born, she would now have the rights of an English-born subject, including being allowed to own land. While it does not seem that Jacquetta bought any land in her initial stay in England, she certainly became a not insignificant landholder in her widowhood.

Bedford seems to have taken Parliament's offer of retirement seriously, for he and Jacquetta stayed in England until July 1434, just over a year since they had arrived. In this time, Jacquetta remains elusive in the records. The only other mention of her comes from the granting of the robes of the garter to her for the Feast of St George at the end of April 1434.[18] If Eleanor Cobham had not yet received her robes, then both women were inducted to the order at this feast. If Eleanor had received hers a few years previously, then it is not difficult to imagine that she may have helped the young duchess to navigate this honour.

It is likely that Jacquetta spent a lot of time at court during this year in England. Bedford, although trialling retirement, was still the most senior leader of the kingdom, with Henry still being in his minority, so affairs in Westminster kept him occupied. Even their home at Penshurst was within a day's ride of the capital, meaning that although it was located in the relaxing countryside, Bedford could be called upon at a moment's notice. As Jacquetta was his wife, and now second-highest lady in the country, it would be reasonable to assume that she would have spent a fair portion of her time at court.

Jacquetta certainly would have known Eleanor, as they were now sisters-in-law, but how much time they spent together is difficult to establish. Bedford and Humphrey were hardly bosom brothers, but they were both working together and based around London. They must have spent time together with their wives in tow. By this time, Joan of Navarre had fully retired from court. Meanwhile, Queen Catherine had been in a relationship with Owen Tudor for several years, which meant she had left the household of Henry VI and rarely visited the court. As such, Eleanor and Jacquetta were the only royal women remaining at court, and it is difficult to imagine that they would not have spent time together. If Eleanor was a kind woman, she may well have taken Jacquetta under her wing, sympathising with this foreign girl who was less than 20 years old and yet thrust into the troubling politics of England. Jacquetta must surely have looked for a mentor to teach her the ways of the English court.

If Jacquetta had started to settle in England by the Garter Feast, then her world was about to be shaken up again. Bedford was growing sick, probably due to the huge strain of the responsibility of maintaining the claims of his nephew in France for the past decade and the constant battles that it required. Nonetheless, he could not accept the retirement offered him; Paris, his home for much of his time in France, begged him for help as the French dauphin's armies had been stopping food convoys into the city. The people were beginning to starve, and it was leading to a collapse in law and order. Bedford could not ignore their pleas, knowing that there was no one else who could do the job for him. As such, in July 1434 he and Jacquetta set sail once again for France.[19]

Jacquetta returned to the opulent Hôtel de Bourbon while Bedford attempted to save matters in Paris. If he was at least partly successful, this did not last long. By spring of the following year, he and Jacquetta were forced to flee Paris for English-held Rouen, as ravaging French troops on the outskirts of Paris had made it dangerous to leave the city walls. By now, Bedford was very ill and his condition cannot have been helped by the sudden downturn in English fortunes. He tried to stabilise Calais by placing his trusted servant, Richard Woodville (senior) as lieutenant of the town.[20]

Richard senior was the Lieutenant of the Tower of London who had argued with Humphrey about releasing Friar Randolph a decade earlier. He was a loyal servant of Bedford, having acted as his chamberlain in the early 1420s. For his service to Bedford, his son was also rewarded; the younger Richard was knighted in 1426 by Bedford alongside the 4-year-old king and Eleanor's father, Reginald Cobham.[21] Richard senior had served under Thomas, Duke of Clarence (Henry V's brother), Henry V and Bedford in France from 1411 onwards, and was a clearly trusted soldier and commander.

In 1434, Richard senior had been part of the meeting of the Great Council at Westminster, and he followed Bedford to France shortly afterwards. It is probable that Richard junior's first meeting with Jacquetta occurred during his father's time at the council. What the two made of each other is impossible to know, but considering the speed of their later relationship, it seems likely there was an instant attraction. Richard was just over ten years older than Jacquetta, but like his father he was an accomplished soldier.

Richard and Jacquetta may have spent some time together in France, as he may well have followed in his father's footsteps and could have been in Bedford's entourage at the time, but their difference in rank would have meant they probably had little interaction, particularly as Richard was there in a military capacity. By May 1435, the same time that Jacquetta and Bedford were fleeing Paris, Richard was away fighting in the Battle of Gerberoy. Here, a French cavalry unit surprised a small vanguard of knights who were travelling with the Earl of Arundel while waiting for the main English forces to arrive. Richard was captured during the skirmish, but was freed at some point during the next year.[22]

Meanwhile, Jacquetta was safe in Rouen with Bedford, who was by now deteriorating rapidly. At the start of August, Bedford attended the Congress of Arras, which included representatives of France and Burgundy. The English intended the congress to be a peace negotiation with France, along similar lines to the Treaty of Troyes. They planned to marry Henry VI to one of the dauphin's daughters, thus unifying the kingdoms – but firmly keeping Henry VI as King of France. As could be predicted, Charles was not content to give up his claim to the throne and the negotiations failed. Worse for the English, though, was that during negotiations the French delegation managed to convince Burgundy to renege on his alliance with the English and join the dauphin's cause. Any attempts Bedford may have made to salvage the important alliance were dashed by his death on 14 September 1435.

This great English prince had finally met his end. For over a decade, he had put all of his time and energy into following his brother's dying wishes to protect the claims of the little boy king. In the end, though, it proved too much. He died seeing the collapse of the union between England and Burgundy, knowing his brother Humphrey and his uncle Beaufort were still at each other's throats and that the power of the French dauphin was growing.

Bedford made sure to look after his beloved young wife, despite the fact that they had been married for less than two and a half years. In his will, drawn up four days before his death, he made Jacquetta his sole heir, granting her all of the lands, tenements, incomes and lordships that he owned in both England and France for the rest of Jacquetta's life, with the exception of a castle and land in the commune of La Haye-du-Puits in Normandy which was to go to his bastard son, Richard. This also included giving her the entirety of his exquisite library.[23] This would have made Jacquetta a very wealthy woman indeed.

However, Bedford's family could not allow such a generous gift for a young foreign woman, particularly when those lands could go to better use – namely, for themselves. Jacquetta was instead granted the customary widow's third. In July 1438 there is a record in the Issues of the Exchequer showing Jacquetta withdrawing 333 marks 'as the third part of 1,000 marks granted to the said late Duke and his heirs'.[24] Jacquetta had still received plenty of properties and sources of income as part of her customary dower, but she was forced to sell many of them within a few years of his death, as will be seen later.

Jacquetta was recalled to England by Henry VI. She was far too important a political pawn now. As a royal duchess of England, she had many privileges, especially with her new-found personal wealth, but she also now found herself restricted as a widow. Royal families at the time were not keen on giving their widows too much autonomy and Jacquetta was not to be allowed to remarry without the king's permission – it could cause far too risky situations for the Crown.

By January 1436, Jacquetta was back in England. If she had wished to return to her marital home of Penshurst then she was to be disappointed, for her brother-in-law Humphrey had claimed the palace for himself. Bedford's goods were already being given away. The younger Richard Woodville had been among the retinue entrusted with bringing Jacquetta back to England, and the pair most certainly hit it off during the journey.

Now the matter of her dower had to be settled. On 6 February, Parliament granted her permission to receive her dower on the proviso that she did not marry without Henry's consent.[25] Records of Jacquetta's movements for the rest of the year are scant, but it is likely she stayed close to the royal court while she was obtaining the lands granted in her dower and figuring out her next move. Perhaps she received some help and guidance from her sister-in-law, Eleanor Cobham, particularly as Jacquetta was now no threat to Eleanor.

One thing that she was doing for certain during the next few months was getting to know Sir Richard Woodville very well. By the end of the year, a scandal had broken. Jacquetta, Dowager Duchess of Bedford and daughter of the Count of Brienne and Saint-Pol, had married the lowly knight, Sir Richard Woodville, in secret. It must be understood what a shock this would have been to everybody on both sides of the

Channel. Jacquetta was of high birth, high enough to marry the heir to the throne of England. She could have, if fate had gone differently, become queen. If she were to remarry, it should have been to one of the highest peers in the country.

Richard Woodville, in the overall hierarchy of the country, was not doing too badly for himself. He was a knight, and his father had climbed through the ranks to be trusted enough to have a place on the King's Council. Although the Woodvilles were therefore an up-and-coming family, in terms of the nobility they were still firmly near the bottom of the ladder. The royal family trusted them, but they would still have been considered very much as servants, not friends – and not even close to equals. For a woman of Jacquetta's position to marry a man like Richard would have been a huge cause for gossip.

While Eleanor and Humphrey had partaken in a similarly scandalous marriage less than ten years previously, the situations were subtly different. In medieval society, it was more accepted for a woman to marry a man of a higher rank than for a man to marry a higher woman. Gender roles and position also have to come into account. As prince of the realm, Humphrey was free to more or less marry who he pleased. Although marrying a knight's daughter would have caused gossip at court, precedents such as that of his grandfather, John of Gaunt, made it a more acceptable decision. While wealth and title were desirable in a wife, a woman of any rank could fulfil the most important role of childbearing.

For a woman like Jacquetta, however, her life depended on the rank of her husband. While she now had a level of personal power and wealth through the dower of Bedford, her quality of life was going to be based on the livelihood of her husband. A husband significantly lower and poorer than herself would not set her up for what was viewed as a suitable life for a woman of her rank. Most importantly, her place as widow in the royal family and the condition that she not remarry without the king's permission made this a very dangerous marriage. She could lose everything by marrying Richard – and lose everything she nearly did.

Any king would be displeased by Jacquetta's actions, but Henry, throughout his life, was to show a particular fury to those he felt had wronged him. She had broken the terms of her dower grant and now her dower was taken away from her. Jacquetta was destitute, with only her husband's limited income to live on. A far cry from her position up to this point.

Her Luxembourg relatives were understandably also extremely unhappy. Her uncle, Bishop Louis, and others of their friends and relations disdained Richard as he was not at all close to the rank of her first husband, Bedford. However, they were powerless to do anything.

Monstrelet is remarkably complimentary towards Richard, describing him as a very well-shaped young man.[26] Richard must certainly have been an excellent man of outstanding character and personality to receive such a compliment in such a scandalous marriage.

Jacquetta ended 1436 on an uncertain note. She had married a man who she was clearly deeply in love with, and would go on to have an exceedingly successful marriage, and so she was experiencing great personal happiness. However, to have had all of her lands and money taken away from her, to be receiving ire from her relatives and friends, to be the topic of scandal and gossip and to be welcomed into a household that, while loving, was far lower than anything she had been used to, must have been a shock. Once the dust had settled, then, she and her new husband set about trying to reclaim what was hers.

Jacquetta and Richard petitioned the king and Parliament to request the restitution of Jacquetta's dower. They submitted themselves to Henry, acknowledging that they had 'offended your seid Hieghnesse' and suffered greatly as a result. They requested that Henry forgive them, that Jacquetta be allowed to receive all the castles, manors, lands, tenements and possessions that had belonged to Bedford. The petition ends emotively to appeal to Henry, but still truthfully – that she had nothing to sustain her without his rightfulness and grace.[27]

Henry needed time to stew, however. It took until 23 March 1437 for Jacquetta and Richard to receive a response. They were to be pardoned on the condition that they pay a £1,000 fine to the king.[28] This was a severe fine. Jacquetta's dower had been assigned at a third of Bedford's £4,000 income in England, alongside a proportion of his lands in England and France. This was twice the qualifying level for an earldom, making her certainly among the wealthiest in the land of any gender.[29] However, to pay this fine she was forced to sell significant portions of her land – one of her generous benefactors being Cardinal Beaufort.

With Beaufort having received significant compensation of land in lieu of a fine to the Crown, Henry was eventually pacified.[30] An official pardon did not come for the couple until October that year, at which point they would finally have been allowed to return to court and Henry's presence.[31] However, while the couple certainly spent time there, particularly for festivities, they were mostly living a quiet life in their new marital home. As Penshurst had passed to Humphrey, the couple needed their own place to live, and here Humphrey's new rival at court, the Duke of Suffolk, came to their rescue. In 1440 he sold them the manor house of Grafton Regis in Northamptonshire, which was then valued at £24 a year.[32]

Although the couple only bought the manor in 1440, it is believed that Richard's family had been living in the manor as tenants of Suffolk and his predecessors for quite a long time.[33] Richard and Jacquetta therefore probably spent their early married life between there and France. Jacquetta needed to sort out her dower lands and rents there, while Richard was also still a soldier and therefore still required to fight.

It is at the end of 1437 that it is believed Jacquetta and Richard had their first child. Although Jacquetta was of high birth, through her marriage to Richard the births of her progeny were no longer deemed noteworthy enough to warrant recording. It has been debated for a long time whether Elizabeth Woodville, their eldest daughter, was also their oldest child, or if their eldest son, Lewis, was born first. Either way, Elizabeth's birth date would be somewhere between 1437 and 1438. Elizabeth may have been born at Grafton Regis, or perhaps in France, but Grafton Regis was the family's main base and so it was her childhood home. Richard and Jacquetta could not have known, upon the birth of this daughter, that their entire fates would be changed because of her.

The birth of this first child may have been what finally encouraged Henry to give the couple their official pardon and welcome them back to court. As with Joan of Navarre, Jacquetta spent most of her marriage in perpetual pregnancy. She and Richard are estimated to have had fourteen children together, with twelve of them reaching adulthood. This resulted in almost a child every year, with their first born around 1437 and their last in 1458. This would have lessened Jacquetta's participation at court, at least for the early years of their marriage, although it does not seem that she minded this too much. English politics were getting messy and dangerous and it was best to stay in her uneventful manor house, ruling her own small territory as lady of the manor.

The next few years were quiet for the Woodvilles. Jacquetta gave birth to several more children and Richard was occupied with English skirmishes in France. In 1439, he was part of an army sent to relieve the commune of Meaux north-east of Paris.[34] By this time, Meaux was the only English-controlled town east of Paris, and in the summer of this year Joan of Navarre's son, Arthur, led a strong French force against the city.[35] Arthur had reneged on his alliance with the English in 1435 alongside the Duke of Burgundy at Arras, and was now Constable of France.

Joan was not the only foreign-born royal woman who had a relative turn against the English. Jacquetta herself suffered the same, for in 1440 her brother Louis, who had become Count of Saint-Pol after the death of her father, also joined the French cause.

Richard was in France once more in June 1441 in the retinue of Richard, Duke of York. York had travelled to Rouen to provide extra relief to the tired forces in France, and it was quite a significant army. There were nearly 1,000 men-at-arms and around 3,000 archers, and there were numerous nobles in the force including two earls and thirty knights, Richard being among them. However, this was not a purely military gathering; many high-ranking women had accompanied their husbands, including York's wife, Cecily, and Jacquetta.[36]

This excursion was not successful, however, and by the end of the year the English had lost many more towns and territories to the French. Jacquetta was very much on the front line of the conflict, showing she was not a shy woman. Perhaps she was used to the conflicts in France from her marriage to Bedford, but she certainly was brave enough to follow her husband as he fought for his country.

The couple did have time for frivolity, nonetheless. During Shrovetide of the same year, Richard had taken part in a two-day jousting tournament at the Tower of London with the Duke of Norfolk.[37] The Woodvilles were to gain a reputation for their jousting skills through their lives, with Jacquetta's son Anthony gaining renown in later years.

Jacquetta and Richard were in France in June 1441, meaning they were not in London when Eleanor made her glorious entry into the city. It is unclear how long the couple were in France and whether they had returned to England by the end of the following month when Eleanor and her alleged accomplices were arrested. They had almost certainly returned to England by the time of Eleanor's trial and penance in October and November, for the Duke of York had retreated back to Normandy in September and winter generally heralded the end of the campaigning season.

How Jacquetta and Richard were affected by Eleanor's trial is impossible to know. It is not even known if the couple were in London, watching events first-hand, or if they quietly and sensibly retreated back to their manor at Grafton Regis. Jacquetta may well have been very concerned watching what was happening to Eleanor, as they had known each and may even have been friends. Regardless of her opinion of Eleanor, to have such a dramatic event hit the heart of the royal family would have completely shaken Jacquetta's world.

Philippa Gregory claims that Jacquetta and Richard would have been concerned for Jacquetta's own safety during the trial.[38] Not only did Jacquetta's family, the Luxembourgs, claim descent from the mythical Melusine, but Jacquetta had also contracted a surprising marriage with Bedford. The couple could well be concerned that Jacquetta would be dragged into events. However, it is necessary to unpack these thoughts, as Eleanor's trial certainly affected Jacquetta – but not quite in this way.

The legend of Melusine comes from European folklore and has connections across various countries of Western Europe. However, the Luxembourg family claimed direct descent from this legend. The story went that Count Siegfried bought the territory upon which he founded the city of Luxembourg in AD 963. Siegfried married Melusine, a beautiful woman who agreed to the marriage on the condition that one day every week Siegfried gave her absolute privacy. The morning after their wedding, Melusine magically made the Castle of Luxembourg appear on the Bock Rock. They had a happy marriage until one day Siegfried broke his promise and spied on Melusine while she was in the bath. Here, he saw to his shock that Melusine was a mermaid. When Melusine realised she had been spotted, she and the bath sank into the rock and never returned.

Gregory says that Jacquetta's claim to be descended from Melusine, a magical mermaid creature, would have made her an easier target for accusations of witchcraft. In reality, there is no evidence that Jacquetta ever advertised this connection. There are no letters, records in chronicles or pieces of heraldry that show that Jacquetta was at all interested in the legend of Melusine. Jacquetta did have a copy of the story of Melusine in her library, but this was a book also held in the libraries of many other noblewomen.[39] This was just one volume of a huge library that, as mentioned, also included the stories of King Arthur that her husband, a prince of England, had owned. As such, it remains a mystery whether she ever read the book or found any interest in it.

Furthermore, legends such as these were accepted pieces of medieval storytelling. Ever since Henry II and Eleanor of Aquitaine in the twelfth century, the English royal family had claimed descent from King Arthur. Edward I had the alleged bones of Arthur transferred to a regal black marble tomb, and his grandson Edward III reinstated the Knights of the Round Table, which eventually became the Order of the Garter.[40] In reality, members of Jacquetta's family at various times claiming their castle had been magically made by a mermaid would never have been considered a legitimate concern.

Then there is Jacquetta's marriage to Bedford. True, the marriage was a surprise (particularly for Burgundy), but it has already been discussed that it was not necessarily a disadvantageous one for Bedford. Although by the time of Eleanor's trial some of Jacquetta's relatives had reneged on the alliance with the English, for several decades her family contributed significantly to the English cause, and she was still the daughter of a count. As such, Jacquetta's marriage to Bedford was hardly comparable to Eleanor's shock marriage to Humphrey.

That being said, Jacquetta and Richard must still have felt some concern with what was happening to Eleanor. Jacquetta was foreign born – always a cause for suspicion and an easy target to point a finger at. She had already angered Henry once by marrying without his permission, so doubt could still be placed on her. Moreover, Jacquetta almost certainly knew some of Eleanor's accomplices to some extent. If nothing else, Thomas Southwell was a canon in the royal chapel at Westminster, where Jacquetta must have attended mass at some point as part of the royal family. Roger Bolingbroke had been part of Eleanor and Humphrey's household and as a scholar he had produced much written material, some of which could well have been in Jacquetta's library from Bedford.

There were, therefore, enough reasons for Jacquetta to at least be mildly concerned. Even if she did not think she was in the line of fire and realised that the accusations were being targeted specifically at Eleanor and Humphrey, it was still a deep scandal at the heart of the royal family, which she was still a part of. By this time, Joan of Navarre and Queen Catherine had both died, and so Jacquetta and Eleanor were the only female members remaining. The accusations would have made Jacquetta feel vulnerable, as she realised that her position would not necessarily be enough to protect her from attack. In this way, it was certainly a lesson that Jacquetta was never to forget – and what she learnt from the attack on Eleanor she was to put into practice herself a few decades later.

After Eleanor was banished and sent for perpetual imprisonment, the English court was a place of uncertainty and power struggles. Humphrey's absence left a hole, and those who remained jostled to find their new place in the hierarchy. If Jacquetta had avoided the court before, she certainly would have distanced herself now to reduce any scandal on herself. She gave birth to another child, probably Anthony, in 1442, and this suggests that she had indeed returned to life at Grafton Regis. She did, after all, have several young children by this time to occupy her. Jacquetta was now the only royal woman remaining in England, and she needed to preserve herself and her family.

For the next few years, little is found of Jacquetta and Richard in the records. However, the winds of change were coming. England was finally to get a new queen, and the course of history was to dramatically alter forever.

10

FROM WOODS TO RIVERS

BY 1444, IT was necessary for the young king to finally marry and provide an heir for the kingdom, particularly now that Humphrey's claim had been so damaged. Margaret of Anjou was decided upon as a suitable match. Accompanying Humphrey's enemy, Suffolk, to the Continent to bring Margaret across the Channel was, among others, Jacquetta. She was chosen for numerous reasons. As Duchess of Bedford, and most senior (and only remaining) woman in the royal family, it was her place to welcome the new queen to the country. Jacquetta was also familiar with the rituals of the English court through her marriage to Bedford and would be well equipped to advise this foreign girl how to behave.

Jacquetta was also likely to be a simple comfort to Margaret. Margaret was just 15 years old, two years younger than Jacquetta had been upon her first marriage, and did not speak a word of English. Jacquetta would certainly have the life experience to be able to help Margaret in her new adventure and sympathise with her position. Moreover, Margaret and Jacquetta were recently related; one of Jacquetta's younger sisters, Isabelle, had married Charles, Count of Maine in 1443. Charles was Margaret's paternal uncle, meaning Jacquetta's sister was now Margaret's aunt. This loose familial connection may well have also provided a sense of security for Margaret when travelling to England.

It seems that during the journey to England, Margaret and Jacquetta hit it off. Although Jacquetta was almost twice her age and by now had five children, with a sixth born that same year, she was still vivacious, entertaining, intelligent and, most likely, exceedingly kind to the young queen.

As Margaret settled in England, Jacquetta was given the honour of being one of her chief ladies-in-waiting. She certainly would have attended the royal wedding on 23 April 1445 and Margaret's coronation on 30 May at Westminster Abbey in her capacity as Duchess of Bedford. Jousting accompanied the festivities, as was customary, and it is very possible that Richard took part, considering his reputation and his place as Jacquetta's husband.

While Jacquetta may have felt invigorated by the arrival of this young queen, the rest of the realm was not so enamoured. Many were on the side of Humphrey, believing that the Armagnac alliance was preferable, and others were frustrated that Margaret brought neither lands, title nor a wealthy dowry with her. In fact, the reality of the marriage alliance was even worse than any in England could have anticipated – so bad that Suffolk and those who organised the marriage had to keep the terms secret from the public as they knew how provocative they would be.

In the marriage treaty, England had agreed to cede to France the territories of Maine and Anjou. These two territories at the time amounted to around a quarter of the remaining French territory in English hands.[1] These were lands for which the English had spilt the blood of thousands across a century. Lands won in the glory days of the king's father and the greatest victories of Agincourt were signed away by a flick of the pen for a marriage that brought no benefit. The government did well to hide the terms for the time being. To reveal them would be to incite riots.

The new queen quickly settled into her role, and she grew to rely heavily on the man who had procured her advantageous marriage. Suffolk had already become Henry's new right-hand man after the destruction of Humphrey and now he courted favour with Margaret. The 23-year-old King Henry was exceedingly happy with his new bride, and Suffolk had been rewarded for the match by having his earldom raised to a marquisate.

Jacquetta seems to have become more involved with the court – or at least her involvement is more evident in surviving records – with the advent of Queen Margaret. In the New Year of 1447, Jacquetta was given a silver cup worth £35 and on 9 May the following year her husband was also rewarded, being made a baron.[2] Richard Woodville chose to take the title of Lord Rivers, although it is not clear where he decided to take this name from.

With the death of both Humphrey of Gloucester and his uncle and rival, Henry Beaufort in 1447, the court was open to domination by Suffolk and his followers. The start of 1450 saw huge shifts across the kingdom. As the second session of Parliament began on 22 January, the Commons were baying for blood. For too long had Suffolk dominated the court and the king's ear, taking for himself whatever he pleased, gathering money, lands and power. Gone were the days of the fights between Humphrey and Beaufort, where at least there was a balance of influence and opinion. The Commons demanded that Suffolk be tried for treason. They claimed that Suffolk had been planning to sell England to the French King, inviting him over to take the throne. After the debacle of Maine and Anjou being ceded, these were credible charges. Suffolk was now in deep danger.[3] By the end of the month he was imprisoned in the Tower of London.

The retribution against Suffolk was delayed time and again by Henry, but eventually he could protect his favourite no longer. Henry, of course, found him innocent of treason, but knew that he could not let him go without consequence. Henry declared Suffolk guilty of some of the lesser charges levied against him and sentenced him to a five-year banishment from the territories of England, to commence on 1 May. Suffolk duly set his affairs in order and, on 1 May, he set sail across the English Channel. However, in the Channel his ship was intercepted by one of the largest ships in the English fleet. Here, the crew dragged him on board, called him a traitor and executed him. Thus, the life of the Duke of Suffolk ended, his body abandoned ignobly on the sands of Dover.[4]

The king and queen were shaken by Suffolk's murder, and Jacquetta must have been there to comfort Margaret. Her husband was soon to be drawn into the affair, however. After Suffolk's murder, various rumours had circulated the realm about who was responsible. One such rumour placed the blame on the men of Kent, and fear of retribution grew among the Commons. By the end of the month, a rebellion was simmering and men from Kent began to make their way to London. A few weeks later, in mid June, the rebels were gathered at Blackheath, 12 miles south-east of London, in their thousands.[5]

The men of Kent said that they had gathered to proclaim their innocence of the murder of Suffolk, but they now brought their own complaints to the Crown. They said that the king was surrounded by corrupt men, the Crown's lands had been given away to the detriment of the royal purse and the kingdom, and taxes were too high.[6] It did not help that many of the men had been stirred up by unpaid soldiers returning from France dissatisfied. Here, the death of Humphrey came back to haunt the court. The rebels also mentioned how unfairly Humphrey had been treated in his last days and they blamed Suffolk for his death. Three years after his death, Humphrey's loyal followers and admirers among the Commons were still honouring his memory.

The rebels demanded that the remainder of Suffolk's followers at court be removed, and instead the king should surround himself with better men, specifically suggesting Richard, Duke of York, as well as the Dukes of Exeter, Buckingham and Norfolk. With thousands of angry rebels so close to the capital, Henry VI found himself in a precarious position. To indulge the rebels would show weakness, but to attack them would be to attack his own subjects and bring great unpopularity. Henry chose the latter. He ordered Buckingham and other upper nobility to punish and arrest the mob.

Among those sent out from London to deal with the rebels was Richard Woodville.[7] In the resulting scuffle, a significant number of Henry's men were slain. Even worse for Henry, many of the soldiers in the royal force began to murmur their support and sympathy for the rebels and their demands.

Henry was not a warmonger, and in the face of such hostility from his own subjects and the death of his men, he fled. Leaving London behind, he took refuge in Kenilworth, 90 miles from the capital.[8] Henry's actions emboldened the rebels. At the end of June, men in Wiltshire dragged the Bishop of Salisbury from his home and murdered him. It seems the main motivation for his murder was that the bishop had been the man who had married Henry and Margaret. The loss of French territory had stung the Commons, and Margaret's dominance at court and connection to the French Crown (the French queen being Margaret's aunt) meant she was increasingly viewed with suspicion. The murder of the bishop meant the rebellions were coming perilously close to the royal family.

Now that Henry had fled the capital, the rebels had free rein. At the start of July they entered London on several consecutive days. Although they initially remained peaceful, by 5 July the leaders had lost control and the mob began to loot shops and the homes of London residents. That night, as the rebels crossed London Bridge, the mayor of London's men joined with sheriffs, citizens and the remaining royal guards at the Tower of London to remove the rebels. The two sides clashed on London Bridge throughout the night, and by the morning the rebels were in a bad state. The Archbishop of York offered a full pardon for all men who would return to their homes in peace, and the Kentish men eagerly agreed, abandoning London in their droves.[9] London was safe once more, but no thanks to the king, who was cowering in his castle nearly 100 miles away.

It is unclear if Jacquetta was in the capital during the rebellion. As the king had been in residence, and her husband was part of the force sent to defend it, it would seem possible that she was also there. If she was, it certainly would have been a terrifying time, particularly when those close to the king and queen were being targeted. However, this year it is thought that Jacquetta gave birth to her ninth child, Margaret, and so it may well be that Jacquetta was safe in her manor at Grafton Regis, either preparing for the birth of her daughter or looking after a newborn. Either way, her husband had survived the disturbances.

The problems in the country did not end with the Kent rebellion. In August, the last English fortress in Normandy, Cherbourg, fell to the French, who had been steadily reclaiming territory since Margaret and Henry's marriage.[10] The English cause in France was almost lost. This month was, however, a proud one for the Woodvilles: Richard was invested as a Knight of the Garter on 4 August 1450.[11] This was the highest honour Richard could receive, and it clearly demonstrates the esteem that Jacquetta and Richard were held in by Henry and Margaret. Richard had risen from a member of a respected gentry family to a baron who was part of the most prestigious order of chivalry in the country. The Woodvilles were on the rise.

In September, Richard, Duke of York, returned from Ireland and landed in Wales. York was descended from Edward III of England, his paternal grandfather being Edward's fourth son, Edmund of Langley. He was also descended through his mother from Edward III's second son, Lionel. York had lost both of his parents by the time he was 4, and this had made him a minor under the custody of the Crown. York's wardship was granted to Ralph Neville, 1st Earl of Westmorland, and when York was 13 Neville betrothed him to his daughter, Cecily. By 1450, York was one of the wealthiest and largest landowners in the country, in control of a dukedom and an earldom, and was a contender for the throne through his direct royal descent on both sides.

York had been acting as Lieutenant of Ireland, a prestigious and highly trusted but undesirable position, since 1447. Now, however, his money was running low and the trouble in England seems to have encouraged him to return to try and help the king. York was a capable military commander, which was why he had been trusted with Ireland, and with news of the king fleeing the capital and men rising up across the country it is easy to see why York thought his services were needed.

York landed in Wales, both for ease of access but also because he owned extensive lands on the Welsh border. He landed at Beaumaris and this was immediately a cause of great concern for the Crown, for Beaumaris was where their valuable prisoner Eleanor Cobham was currently residing.[12] Initially, it may seem strange that Eleanor could be considered a target for York. Indeed, it is extremely unlikely that York had any plans to seize Eleanor, particularly as there were no attempts in the next few years by York to free or reinstate her. However, it may well have been in the minds of Henry and Margaret that just a few months previously the rebels of Kent had invoked the memory of Eleanor's husband, Humphrey. Humphrey's memory still held political currency, and so the Crown may well have therefore considered Eleanor a danger.

In the event, York's landing was the start of a conflict that would engulf the country within a decade. Though he likely came with good intentions, he soon received rumours that the king was looking to arrest him. He raised a defending force and travelled to London, bursting in on the king in his chambers to plead his innocence from any nefarious deeds – necessary, in part, because of the rebels' demands that he be placed near the king. Henry reassured York that he had never intended to arrest him and he could go in peace.

York was unfortunately implicated in whispers against the Crown again, however – this time in Parliament. An MP from Bristol, Thomas Young, proposed that York should be officially recognised as Henry's heir, considering his five-year marriage to Margaret was still childless. For such an outrageous suggestion, Young was sent to the Tower of London, and York became unpopular.[13]

The following year was to see law and order continue to disintegrate under Henry's rule. Henry was now nearly 30 years old, and yet he had not properly taken up the reins of government. There did not seem to be an ounce of his father's courage, war acumen or authority, and the government was floundering. Favourites such as Suffolk may have been unpopular and greedy, but at least they gave the Crown some direction. Henry was easily guided to whatever his favourites or his wife wanted him to do. There was also a new favourite in town, the Duke of Somerset, who very quickly turned out to be as bad – if not worse – than his predecessor. Personal rivalries picked up, and 1451 saw lots of petty squabbles among the nobility looking to settle scores with private armies rather than defer to the Crown's judgement.

Jacquetta of Luxembourg and Richard Woodville had weathered the storms well so far. They had survived their scandalous marriage, and with the arrival of a new queen they had risen through the ranks of royal favour and position. Although they received generous gifts from Margaret, and Jacquetta was often at court alongside her in her capacity as lady-in-waiting, it does not seem that the Woodvilles were viewed as being influential enough to be a threat at court. They were not targeted in any of the discontented stirrings across the country at all levels of society, and so they were able to generally continue their quiet life uninterrupted.

In October 1450, Richard had been sent to Aquitaine in his position as seneschal of the region, and letters of protection were granted to many men to accompany him.[14] The following year, Henry asked Richard to take 4,000 men to Bordeaux to help fight against the French King. However, due to the dire financial circumstances of the Crown, the soldiers could not be paid and so the expedition was delayed.[15] This led to the capture of Bordeaux in the summer, creating more unrest in England and making the Crown even more unpopular. Numerous orders were issued at the end of the year for Richard to take men to Bordeaux, with Richard being appointed seneschal of the region in October, but still no expedition was launched and Richard seems to have remained in England.

By 1452, Jacquetta and Richard had now had ten children, although their first son Lewis had died in childhood. This still left them with nine mouths to feed beyond their own, the youngest being around 1 year old, the eldest, probably Elizabeth, around 15. They needed to start marrying off their children, and Elizabeth was at a perfect age to do so. Her chosen groom was Sir John Grey of Leicestershire.

John's parents were both of the baronage, his mother being Elizabeth Ferrers, 6th Baroness Ferrers of Groby, and his father being Sir Edward Grey, son of the 3rd Baron Grey de Ruthyn. John had been born around 1432, making him about five years older than Elizabeth.[16] The marriage was certainly solemnised by 1454, but as is so often the case, the exact date of their marriage is unknown. It is possible that Elizabeth had been lodging with the Grey family for several years, as was common for girls of her rank.[17] If she were to board in another house for her education, it would make sense for her to do so in the household of a potential spouse. If she had remained at Grafton Regis, however, the marriage would have seen Elizabeth move out of her family home which had been her main base for most of her life.

John Grey's family home was Groby Hall near Leicester, passed through John's mother's side. Groby Hall was within a day's ride from Grafton Regis, so Elizabeth had not gone too far from home. The hall had been built by the family and was situated close to the castle. It was a comfortable manor home with a grand hall and would have been a sufficient place for Elizabeth to begin her married life.

There was change in the royal family at this time as well. By summer of 1453 it was clear that Margaret of Anjou had finally conceived a child. This would have been a welcome relief to the king and queen, for an heir was much needed to try and stabilise the regime and provide a counter to the claims of the Duke of York. Disturbances were still rife, however, and in the midst of Margaret's pregnancy the realm was running wild. Nobles were settling private scores among themselves with little intervention from the king, and when he did intercede, his favourites were clear. One such example was in the West Country, where the

Duke of Somerset and Richard Neville, the Earl of Warwick (grandson of York's guardian, Ralph Neville), both laid claim to an array of territory. Warwick had been in control of the area for ten years, which in many eyes (including his own) would give him right of ownership; Somerset contested this, and Henry of course sided with him. Warwick refused to agree and fortified himself in Cardiff Castle. Somerset duly raised an army to force him out.[18]

All-out war was imminent between Somerset and Warwick, both powerful men with large lands, resources and men at their disposal, and for once Henry knew he had to act personally. He began to march west from London with men of his own to settle the squabbles between the two great magnates. In early August 1453, King Henry VI arrived at the royal lodge of Clarendon in Wiltshire, within a few days' march of Cardiff Castle. Here occurred the first great disaster of his reign, which was to mark the beginning of the end. For it was at Clarendon that Henry was struck by an unknown affliction that left him catatonic.

A contemporary chronicler records that Henry was 'so incapable that he was neither able to walk upon his feet nor to lift up his head'.[19] This was an unprecedented disaster for England. No king had ever before been so completely invalid. At first, the King's Council kept all information about the king's state secret, hoping that he would regain consciousness. By October, however, it was clear that Henry was not going to recover any time soon – if ever. A Great Council was summoned, calling together the great lords of the realm.

York was included in the invitation for the council, a quick reversal in his fortunes. After his various conflicts with the king and Somerset across the previous few years, York had fallen. He had already lost much of his money through the expenditure of his post as Lieutenant of Ireland, and he was increasingly scorned by the king. However, he was still of royal blood and one of the most powerful and capable men in the land, and the council could not ignore his invaluable input at this time of crisis.

On 13 October 1453, Queen Margaret gave birth to a healthy baby boy. Usually, this would have been the greatest news she could have hoped for. After over eight years of marriage she had finally provided a child, and the best kind – a future King of England. Her position was secure and England finally had a direct male heir. However, there was a problem: the child had to be recognised by his father, the reigning king, in order to be a legitimate child and thus contender for the throne. Despite being presented with the child and informed of its birth, Henry was still completely unresponsive.[20] Prince Edward was not yet legitimate.

The King's Great Council attempted to rule the kingdom in his name, and Henry's condition continued to be kept secret from his citizens. Life continued as normal. On 18 November, Queen Margaret had her churching ceremony. Ten duchesses, eight countesses and a plethora of ladies attended the queen on the occasion, including Jacquetta of Luxembourg, as well as Elizabeth Woodville's mother-in-law, Lady Elizabeth Ferrers.[21]

The churching ceremony was very important for Queens of England. The practice originated in the Jewish community, where a woman was considered 'unclean' after giving birth and had to be ceremonially cleansed. In the Bible, the Jewish Virgin Mary went through a purification after giving birth to Jesus. Christian monarchies took up the practice from there. When medieval English queens had given birth, they stayed hidden away from the world for several weeks, being waited on only by women. After a period of time, the queen re-emerged to the world through the churching ceremony, where she and the women around her would celebrate the birth of the child, she would be blessed by the Church and she would once again enter the court and resume her duties.

That Margaret had her churching showed not only that she was respecting custom, but that she was trying to follow protocol closely to emphasise the legitimacy of her baby and government was running as normal.

The churching would have been a time of joy for Jacquetta. Her dear friend had finally produced the child she would have longed for, and a healthy birth for mother and child was always to be celebrated. Moreover, a gathering of so many women at court was an anticipated social occasion and would have been enjoyed by all. It was also a chance for Jacquetta to see her daughter's mother-in-law and check in on Elizabeth's well-being.

The court and government kept up pretences across winter, muddling through the running of the country with an unresponsive king. In November, Somerset was sent to the Tower of London, presumably a move by the council to placate York, who was a far more valuable member of the council. Somerset had also caused problems around the birth of Prince Edward, for rumours had circulated that Somerset was the real father of Margaret's son due to his closeness to the queen.

In January 1454, Margaret of Anjou made a bold move. Perhaps reassured by her newly increased status as mother to the heir, Margaret produced a bill of five articles. These articles proclaimed her desire to be given the regency of England, the power to grant the offices of government, control of the Privy Seal and be allowed to allocate all benefices of the Church.[22] These requests would effectively give Margaret the power to rule as if she were Henry.

This proposal horrified the government. Queens had acted as regents of England before, but usually this was for short periods of time when the king was abroad fighting wars and an end was in sight. Perhaps the greatest exception to this had been Isabella, wife of Edward II, who ruled for four years from 1326 to 1330 in the name of her son, Edward III. Isabella, however, had initially been welcomed in England as a force of good against her despised husband, and had been in control of an army which allowed her to fortify her power in government. Margaret was hated and mistrusted across the realm for her French connections and her favouritism of loathed men such as Suffolk and Somerset. She had implicitly been targeted in attacks on these favourites, and no one in the realm would want to give her control of government.

The government denied her requests and England continued to be ruled by the Great Council until March 1454 when the chancellor died. Constitutionally, only the king could replace him, but Henry was still unresponsive to any attempts to communicate with him. Finally, the government's hand was forced. They needed someone to act as king. They had to turn to York. Parliament officially invited York to take the position of Lord Protector, and in early April he accepted. Everybody in government, York included, proceeded exceedingly cautiously. No one wanted to be accused of trying to seize power for themselves. York himself announced in Parliament how reluctant he was to take up the control of government.

York brought together a large council filled with experienced men of noble blood, and there was not a single meeting of the council that met with fewer than twenty members – this ensured that it was clear that power was being shared.[23] York and his council set about restoring law and order to the kingdom, brokering peace between warring families, reducing the expenditure of the royal household and tightening up finances.

York needed people on his side to help him in this difficult position, and for this he turned to the Nevilles. The Nevilles were his wife's family and had looked after him and his lands well during his minority. The Earl of Warwick had clashed with York's enemy, Somerset, and the classic adage of 'the enemy of my enemy is my friend' certainly applied here.

The Nevilles made sure to pledge their support to York and, gratefully, he quickly placed many of the Neville family in positions of power in the government. Whereas the Nevilles had been pushed to the side and overlooked by Henry VI, York gave them recognition as the powerful family that they were and they were happy to give all their resources to York's government. They gave money and men to help York reinforce Calais, one of the last remaining strongholds of English power in France that was close to breaking point, and the territory was secured. For the rest of the year, York ruled with exceeding popularity at all levels of society, acting 'most admirably, and wonderfully pacifying all rebels and malefactors according to law … with great honour and the love of all'.[24]

On Christmas Day 1454, a Christmas miracle occurred: King Henry VI woke up from his stupor. The court was overjoyed, and Henry finally met his son who was now over a year old. Prince Edward was recognised as Henry's child and England formally had an heir once more. Henry very quickly took control of the government again and there was a significant about-turn. Infuriated that Somerset had been locked away in the Tower without trial for a year, Henry immediately released him and restored him to his previous position of power. York and the Nevilles were removed from their positions in government and everything went back to how it was before.[25] Now, however, there were two crucial differences. Firstly, York had gained the allegiance of the Neville family. Secondly, England had spent a year experiencing an efficient, strong and fiscally responsible government. It would not forget this.

The year of 1455 saw the start of the Wars of the Roses, a bloody series of civil wars on English soil. The restoration of Henry's favourites was unpopular, and it did not take long for tensions to reach breaking point. At the end of May, a meeting of the Great Council was called and York became paranoid that the council was planning on moving against him. Supported this time by the Nevilles, York raised an army in the north and across parts of the Welsh border. The joint force blocked the arrival of the Great Council and surprised Henry and Somerset, who had very little time to rally a defending army.

On 22 May 1455, the king's poorly equipped force of around 2,000 men met with York's far superior forces at St Albans, around 20 miles north of London. This First Battle of St Albans was a resounding victory for York. His great rival Somerset was killed in the battle, along with other leading supporters of the king's regime.[26] Henry was abandoned by his advisors and bodyguards and was captured by York's men. He seems to have also suffered another mental break, understandable considering the circumstances. Henry had also been wounded in the neck, which would have only added to the stress of his mental state.[27] With the king in his possession and again indisposed, York was once more appointed Protector.

With all this chaos in the kingdom, it is a wonder that life carried on as normal, but it did. This year, 18-year-old Elizabeth Woodville gave birth to her first child by her husband, John Grey.[28] The child was a boy and they named him Thomas. By the time of Thomas' birth, it is likely that Elizabeth and John had moved to the Grey family's second principal manor house at Astley in Warwickshire.[29]

Elizabeth and her husband were still in the midst of the turmoil, however; the Great Council that never met had been summoned to meet in Leicester, 20 miles from Astley and just 5 miles from Groby. Whichever house they were living in at the time, York's men had walked right past them and their families on his way to blocking the arrival of the council. It certainly would have been a terrifying time for Elizabeth, who would have probably been in the midst of pregnancy or possibly had already given birth.

With Henry in his custody, York returned to rule. Warwick once again took power and was appointed Captain of Calais. Although York did not yet have widespread support, some members of the nobility were won to his side, particularly considering his stable government of the previous year. Margaret of Anjou was side-lined and reduced to looking after her infant son.

York ruled until February the following year, when Henry regained his senses. Once again, he set about undoing York's actions. Although London had become the traditional base for the king and his court, Margaret was aware that the citizens of London were becoming increasingly frustrated with Henry's government and that he was very unpopular there. As such, spring 1456 saw the court move to the Midlands where the royal couple were popular.[30]

The Woodvilles continued to loyally serve the king and queen during this period of retreat. By 1457, Jacquetta had given birth to thirteen children, the youngest around a year old, and yet she continued to be at Margaret's side. On 31 May, Jacquetta and Richard accompanied Queen Margaret as she travelled from Kenilworth Castle to Coventry for the feast of Corpus Christi.[31] Here, they watched the various pageants and plays being performed, enjoying the festivities. Margaret received numerous gifts from the mayor and the citizens of Coventry, showing that the king and queen still had great support in parts of the realm.

This year also saw Elizabeth give birth to her second child, another son, Richard. At 20 years old, Elizabeth had already fulfilled her duty to provide heirs for her husband. She was kept company in this by her mother who, at the age of 40, was still producing children. Elizabeth and John seemed to be building up a contented life together, living in relative comfort with their own small family. An uneasy peace had broken out across the kingdom, and so, compared to previous years, 1457 was a quiet one.

Although Jacquetta and Richard were still firmly in the favour of the royal circle, they had suffered personally through the poor governance of Henry and Margaret. The almost complete loss of English territory in France had meant that Jacquetta had lost all of her dower lands (and thus income) which had once belonged to her first husband, Bedford, in the country. Jacquetta had also been entitled to receive a monetary income from the Crown, as seen previously, but the staggering debt of the English Crown meant it was more and more difficult to obtain payments from the Chancery. The couple were still living in relative comfort, particularly when they received gifts from the Crown, but by 1461 Jacquetta and Richard only owned eight manors across England; a far cry from Jacquetta's noble birth as the daughter of a count and someone married to the heir to the throne of England.[32]

Spring 1458 arrived and Henry decided to capitalise on the unspoken truce across the warring nobility. Tensions were still rife, with the heirs of those magnates killed at the First Battle of St Albans wanting revenge and those on York's side still disillusioned with Henry's reign. In an attempt to unite the realm, Henry organised a reconciliation. At the end of January, he issued summons to London for a Great Council. Over the next month all of the significant magnates made their way to the capital, each arriving with a force of several hundred soldiers for personal protection.[33] York, Salisbury and Warwick came from the Yorkist side, with Exeter, Somerset and Northumberland, as well as some of the Percy family, on the opposing side. To guarantee the safety of all involved, Henry summoned an independent force to protect London. Despite this, the Londoners were reluctant to allow so many soldiers into the city and many pitched up outside.

In mid March, Henry began negotiations between the lords to try and make a peace settlement. Eventually an agreement was reached. The Yorkists were placated to an extent when Warwick was made Admiral of the Seas. However, the blame for the Battle of St Albans was placed solely on the Yorkists, who were made to pay fines as recompense to the heirs of those killed. York was instructed to pay 5,000 marks to the new Duke of Somerset and his mother, the previous Somerset's wife.

To seal the agreements, on 25 March 1458, the Feast of the Annunciation, Henry led a parade through London.[34] The procession was formed of Henry, Margaret and all of the concerned lords. Richard and Jacquetta may well have been involved in the parade, for although they had not been involved in the quarrels, Richard's position as soldier and Jacquetta's place as one of Margaret's ladies-in-waiting would have afforded them a place. The group of nobles proceeded to St Paul's Cathedral for a religious ceremony to seal the peace, although the presence of soldiers still accompanying their masters somewhat undermined the sincerity of this.

If Jacquetta and Richard were not involved in the parade itself, they were certainly involved in the celebrations afterwards. To seal the peace, during Whitsun week there were great celebrations, and jousting was held at the Tower of London. The new Duke of Somerset took part, alongside Jacquetta and Richard's son Anthony, who was now 18, battling against esquires of the queen. A few days later, more jousting was held at the palace at Greenwich.[35]

Peace reigned on the surface, but below ground bitterness still festered. The children of those slain at St Albans still had not forgotten, and Queen Margaret was slowly gaining more power – and the Yorkists were her enemies. It was this year that Jacquetta gave birth to her last child with Richard, a daughter called Catherine.

At the start of 1459, then, Jacquetta was 43 years old with another baby to care for. Summer saw fighting return to England once more. A Great Council had been summoned at Coventry, but again in fear for their safety, York, the Nevilles and others of their allies did not appear. Margaret took this opportunity to strike at the threat to the throne.

'As a result of the advice of the queen', York and his supporters were accused of treason.[36] Skirmishes broke out across September between the Yorkists and Lancastrians, with victories and defeats on both sides. The Battle of Ludford Bridge in October, however, was a huge loss for the Yorkists. Many defected to Henry, unwilling to take the step of fighting the king in a pitched battle, and York, Salisbury and Warwick were forced to flee. York went to Ireland, where he still had great support as a result of his time as lieutenant. Meanwhile, Salisbury, Warwick, and York's eldest son Edward, the Earl of March, went to Wales which also had strong Yorkist support.[37] They travelled from there to Calais.

Now that York and his supporters were named as traitors, all of their lands and titles were forfeit to the Crown. All that was left was to capture the offenders. Henry had Somerset try to launch attacks on Calais to reclaim it from Warwick, but he was unsuccessful. In January 1460, Henry turned to Richard Woodville, Lord Rivers. Richard gathered his own fleet to help Somerset in his attempts to reclaim Calais, and his men gathered at Sandwich on the south-east coast.

According to a contemporary account, Richard and his son, Anthony, who was now around 20 years old, were sleeping soundly in their beds when the Yorkists from across the Channel unexpectedly attacked.[38]

Sometime between 4 and 5 a.m. a force led by John Denham surprised Sandwich and seized the pair. The Yorkists took Richard and Anthony to Calais, where Warwick, Salisbury and Edward were staying. There, they were subjected to a bizarre spectacle.

Surrounded by 160 torches, Richard and Anthony were brought in front of the men and 'rated' for their low birth. Richard was called a knave's son and taunted that his father was no more than a squire. They berated him for daring to call them traitors when he was of such low birth and they were the 'Kyngs treue liege men'. His marriage to Jacquetta was also brought up, and Richard was heavily criticised for having been a social upstart who only rose through the ranks because of this marriage. Anthony, as his son, was insulted in a similar fashion.

This must certainly have been a terrifying experience for the Woodville men. Much blood had been spilt during the conflicts of the previous years, and they were now in enemy hands in enemy territory. They could well be killed by the Yorkists. Luckily for them, the Yorkists seem to have seized them purely for this strange rating session and the men were left unharmed.

The esteem in which the Woodville family was held by the royal family is evident as the chancellor rode hastily to Henry to bring him the news of Richard's capture. Henry then made his way to London, gathering men as he went.[39]

At some point, although it is not clear when, Richard and Anthony were released by Edward and his men and they returned safely to England. It must have been quite an emotional reunion with their family. The fear that Jacquetta would have felt, especially with so many children under her care, is unimaginable.

In June, Edward finally made his move. Alongside Warwick and Salisbury, he crossed the Channel with an army and was welcomed in Kent. The legacy of the rebellion and Henry's treatment of the Kentish men was still remembered. They swiftly made their way to London, where the disaffected citizens opened the gates willingly. The right-eousness of their cause seemed apparent, as they had gained an ally in a papal legate, Francisco Coppini. Coppini had initially been given the diplomatic mission of ending the Wars of the Roses and bringing peace to England, so that Henry could then join the latest Crusade. However, Margaret had refused his attempts to raise a tithe on the people of England for the Crusade and so he turned to Edward. In return for a promise of support, Coppini accompanied the Yorkists on their journey to London. He procured papal bulls which said that the pope had excommunicated all those who resisted the Yorkist forces.[40] This was quite some support to have.

All-out war was once again on the table. Henry summoned a force and marched south from Coventry, leaving Margaret and their 6-year-old son Edward behind. On 10 July 1460, Henry's forces met Warwick's army at Northampton.[41] Warwick's forces were greatly aided by the betrayal of Edmund Grey, Earl of Kent. Kent had secretly corresponded with Warwick, saying he would join the Yorkist cause if Warwick helped him in a property dispute and possibly in return for promotion of office. During the battle, then, Kent ordered his men to lay down their weapons when Warwick's men approached their flank, allowing Warwick easy access to the camps where Henry was. Kent was, in fact, the cousin of Elizabeth's husband, John Grey. The Wars of the Roses split families in half.

After the betrayal of the Earl of Kent, the battle was swift and decisively in Warwick's favour. Lancastrian soldiers were slain and numerous lords, an earl and a duke all died trying to defend Henry in his tent. Ultimately, they were unsuccessful. Henry VI was once more in the hands of the Yorkist party. Edward and the Nevilles brought Henry back to London with them and once the dust had settled and their control seemed certain, Edward's father, York, finally returned from Ireland.

It was now September, and York was confident. He began to act in a very royal – essentially kingly – manner. He marched to London bearing the arms of his maternal ancestor, Lionel of Antwerp, emphasising his royal blood, and he displayed a banner of the coat of arms of England. He took up residence in the king's palace alongside Henry and even took Henry's place in Parliament.[42]

In October a Parliament was called, and at the end of the month the Act of Accord was agreed.[43] Despite all that had happened, Parliament was not willing to remove Henry VI as king as it had removed Richard II in favour of Henry IV less than a century previously. A compromise was therefore reached: Henry would remain king for the rest of his life, with York swearing to do nothing to cut Henry's life short, and after his death the throne would pass to York and his heirs. This disinherited Henry's own son, Edward. The agreement was similar to that made at Troyes by Henry V and the French king.

To recognise York's new status as heir to the throne, he was given various castles, manors and lands worth 10,000 marks a year. This was a huge amount, equal to Joan's dower earlier in the century – although Queen Margaret had been living on a more lavish income. Of this 10,000 marks, 5,000 were for his own use, 3,500 was to go to his eldest son, Edward, and the rest to his second son, Edmund. It was also proclaimed high treason to kill York, putting him on the same rank as the king and queen. He was once more made Protector of England. York was king in all but name.

After Henry's capture, Margaret fled to Wales with her son for safety, as there were still Lancastrian strongholds there. It is highly unlikely that Jacquetta followed, for she had her own family and lands to protect, but Richard may well have followed to serve her in a military capacity. It is likely that their son Anthony remained in England, because by March the following year he was married.[44] He had married well for his status, his bride being Elizabeth, Baroness Scales. Elizabeth's father had been killed in July under the Yorkist occupation of London, and that made her a wealthy heiress and a good Lancastrian ally for the family.

At the end of 1460, York seemed on the top of the world. He had secured his succession to the throne of England, had gained lands and riches, and now was effectively acting as king. However, Queen Margaret had been working hard on the outskirts of the kingdom. She had consolidated Lancastrian power in Wales, and had made an alliance with the Queen Regent of Scotland to gain troops and funding for her armies. Meanwhile, leading Lancastrian nobles were gathering in the north of England. A huge force began to gather in Hull formed of thousands of men and an array of dukes, earls and lords.

York now had to defend his newly won position. He sent his eldest son Edward to deal with the forces gathered in the Welsh Marches, while he travelled north with his second son, Edmund, and Salisbury to face the main army. Warwick was left in charge of London. Although York and the Nevilles had significant estates in the north, most of the territory had now returned to the Lancastrian cause.

On 30 December 1460, York's army met with the Lancastrians near Wakefield and was destroyed.[45] It was vastly outnumbered and completely surrounded, with nowhere to run. During the battle and its immediate aftermath, York, his son Edmund, Salisbury and Salisbury's son were all killed. A decade-long conflict between York and the Crown had seemingly come to an end.

Despite the death of his father and brother, the 18-year-old Edward decided to continue to champion his father's cause. Under the Act of Accord, Edward was now heir to the throne, and this was not something he was going to give up. At this point, there was no turning back anyway. Edward defeated a Lancastrian army in the Welsh Marches led by Jasper Tudor (Henry VI's half-brother) in February 1461. Meanwhile, Queen Margaret was marching south with her own army, but as she had no money to pay the soldiers she allowed them to plunder riches from territories of the south of England.[46] Warwick, who was still in charge of London, used this as propaganda against the evil reign of the Lancastrians, and it worked: many territories in the south that had held out loyally now switched to the side of the Yorkists. Coventry, which had housed Henry and Margaret for so long, and which had bestowed generous gifts during the feast of Corpus Christi just three years previously, now pledged its allegiance to Edward.

As Margaret approached London, Warwick sent out his army to blockade the road north of St Albans. However, Margaret had intelligence of their fortifications, which only faced north, and her army skirted around them and attacked them from behind. On 17 February, they captured St Albans then moved north to attack Warwick's main force. Caught unaware and struggling to remove itself from its own fortifications, Warwick's army was easily overwhelmed.

Eventually, Warwick had to concede defeat and he retreated to Oxfordshire with his remaining forces. He had brought King Henry to the battlefield and was forced to leave him behind in the haste to retreat.[47] Henry may have suffered another mental breakdown, for it was said that during the battle he had been sitting under a tree singing.

The Second Battle of St Albans had been a resounding victory for Margaret and the Lancastrians, not least because the body of the king was once more in their possession. This would allow them to take back control of the government, particularly now that York was dead.

However, there were still losses on the Lancastrian side, and one in particular which was devastating for the Woodvilles. It was at this battle that Elizabeth Woodville's husband, John Grey, had been killed. At 23 years old, Elizabeth was now a widow.

Jacquetta of Luxembourg was also in a difficult position. She was staying in London while these events were transpiring – curious, considering she was a Lancastrian and the city was in Yorkist hands – and now the citizens called for her help. It was no secret by now that London and Margaret hated and mistrusted each other, and Margaret's reputation had preceded her with all the reports of her soldiers' plundering of the south. The city was terrified that it was going to be despoiled, raided and destroyed by Margaret, so they turned to Jacquetta. Knowing how close she was to Margaret, they hoped that she would be able to convince Margaret to spare them.

The city of London barred its gates, and the following day Jacquetta, alongside Anthony's wife, Lady Scales, Anne Neville, Duchess of Buckingham and various men of the city travelled to St Albans to meet with Margaret. Here, they pleaded for the king and queen to be 'benevolent and owe good will to the City' and leave them alone. It was agreed that they would leave London in peace if it sent some money (sorely needed to pay soldiers), but in the event the Londoners refused to allow entry to a small contingent of soldiers sent to collect the supplies.[48]

Margaret was not able to push London, for news had arrived of Edward's victory against Jasper Tudor, and as London had barred its gates Margaret was not prepared to besiege it. There were more pressing matters at hand. Margaret and Henry moved north once more, which turned out to be a mistake when, at the start of March, Warwick and Edward returned to London and were welcomed with open arms. Edward's victory was swift – the Londoners proclaimed him King Edward IV on 4 March 1461, and this was soon approved by Parliament.

Edward's appointment was unofficial, however, as he declared he would not have a formal coronation until Henry and Margaret were removed. He did have a small ceremony at Westminster Abbey where lords paid homage to him and the people of London clamoured their desire for him to be king.[49] Edward had honoured his father and achieved what he could not; he was now implicitly King of England.

All that was left was to get rid of the competition. Edward and Warwick marched north to meet Margaret and Henry in battle one last time. The two armies, the Yorkists and the Lancastrians, met near York at the Battle of Towton on 29 March 1461.

The Battle of Towton is widely regarded as the bloodiest battle ever fought on English soil. Around 50,000 soldiers are believed to have taken part, with a numerical advantage on the Lancastrian side. It is thought that three-quarters of the peerage of England were involved in the battle.[50] Despite it being the end of March, there was heavy snowfall. This worked to the Yorkists' advantage, for the blizzard winds drove the arrows from their archers further than the Lancastrian arrows, allowing them to attack the enemy without being hit themselves. Hand-to-hand combat ensued, but both armies were exhausted by the heavy snow and fighting was bitter. Edward's forces were outnumbered and both sides were taking heavy casualties.

Edward then received fantastic news: the Duke of Norfolk, who had been delayed in his arrival, had finally reached the battlefield. Whereas the forces currently battling had been fighting for hours and were completely drained, Norfolk's men were fresh and ready to fight. This invigorated Edward's side and slowly the battle fell into their favour. Lancastrian troops started to flee, and many were slaughtered as they ran past Norfolk's troops. Those who were not killed by the Yorkists drowned as they tried to cross the nearby river, with others being trampled to death. Modern estimates place the dead at 20,000–30,000 men, with the majority on the Lancastrian side.[51] This was 1 per cent of the total population of the country killed in one day.

Margaret and Henry had not been present at the battle, choosing instead to hide in the city of York. When news reached them of the disaster at Towton, they had no option but to flee to Scotland. There were no more men left to fight. York had won.

The Lancastrians who had survived the battle either fled into exile with Margaret and Henry, or finally accepted defeat and defected to King Edward. The Woodvilles would have been waiting with bated breath for news from Towton. Not only were they Lancastrians desiring, in all likelihood, the success of their patrons for the past twenty-five years, but they were personally invested in the battle. Fighting at

Towton had been Richard Woodville and his son Anthony. Were they among the tens of thousands slain?

The family had lost John Grey during the Second Battle of St Albans, but thankfully they did not now need to bury more men, for both Richard and Anthony managed to survive the battle. However, they were now at the mercy of the new king, Edward. Elizabeth had by now returned to Grafton Regis to be with her mother and siblings.[52] The family must have gathered anxiously, waiting for news of what was to happen. Thankfully, the news was good. Edward, secure in his victory, was willing to give reconciliation to Lancastrians who would pledge their allegiance to him. The Woodvilles had supported Margaret and Henry to the end, but now they saw that there was no alternative and they would have to change their support to the new regime. On 12 July, Richard received his official pardon from the Crown, followed on the 23rd of the month by Anthony.[53]

Despite Edward's admonishments of Richard and Anthony's low status the year before, the defection of Lord Rivers and Lord Scales were notable among the kingdom, for they were renowned for their devotion to the Lancastrian cause. At the end of August, the State Papers of Venice record a letter from Count Ludovico Dallugo to the Duke of Milan reporting on affairs in England. Here, he mentions the defection of the lords previously loyal to Henry, including chiefly Richard and Anthony, 'men of very great valour'. It is clear that Richard had lost all hope that Henry would return as king, for when Dallugo questioned him about Henry's cause, Richard replied, '… the cause was lost irremediably'.[54]

The Wars of the Roses thus came to a temporary end. Margaret and Henry took up residence in the Scottish court of James III, joined by some of their noble Lancastrian supporters. Other Lancastrians hid out in Wales, and some stayed staunch in their northern homes. At the end of June 1461, Edward IV had his official coronation.[55] The Woodville family regrouped and licked their wounds, shaken but having survived the ordeal. Elizabeth was left to grieve the loss of her husband and to try to put her affairs in order so that she could properly provide for her two young children. Jacquetta had won the love and support of the city of London for helping to protect them from the ravages of Margaret's army, while Richard began to ingratiate himself with the new king. Grants at the end of 1461 confirming Richard's positions as steward of the king's forest in Northampton show that the two had at least been superficially reconciled.[56] Richard Woodville had risen from relatively humble beginnings to become Lord Rivers, survived a change in regime and was now a respected member of the nobility. The next decade was to see his family soar to even greater heights – but with greater heights come greater falls.

II

A COMMON NOISE
OF WITCHCRAFT

IF ELIZABETH WOODVILLE had been deeply upset by the death of her husband while fighting for the Lancastrian cause, then the subsequent actions of her in-laws were to make matters worse. Elizabeth was widowed in her early twenties and had two young boys, who were heirs to the Grey lands, and the baronage of Groby to look after, but her marital family were not to make matters easy for her. By May 1462, Elizabeth's mother-in-law, Baroness Ferrers of Groby, had married her second husband, John Bourchier. Whether Baroness Ferrers had never much liked Elizabeth or something happened after John Grey's death to cause a falling out between the two is unknown, but the baroness showed shocking disregard to the widow of her son.

After John and Elizabeth's marriage, the Grey family had bestowed three manors upon the couple – Newbottle, Brington and Woodham Ferrers – which gave a combined annual income of 100 marks. This was intended to sustain them, starting them out on their married life together. The manors were put in trust to numerous independent men to administer, and John, Elizabeth and their heirs were to receive the income every year. Now that John was dead, however, the baroness attempted to reclaim these three manors, which would deprive Elizabeth of any income to provide for herself and her two children.

Elizabeth was not going to give up easily. She may have been young, but already her determination and strength had shone through. Both the baroness and Elizabeth petitioned the chancellor for a resolution, both sides claiming the manors should go to them.[1] The three remaining trustees were duly summoned and, luckily for Elizabeth, two of the trustees sided with her, while the third said they could not remember the specifics of the agreement.[2] The trustees had therefore confirmed that even though John had died, Elizabeth was still entitled to the income. The outcome was recorded officially on 26 May 1464, although the situation may well have been resolved earlier than this.[3]

This victory must have been of great relief to Elizabeth, for in her current position an income of 100 marks a year was very respectable. Elizabeth seems to have remained at her parents' manor of Grafton Regis with her children after her husband's death and, considering her clearly acrimonious relationship with her mother-in-law, it is easy to see why.

The financial situation of her parents was somewhat allayed at the end of 1461 when Jacquetta's dower from the Duke of Bedford was confirmed by Edward, alongside grants of lands and manors to the couple throughout Henry VI's reign.[4] The values of the land and incomes listed totalled over £800 a year. Despite having to give away many parcels of land to pay for their marriage pardon decades previously, and the loss of the dower properties in France, the couple had been sufficiently recompensed by grants from Henry and the remainder of Bedford's dower to afford them a more than comfortable income. It still did not make them among the richest of the nobility, but they were certainly doing well for themselves.

King Edward seemingly came to appreciate the usefulness of a loyal servant like Richard. He was also perhaps beginning to realise a few months into his reign that he did not have as much support among the nobility as he had initially anticipated. Richard must have spent the following year building his esteem in Edward's eyes, for by 1463 he was given a place on the Royal Council.[5] This was a highly trusted position, particularly for a formerly staunch Lancastrian, and shows not only Edward's willingness for reconciliation, but that Richard must have been a very capable advisor. Despite this, however, Richard does not seem to have had much influence over Edward.

He procured very few personal favours and the rest of his family did not see any advancement.

At the start of 1464, the majority of England was finally settled. The new king proved popular, and the commons seemed relieved to finally have a capable leader, despite Edward's young age of 22. Edward handsomely rewarded those who had supported his rise to the throne, but by bringing former Lancastrians into his government Edward was showing favour to all. There were still sporadic rebellions by the Lancastrian nobility, with one led the same year by the Duke of Somerset. The rebellions were all easily quashed by Edward and the Nevilles, with Warwick's brother John Neville defeating Somerset in May. Somerset was executed for his crimes, joining his father in dying for the Lancastrian cause.

Little more had been heard from the Woodvilles, who had returned to their quiet life at Grafton Regis. While Richard was involved in government, there is no evidence that Jacquetta had returned to court, particularly as there was now no queen to serve. Early in the year, however, Elizabeth was once more having problems with her Grey relatives. If she had already secured her three manors and annual income, Elizabeth now seems to have grown increasingly concerned about the inheritance of her two sons. Baroness Ferrers had been remarried for several years now, and although she was in her early forties, Jacquetta had proven that a woman of her age could still produce children. Elizabeth was seemingly concerned that any children borne from the baroness' second marriage might replace her own children in the inheritance of the Ferrers-Grey estates, particularly considering how the baroness had already tried to reclaim property from her.[6] Whatever the cause, she was desperately searching for a powerful ally to champion her cause.

Elizabeth resolved to protect her sons by appealing to the Crown. A neighbour of the Greys at Groby was Lord Hastings who, conveniently, was a very close friend of Edward IV. After Edward's accession, Hastings had been made Lord Chamberlain, one of the principal roles of the royal household and one which controlled access to the monarch. The following year, he had been given the honour of being invested as a Knight of the Garter. Hastings would be an excellent ally against her mother-in-law, and his proximity to the Grey estates gave him a vested interest.

On 13 April 1464, Elizabeth signed an agreement with Lord Hastings. The document favoured Elizabeth in her current predicament – if fate was on her side. Otherwise, it was a potentially punishing agreement for her and her children. Hastings agreed to share the rental income of the Grey lands with Elizabeth while her eldest son, Thomas, was under the age of 12 (thus implicitly agreeing to champion her rights to hold them over the baroness). In return, Thomas (or Richard, in the event of Thomas' death) would marry one of Hastings' as yet unborn daughters or nieces. For the marriage, Hastings would give Elizabeth a dower of 500 marks, a significant amount to her but, crucially, if both of Elizabeth's sons were to die, or if within six years neither Hastings nor his relations had a daughter to marry to the boys, then Elizabeth would instead have to pay Hastings 250 marks.[7]

Considering the lands Elizabeth was arguing over gave an annual income of 100 marks, this was clearly a punishing loss for her, were it to happen. It shows the desperation that Elizabeth must have felt to try and save the lands for her boys. Elizabeth now had a powerful ally, and if the matter of the three manors had not yet been settled, then Hastings certainly pulled through for Elizabeth, considering the official settlement of Elizabeth's estates is dated to the following month.

Elizabeth Woodville now seemed settled in her widowhood. The immediate inheritance of her children was secured with her dower lands, and if Hastings' family could provide a daughter then she would be tied by marriage to a very powerful man. This would be quite the rise for the daughter of a humble knight. Her parents had retained their position of respect in the government and continued to enjoy the income they had received under the king's predecessor. All but two of Elizabeth's siblings were still unmarried, and this must have started to be quite a drain on the family's resources. However, they were reaching the right age to begin to find suitable spouses and the family may have started to look among the ranks of the baronage for men and women of a similar rank to the Greys.

This was not meant to be, for in September 1464 the country received shocking news: King Edward IV of England had married Elizabeth Woodville. The circumstances of Elizabeth and Edward's marriage remain a mystery to this day. The issue of Edward's marriage had been a topic for government since his accession. As with all previous monarchs, a foreign princess was considered the worthiest bride for the King of England. This would bring money into the kingdom through a dowry and provide important diplomatic ties and alliances with powerful foreign nations. Various brides had been suggested across the past few years, but Edward either rejected them or the plans fell through. Warwick had, for some time, been pushing the idea of a French alliance, and by the summer of that year the French King Louis XI was keen to make an alliance with England. Warwick had invested time negotiating with Louis and talks were looking promising. The same year, Henry of Castile had offered his sister Isabella as a bride, while the Duke of Burgundy also seemed keen to make an alliance with the English.

In 1464, then, the marriage prospects of the young king were certainly in his favour, with a plethora of brides to choose from. In September, the King's Council met at Reading to clarify the king's desires. They were keen to press on with the various alliances on the table and they needed to know whether the king would consider a marriage with any of the concerned parties so that they knew what to bargain for. Edward seemed hesitant to give a clear answer, and so his councillors had to push for one. Finally, he gave his reply: he could not marry a foreign bride – because he was already married to the daughter of Lord Rivers.

The shock in the room must have been overwhelming – silence, followed by protests of indignation and lack of understanding roaring out. How could the king already be married to an Englishwoman? As details of the marriage came to light, the men voiced their deep disapproval. They told Edward that while Elizabeth might be beautiful and good, she was no match for a prince such as he. For she was not a daughter of a duke or a count, but she was a widow with two children. Even her mother's previous position as Duchess of Bedford was not considered acceptable.[8] They must have felt helpless, for they could in reality do nothing. The marriage was solemnised and consummated and there was no legal reason they could get it annulled.

The reaction to the marriage and its subsequent acceptance tells a lot about the shifting politics and opinions of the time, and the blurred lines as to the status of the Woodvilles. Richard Woodville was a social upstart. His father had been a knight, but Richard had climbed through the ranks to a baronage, holding important military offices, becoming a

Knight of the Garter and sitting on the Royal Council. In technicalities, therefore, Richard was now reasonably high up the ladder of nobility; although still not close enough to the heights of dukes, who would be far more suited to a royal marriage.

On the other hand, Elizabeth's mother was certainly well placed in blood for a royal match – as she herself had been. The daughter of a count, related to various royal and noble families of Europe, Jacquetta had been considered of high enough blood to marry a prince of England. Why, then, should her daughter not also be? This is where the difficult delineations of social class and status of medieval England come into effect. Usually, spouses were of similar social status or the husband was of higher status than his wife. In these cases, the children always took the status of their father.

In cases where the wife had married below her station, however, the situation was more complicated. People were still inclined to give children the status of their lower father, but the high blood of the mother could not be ignored, giving the children a somewhat raised status. Usually, this lack of clarity was not too much of an issue, but in this case, it was deeply important. Was Elizabeth considered a good enough match for Edward because of the high blood of her mother? Or was she the lowly daughter of a knight through her father?

The question of Elizabeth's status was not the only problem with the marriage. Elizabeth was a widow and, more importantly, a widow with children. It had become the tradition that the king should marry a virgin, bestowing implications of virginity, chastity and holiness onto the royal union. The bride was also usually young – in her teens – which allowed her to be moulded by her new country to fulfil the correct role expected of her.[9] Elizabeth was not only 27 years old, but she was older than her new husband, who was just 22. These were all important factors that broke all the traditional patterns. Her previous children could even be viewed as a threat to the monarchy.

The starkest problems with the marriage, however, came from the loss of the clear benefits of a foreign marriage. England would now not receive a wealthy dowry from a foreign land to replenish the still-low coffers, nor would England receive the diplomatic benefits from an alliance with a strong nation. The marriage was also a gross insult to the council. A monarch was expected to consult his people during important decisions and Edward had gone ahead with the union without anybody's knowledge.

Elizabeth was now the first English-born Queen Consort of England since the eleventh century. However, the marriage was not quite without precedent. The previous century, the Black Prince – eldest son of Edward III and father to Richard II – had married an Englishwoman, Joan, Countess of Kent. The marriage was shocking for many reasons: Joan was the first cousin of Edward III, a widow, a mother of four children and two years older than the prince, as well as being English-born. Here, at least, her blood status was no issue, as Joan was granddaughter to King Edward I, but the similarities between this marriage and Edward and Elizabeth's is striking. Yorkist propaganda was to link Edward IV with Edward the Black Prince, and so this precedent was important for getting his own marriage accepted.[10]

There were other royal precedents, such as the marriage of John of Gaunt to widow and mother Katherine Swynford a century previously, and the marriage of Henry IV to widow and mother Joan of Navarre. These two situations were more acceptable, however, for John was not a reigning king nor expected to become one, and Henry IV already had heirs and so his second wife was less important.

Edward and Elizabeth were truly pioneers. In fact, their marriage paved the way for their successors, reflecting the changing attitudes to the monarchy towards the end of the Wars of the Roses. One of Edward's successors, Richard III, was married to an Englishwoman, as was *his* successor, Henry VII (albeit to a princess). Henry's son Henry VIII married four Englishwomen, while his daughter Elizabeth I did not marry at all. Attitudes towards marriage and what was expected of a queen were changing. But, for the meantime, Edward and Elizabeth's marriage was still a shocking first.

It is not clear when the marriage between Elizabeth and Edward was contracted. The two may well have met each other at times during their childhood, with both sets of parents being prominent at court and often working alongside each other. However, Elizabeth was married when Edward was just 10 years old and so it is unlikely they knew each other well at all. The traditional wedding date given for the pair was 1 May 1464, though, as will be seen, this is unlikely to have been the case.

The story of their marriage is presented through numerous chronicle accounts.[11] The tale went that Elizabeth had heard that the king was hunting nearby and, determined to obtain the rights for herself and her sons being denied to her by Baroness Ferrers, she decided to petition the king himself. She took her two young sons with her to an oak tree on her family's estates at Grafton Regis, where she knew the path of the hunt would take the king. As Edward rode by with his men, he was struck by the sight of a beautiful woman standing with two young boys by her side, looking quite downcast. He stopped to talk to her, and Elizabeth then pleaded with the king to restore her lands to her. Enchanted, he could not refuse her offer.

After speaking further with Elizabeth, he realised that no other woman had 'such constant womanhood, wisdom and beauty, as was Dame Elizabeth'.[12] Edward resolved to woo her, but the chaste Elizabeth would not submit herself to the king. After continued meetings, the king fell deeply in love with Elizabeth, but still she would not stoop to have sex with him. In some versions of the story, one time Edward decided to try and pressure her more forcefully, but Elizabeth held a dagger to her throat and said she would rather die than become his mistress.

In all versions, Elizabeth's consistent refusal to be his mistress only raised her in his esteem so that 'she rather kindled his desire than quenched it'. Eventually, Elizabeth told Edward that while she was of too high birth and character to become his mistress, she knew that she was 'too simple to be his wife'.[13]

Elizabeth had proven herself to be chaste, wise and well-mannered in her rebuffs of the king, and of excellent character, and Edward, deeply in love, decided he had to marry her. One morning, therefore, he snuck away from his lodgings with the royal party to meet her. At her family home of Grafton Regis, Edward and Elizabeth were married in a secret ceremony on 1 May with just Jacquetta, a priest, a man to help the priest sing and two gentlewomen present. After spending a few hours in bed with Elizabeth, Edward returned to his men pretending to have been out hunting. Over the next few days, he continued to meet her in secret with the help of her mother and the knowledge of no one else.

The story of Elizabeth and Edward's marriage circulated in this form within a few years of their marriage, with details added and changed over time, but the essential essence staying the same.[14] The fact that versions of this story were spreading across the country and beyond within a few years of their marriage suggests that there were certainly elements of truth to the story. Undoubtedly, that the marriage was concluded in secret at Grafton Regis with just a handful of people is true. Other details are more debatable. The story is romantic, and always emphasises the chastity and purity of Elizabeth. These are elements that were necessary, due to Elizabeth's status as widow. She was not a pure, untouched virgin bride and so her purity had to be shown through different means. It is therefore a convenient part of the story that makes up for Elizabeth's otherwise deficient qualities.

The traditional date given for the marriage, 1 May, also does not quite hold up to scrutiny. May Day was traditionally seen as a day with romantic connotations and, given the romantic aspect of their courtship and wedding stories, it seems a little too apt that the couple would have married on this day.[15] There also stands Elizabeth's agreement with Hastings. The document detailing their alliance in order to protect Elizabeth's Grey lands was dated to April that year. If Elizabeth knew that a romance was blossoming with Edward – enough for them to get married around two weeks later – why would she enter into such a dangerous agreement with Hastings? Even if Elizabeth did not consider that Edward might take her for a bride, his clear affections for her would have been enough for her to get Edward to rule in her favour on the matter, without needing Hastings' influence.

The date in May also would mean that Elizabeth and Edward kept their marriage a secret for four months. While not impossible, it seems quite unlikely that they would have been able to maintain secret liaisons across this time without any suspicions being raised. For these reasons – the Hastings situation, in particular – it seems more likely that the couple were married sometime in late summer, closer to Edward's September announcement.

One aspect of the story is difficult to deny, though: Edward had fallen completely in love with Elizabeth. It is clear that the marriage happened in haste, with Elizabeth oblivious in April to any potential match with the king, and the simplest explanation for this haste was affection. It has been debated at length for decades how much the marriage was actually sensible on Edward's behalf, and how much it was the rash decision of a young man in love. However, Edward could not have been quite so naïve. He knew the importance of a good bride for him. Not only had the lords of the realm been debating potential matches for years but even at 3 years old it had been proposed that he would marry a daughter of the French king.[16] That Edward conducted his marriage in utter secrecy showed that he was conscious enough of his actions to know that it would not be accepted by his peers.

Marrying Elizabeth certainly was wise on some fronts. It is clear from Elizabeth's later actions as queen that she was an intelligent, pious, cultured woman who knew how to navigate court and common opinion and portray an excellent image of herself. At 27 years old, these traits would certainly be clear, and Edward would easily recognise that these were the qualities to be highly desired in a queen, particularly one of a fractured realm.

Although marrying Elizabeth would lose the benefits of a foreign alliance, Edward may well have married her for this exact reason. Henry VI's marriage to Margaret of Anjou had turned out to be disastrous for the realm. She brought no dowry, the marriage did not prevent the loss of English territory in France, and unpopular opinion of her towards the end of the realm as a greedy, grasping, power-hungry foreigner only reignited hatred of foreigners, and the French in particular. While Edward did not have to choose an alliance with the French, as Warwick had hoped, any other foreign alliance may still bring great suspicion onto the new queen. An Englishwoman could never have her loyalty to her country called into question.

The final obvious benefit to marrying Elizabeth was her Lancastrian connection. Her parents were among the most renowned loyal Lancastrian nobles – particularly after so many had died during the Wars of the Roses – and to bring Elizabeth into the royal family would unite the two warring strands. Elizabeth also had a plethora of unmarried brothers and sisters. Edward could utilise these familial connections to bring other nobles closer to his government. Considering the discord still rumbling across the country, this would be much needed to bring stability and loyalty.

The extent to which Edward weighed up the pros and cons listed by historians over the years is impossible to know. Whether it was the combination of love with shrewd analysis that made Edward believe Elizabeth was the right choice, or if he simply blindly followed his emotions, is lost to history. What is clear is that Edward loved Elizabeth and made sure that there were no obstacles to their marriage by marrying first in secret. How far Elizabeth loved Edward at this point is also unclear, but their marriage in future years was strong, loving, respectful and unwavering. In all likelihood she had fallen deeply for him too. How could she not when Edward was young, 6ft tall, brave, strong and had already proven himself a capable leader?

The lords of the realm did not have much time to come to terms with Edward's revelation at the Royal Council meeting, for he was keen for them to meet his bride at last. One can imagine him beaming with pride when, on 29 September, Elizabeth was formally introduced to the court at Reading Abbey. Escorted by Warwick and the king's brother, Clarence, Elizabeth entered the chapel of the abbey.[17] While Edward may have been overjoyed and relieved to finally have the secret of his wife in the open, Elizabeth must surely have been filled with fear and apprehension at this presentation. She would not have been oblivious to the criticisms and displeasure of the lords assembled before her, and she would have been conscious that her every move was to be judged to see if she was worthy to be queen.

Nonetheless, the couple found time for pleasure during their time at Reading, which acted as their official honeymoon. They stayed together at Reading for the duration of the Royal Council, then after it disbanded they travelled to Windsor. Edward and Elizabeth spent their first Christmas together as husband and wife at Eltham Palace – the same place at which Joan and Henry IV had honeymooned sixty years previously.[18]

It was not long before Edward started to address the marriages of Elizabeth's siblings. Her sister Jacquetta had been married around the age of 5 to Baron Strange of Knockin, while Anthony was married to Baroness Scales.[19] This left nine Woodvilles who were suddenly prime marriage material. Before Edward and Elizabeth had even left Reading Abbey, organisations began to make important alliances.

The first sibling to find a spouse was Margaret, who was betrothed to Lord Maltravers, the heir of the Earl of Arundel, although it does not seem that they were married until February 1466.[20] The next marriage was far more shocking. In January 1465, Elizabeth's brother John was married to Catherine Neville, Duchess of Norfolk. John was only just turning 20, whereas Catherine was approaching 65 years old. It was not entirely unusual for younger men to marry a wealthy, older dowager, but the significant age difference between the two was distasteful to many. Not least among these was the Earl of Warwick, for Catherine was his paternal aunt. It is easy to see why Warwick would bridle at this marriage, which was so clearly made to grasp an easy inheritance for John from a woman who could easily be expected to die within a decade.

Now that two of Elizabeth's siblings had made good marriages, with talks now likely in the works for the rest of them, it was time to turn to Elizabeth's coronation. The secret marriage of Edward and Elizabeth meant that the public had been denied the spectacle of a royal wedding. This meant, in turn, that the monarchy had missed an important public relations opportunity, necessary for legitimising a new king who had usurped the throne just a few years earlier. Whereas Joan's marriage to Henry IV at the start of the century had done just this, showing the wealth and might of the new king and including thousands of nobles in the festivities, no such event could now be held for Edward. As such, full advantage was to be taken of Elizabeth's coronation.

Having an elaborate coronation not only gave Edward a chance to show how successful his reign was, but it gave legitimisation to Elizabeth too. While some in the realm may have been taken in by the romantic story of love, many would still hold the view that Elizabeth was not worthy to be queen. All efforts had to be made to show why Elizabeth was entitled to the Crown and to emphasise her noble blood.

Edward took charge of the coronation to ensure that everything was perfect. On 13 April, Edward wrote to the Mayor of London telling him that he had finished making arrangements for 'the Coronacion of our moost dere and moost entierly beloved wiff the Quene'. The coronation was to take place at Westminster Palace on the Sunday before Whitsunday, and Edward invited the mayor and his men to attend.[21] On 23 May, Edward started celebrations at the Tower of London. Here, he made forty-three men Knights of the Bath, including two of Elizabeth's brothers, Richard and John.[22] This was an elaborate ceremony, reserved by this time for the most special of occasions and involving the invested men taking a spiritually cleansing bath, embarking on an all-night vigil then being knighted by the king.

The following day, Elizabeth left Eltham Palace and travelled to the Tower of London in a marvellous procession, bedecked in jewels, precious stones and silks. London's mayor and aldermen had followed Edward's instructions and met Elizabeth dressed in scarlet in order to escort her across London Bridge. The bridge itself was elaborately decorated for her arrival, heavily painted and covered in stages. Pageants and singing met the queen as she progressed across the bridge. At Tower Bridge, a man dressed as St Paul met her – in all likelihood, a reference to Elizabeth's descent from the Counts of Saint-Pol through her mother, Jacquetta.[23] To further this connection, Jacquetta's brother, Jacques of Luxembourg, had travelled to London to represent the Duke of Burgundy. His attendance served to remind those present of Elizabeth's high birth through her mother.

The expense was significant, but the coronation celebrations were only just beginning. Elizabeth met Edward at the Tower of London, and the following day Elizabeth's procession left the Tower, now bolstered by the Knights of the Bath. Edward stayed behind, for it was tradition for the king not to attend the coronation of the queen. The newly invested knights must have been a stunning spectacle, cloaked in bright blue gowns and white silk hoods. Elizabeth made her way to Westminster Palace to make the final preparations for her coronation the next day.

On Sunday 26 May 1465, the royal party entered the hall of Westminster Palace.[24] Leading the party was the king's brother, the Duke of Clarence, on horseback 'trapped hede & body to the grounde' with richly embroidered cloth garnished with gold. The Earl of Arundel and the Duke of Norfolk followed in a similar manner, in order to hold back the crowds. Elizabeth then entered the hall in full queenly regalia. She walked under a canopy which was held up by four Barons of the Cinque Ports.

Elizabeth was wearing a mantle of purple with a coronal (a type of crown) on her head, accompanied by the Bishops of Durham and Salisbury and the Abbot of Westminster. Following Elizabeth were her ladies, the Duchess of Buckingham (Edward's maternal aunt) who held her train, followed by the Duchess of Suffolk and

Lady Margaret, both of whom were Edward's sisters, and Elizabeth's mother, Jacquetta of Luxembourg. Behind them were thirteen duchesses and countesses, fourteen baronesses and twelve ladies. Elizabeth was then crowned with all usual reverence and ceremony. Afterwards, Elizabeth was led from the monastery to her chamber where she dressed in a purple surcoat.

A celebratory feast followed the coronation, and consisted of three courses: the first had seventeen dishes, the second nineteen and the last fifteen.

The most notable absences were the Earl of Warwick and the king's mother, Cecily. Warwick had been sent by Edward on a diplomatic mission to Burgundy for the course of the coronation, presumably to save him some enmity in watching Elizabeth be crowned after he had pushed for a French alliance.[25] The absence of Cecily must surely be viewed as her disapproval of this common woman taking the throne and her eldest son, although the presence of two of Edward's sisters and his aunt showed that at least some of his family members supported him in his match.

The coronation had been a resounding success. Elizabeth had not put a foot wrong and had acted as an exemplary queen. No one could criticise her. Edward had organised everything perfectly, and the plethora of nobles, expensive materials, excess of food and adherence to tradition served to bolster his own reputation while legitimising his wife's right to her new position. Wearing the regal purple of the monarchy, Elizabeth was a queen to be reckoned with.

Prior to Elizabeth's coronation, Edward had set about providing for her. On 22 April, he gifted Elizabeth the manor of Greenwich, along with its tower and all of the parkland, as well as Ormondes Place in London. Humphrey and Eleanor's palace of La Pleasaunce was finally removed from the hands of those who had been responsible for their downfall. In July the following year, Edward gave her the palace at Sheen.[26]

Elizabeth soon set about establishing herself in the court and government. Like Joan of Navarre before her, she set up offices at Westminster in the New Tower, next to the king's Exchequer, so she could easily conduct her business.[27] As a previously loyal Lancastrian, Elizabeth immediately set about reconciling former Lancastrians to the new regime. Much of her dower land had been confiscated from the Duchy of Lancaster, and Elizabeth ensured that many of the same officials who had held offices under Henry VI remained in place. She also started organising her household, with accounts from 1466–67 showing that she had 100 household staff and five ladies-in-waiting.[28]

By all accounts, Elizabeth easily settled into her new role as queen. While it must have been daunting at times, and she must have still been subjected to whispers at court regarding her status, her mother had prepared her well. While Jacquetta could never have imagined her daughter with Richard Woodville would one day become queen, it is clear that she had educated her children well. Jacquetta had received an education worthy of her status and she passed this knowledge on to her children. Elizabeth was able to read and write at least in English, if not other languages – most likely French.

This year also saw a tremendous victory for Edward IV. After a failed invasion attempt by Queen Margaret and Henry VI, Henry had been hidden by the Scots and still-loyal Lancastrians across Scotland and rural parts of northern England. In the meantime, Margaret continued to petition the Scottish and French for help, travelling to Paris in October to gain financial help and troops.[29] However, Henry's hiding place had been discovered and, to Edward's joy, Henry was captured by the Yorkists once more.[30] Henry was brought to the Tower of London for safekeeping. Edward's reign was now the most secure it had ever been. With his rival king in his possession, Margaret now lost a lot of clout for rallying support, although she did still have Henry's heir, their son Edward, who was now 12 years old.

The Woodville family rose to greater heights in 1466. On 4 March, Richard Woodville was given the prestigious position of Lord Treasurer of England.[31] This meant he was now in charge of the king's money, supervising the royal accounts, making him one of the most important officials in government. He was further rewarded at the end of May when he rose from Lord Rivers to Earl Rivers.[32] Richard was now among the top echelons of the nobility.

More of Elizabeth's siblings found marriages this year with the help of Edward. In February, Elizabeth's sister Anne married Henry Bourchier, the heir of the Earl of Essex. Around the same time, her sister Joan (sometimes known as Eleanor) married Anthony Grey, the eldest son of Lord Grey of Ruthin, whose defection had been so crucial to the Yorkist victory at Northampton. September of this year saw a third sister, Mary, marry William Herbert, Lord Dunster, who was made Earl of Pembroke two years later.

In October this year, one of Elizabeth's own children was married. Elizabeth's marriage to Edward had somewhat invalidated her agreement with Hastings made in spring 1464. Her eldest son, Thomas, instead married Lady Anne, the heir of the Duke of Exeter and the niece of Edward IV. The previous year, Elizabeth's youngest sibling, Catherine, had married Henry Stafford, Duke of Buckingham. Catherine was just 8 years old and her groom was 11.[33] By the end of 1466, one of Elizabeth's children and eight of her siblings were married.

Much debate has been had as to how damaging or beneficial the Woodville marriages were to the family and the monarchy, and as with many aspects of this tumultuous period, the real answer lies somewhere in between. No doubt the marriages would have offended some. This would have invariably been because the Woodvilles were still seen as social upstarts, forcing those of higher blood to marry below their station, or because the sheer number of children that Richard and Jacquetta had meant that many marriages were procured in a short space of time.

On the other hand, there is ample evidence to show that the nobility was not as affronted by the Woodville marriages as had long been thought. While Edward did tempt families with grants of land and money, in some cases this would have been in part because Elizabeth's family was not rich enough to provide an appropriate dower for their daughters in such significant marriages. Edward was merely providing it for them. There do not seem to be any contemporary accounts of the marriages themselves that show the nobility complaining about being 'forced' to marry the Woodvilles.

Moreover, during this period, the nobility was always fighting for access and ties to the king in order to gain favour, lands and power from him. Henry VI's reign had been characterised by favourites climbing to greater and greater heights due to his support. Although Edward was more careful to be even-handed in his patronage, few nobles would give up the chance to marry a sibling of the queen for the benefits it would bring.

Warwick himself, however, was aggrieved by the marriages. Not only was the marriage of John Woodville to his aunt a clear move to gain easy wealth for John, but the marriage of Thomas Grey to Anne disregarded the fact that Anne was currently betrothed to Warwick's nephew.[34] Warwick may have been able to get over these insults, but the marriage of so many of Elizabeth's female relatives across the space of two years had completely depleted the marriage market. Warwick had two daughters, aged 15 and 10, making them the perfect age to complete marriages of their own.

Warwick's rank meant that his daughters could only find acceptable marriages among the top echelons of society, but all of the available men had been taken by the Woodville clan. As such, Warwick turned to the idea of marrying his eldest daughter, Isabel, to Edward's brother, Clarence. This would bring Clarence great wealth, would tie Warwick even closer to the royal family and, in reality, it was the only suitable match left for his daughter. Edward, however, would not even entertain the idea of the marriage and refused time and again to consent to it.[35]

The fate of Elizabeth's siblings had largely been satisfied. Edward had ensured they would have wealthy lives among the upper echelons of society, but he still had his characteristic reserve. Beyond the marriages and Richard's promotions in government, the Woodville family saw very few favours bestowed upon them.

The royal family experienced great joy this year. On 11 February 1466, Queen Elizabeth gave birth to her first child with Edward, a daughter also named Elizabeth, at Westminster Palace. The healthy birth of a first child was cause for great celebration at court. Within two years of marriage, a child showed that Elizabeth and Edward were likely to have more. Even a daughter was a legitimate heir with whom Edward could start to build his empire, and a sign of blessing on their union. The birth of Elizabeth seems to have reconciled the court somewhat. Edward's mother Cecily put aside any animosity she may have had during Elizabeth's coronation the previous year and came to court to see the baby. The child was christened at Westminster Abbey, with Jacquetta and Cecily serving as Elizabeth's godmothers and Edward's cousin, Warwick, standing as her godfather.[36] Seemingly, all the discontented strands of the royal party had finally been reconciled.

The account of Elizabeth's churching ceremony, recorded by Gabriel Tetzel from Nuremburg, has been a source of controversy for decades.[37] Gabriel was travelling in the retinue of a Bohemian nobleman named Leo of Rozmital, and the two men's presence at court at the occasion of the queen's churching afforded them an invitation to proceedings. Tetzel reports that Elizabeth went to church in the company of many priests and scholars, who bore relics and lights and were singing on the way. Following her were a plethora of ladies who had been summoned from across the realm, as well as many more musicians and singers, pipers and trumpeters. Sixty counts and knights were also in the retinue, with Elizabeth following and escorted by two dukes.

Behind Elizabeth came Jacquetta and sixty ladies. The church ceremony commenced, and afterwards the huge procession continued to a great feast – so large it filled four huge rooms. Tetzel enjoyed his dinner alongside his lord in a room reserved for the noblemen, which was supplied 'in such costly measure that it is unbelievable that it could be provided'. After they were done, they were moved to 'an unbelievably costly apartment' where Elizabeth was about to start her meal. The men stood in an alcove which allowed them to observe the event without taking part.

Elizabeth sat alone at a table on a golden chair, with her mother and one of Edward's sisters standing 'some distance away'. If Elizabeth spoke to either of them, they had to kneel before her, and they could not take their seats until Elizabeth had been served her first dish. The rest of the women who were present had to kneel throughout the rest of the meal, which took three hours. Everybody was silent during this whole time and the male nobles who were observing had to stand the entire time.

After the meal, events seemed to perk up. Dancing began, although Elizabeth remained seated with her mother kneeling before her – but 'at times the Queen bade her rise'. Edward's sister, meanwhile, danced a 'stately dance' with two dukes. The room was filled with 'exceedingly beautiful maids', including eight duchesses and thirty countesses. Afterwards, Edward held mass in his chapel with many of the noblemen and the ceremony was seemingly over, for Edward showed Tetzel and his lord his collection of relics, then two earls invited the men and their retinue to have dinner at their house.

Tetzel's whole account is filled with wonder and awe. Every woman was beautiful, the choirs sang so that he did 'not think that I have heard finer singing in this world', and no expense was spared. There is not a hint of criticism anywhere in his account, even if the rituals were not ones he was familiar with from his homeland. Despite this, many modern historians have often used this account to decry Elizabeth's haughty nature, her vanity and sense of self-importance and grandeur. Even her mother was made to kneel before her for hours. For Elizabeth 'had seldom a wise or good end in view' and was 'to prove a woman of designing character, grasping and ambitious for her family's interests, quick to take offence and reluctant to forgive'.[38]

These historians have been quick to seize upon later negative propaganda that vilified the entire Woodville family. If Elizabeth's behaviour at this churching ceremony was considered the epitome of her pride, then Tetzel's account surely would not have been so adoring. Even a foreigner unacquainted with the customs of the kingdom would have picked up on a feeling that the ceremony was not usual. He, at least, would have heard criticisms among the noblemen with whom he spent time during his visit to London to inform him that Elizabeth's ceremony was out of the ordinary.

Instead, Tetzel does not give a hint that this was not the usual custom of the churching ceremony in England. Considering Elizabeth and Edward's adherence to tradition in other ceremonies – such as her coronation the year before – it is more than likely that this was the usual performance of the churching, at least for a first child and legitimate heir. When Edward's reign was still just in its fifth year, and with Margaret still prowling the borders with foreign armies waiting for her chance to invade, Edward would hardly have wanted to antagonise the nobility with an inordinate ceremony that made his wife show disdain to those around her.

Tetzel's account even gives us a hint that Elizabeth herself may have been uncomfortable with the ceremony, when she asked her mother to stand instead of kneeling. Considering the fact that Jacquetta and Elizabeth's extremely close relationship is one of the certainties of history, it would seem uncharacteristic to then make her mother kneel for hours on end because she felt superior to her. This account, then, is hardly indicative of Elizabeth's overweening pride, but more another example of the Yorkists trying to gain legitimacy by sticking to tradition and showing the grandeur of their government.

Across this year and the next, the English court was a flurry of activity as ambassadors from all across Europe gathered. Despite the nobility's worries that Edward's marriage to Elizabeth was detrimental to their diplomatic plans, those who had been looking for an alliance in 1464 were still keen to gain England as an ally. Edward had an unmarried sister, Margaret, and it was to her that they now looked. Margaret was now 20 years old, and an excellent pawn in Edward's dynastic ambitions. Warwick once more took the line of a French alliance, while the Woodvilles instead favoured one with the Duke of Burgundy, for he had kinship ties with Jacquetta's family. Edward himself seemed more inclined to favour a Burgundian alliance, probably still wary of the unpopularity of the French and the fact that King Louis XI had given Margaret (albeit limited) help in reclaiming the throne from him.

Despite this, Edward seemed open to negotiation – particularly as the representatives of each territory brought eager gifts and proposals to sweeten the deal. In May 1467, Edward sent Warwick to France to negotiate with Louis. Louis lavished Warwick with expensive gifts, including a cup which cost 2,000 livres given to Warwick personally. He also offered very generous terms for an alliance.[39] Warwick had seemingly got the terms already laid out: the two countries should have perpetual peace, with Edward renouncing his claims to the French Crown; Louis would give one of his daughters in marriage to one of Edward's brothers, whereupon Louis would give part of the territory of the Duke of Burgundy as her dowry to the English. The two countries would then wage a joint war on Burgundy, splitting up the territory between them.[40]

While, on the surface, preparations for a French alliance seemed well met, underneath there was great intrigue and deception. The French were very much aware that Edward was also in negotiations to marry his sister to Louis' enemies in Burgundy. While Warwick was in France treating with King Louis, a Milanese letter dated to 19 May suggests that Louis was securing a back-up plan for himself. The letter said that if Edward were to choose a Burgundian alliance, then the French had 'talked of treating with the Earl of Warwick to restore King Henry in England, and the ambassador of the old Queen of England is already here'.[41] Warwick, then, may well have been considering his loyalty to Edward at this point.

Around the end of August, Warwick returned to England with a delegation of French ambassadors, laden with gifts from the French king and most likely full of hope that his hard work would now pay off. He could not be further from the reality. Much had happened in his absence. In June, Edward had invited the 'Bastard of Burgundy', Antoine de Bourgogne, to England. Antoine was the illegitimate son of Burgundy, and while the visit was veiled as a pleasure trip, in reality much negotiation must have gone on behind the scenes.

Antoine's visit was ostensibly in order to take part in a jousting tournament with Anthony Woodville, now renowned for his skill in the sport. On 11 June 1467, the jousting tournament arrivals began.[42] The tournament was a particularly noteworthy one, not least for the multitude of princes, dukes, earls, barons, knights and men of other significant rank attending. Anthony's arrival was positively royal. On the first day of the tournament, he rode to the field followed by nine men on horseback, who were all decorated in the most elaborate attire: clad in damask, velvet, satin and ermine with gold embroidery and tassels, they were in an array of colour from purple to blue, crimson, green and yet more gold. Anthony himself rode a horse draped in white cloth of gold which was embroidered with a crimson velvet cross of St George and bordered with a fringe of gold half a foot long. His pavilion was made of blue satin, embroidered with his letters and hung with eight banners.[43]

The tournament demonstrated the eminence of members of the Woodville family at court and, possibly, that the Woodvilles were starting to eclipse Warwick in his influence over the king. The visit of the 'Bastard' was cut short, however, when news arrived that on 15 June, Philip, Duke of Burgundy, had died. The Burgundians needed to return home to sort out matters in their kingdom. The tournament had, however, shown great favour to the Burgundian cause and, as such, was an embarrassment for Warwick upon his return.

Another event happened during Warwick's absence that would have caused him much aggravation. Just prior to the commencement of the tournament, on 8 June, King Edward had relieved the Archbishop of York from his position as chancellor. As the archbishop was Warwick's brother, this was the first concrete suggestion that the Nevilles had lost their place at the top of the York family esteem, which they had held for over a decade. It is not recorded what had aggrieved Edward enough to remove the archbishop, but he had obviously become disillusioned enough to act personally. In the presence of his brother, Clarence, and numerous lords of the realm, Edward himself instructed the archbishop to deliver the great seal into his own hands.[44]

On 12 September 1467, the Milanese ambassador in France wrote of the return of King Louis XI's ambassadors to their country. He explained that 'the Earl of Warwick met with many opponents to his plan' and so the ambassadors 'found him unable to effect what he had promised on his departure'. Even worse, King Edward 'seems very averse to France, and Warwick; they are constantly at strife'. As such, Warwick had returned to his estates to raise troops.[45]

Though Warwick had returned from France with gifts, ambassadors and the promise of an excellent treaty with the French, he found his family snubbed from government, the Burgundians lauded and the Woodvilles at the helm. Edward had all but ignored the ambassadors he had brought back from France, refusing to meet with them to discuss matters and sending them back to the French court with scarcely a gift in return for all the expensive gifts sent. No wonder he retreated to his estates, humiliated.

Christmas passed quietly. August had seen the birth of a second child for the royal couple, another daughter, Mary, and so Edward and Elizabeth spent the festive season filled with joy for another addition to their family so quickly. In January 1468, however, a mob attacked and pillaged some of Richard Woodville's estates in Kent.[46] The source of their discontent was unclear, but the mob may well have been stirred by Warwick or his followers. On 7 January, Warwick refused a summons to court, saying he would not go to see Edward as long as Richard and Anthony Woodville or Lord Herbert were in his presence.[47] This was the first time Warwick had publicly vocalised his growing hatred for the Woodville family. By the end of the month, however, his brother, the Archbishop of York, and Richard Woodville organised a reconciliation between Richard and Warwick.[48] On the surface, then, Warwick was back in the fold.

In July, Edward's sister, Margaret finally set sail to get married. After much negotiation, Edward had agreed to a Burgundian alliance

– although the new duke was a much harsher negotiator than his father. In return for marrying Margaret, Burgundy would receive a dowry of £41,666, a staggering amount for the English finances. Understandably, it had taken about five months to gather so much money, but at last 22-year-old Margaret was to leave for her new life. Warwick took a starring role in her journey to the coast, with he and Margaret riding on the same horse as the entourage left London.[49]

In reality, however, the Woodvilles' input to bringing about the marriage alliance took centre place. Warwick stayed in England as Margaret sailed to Burgundy accompanied by Anthony Woodville. Anthony also took part in the jousting celebrations for the wedding in Burgundy – though not against the 'Bastard', as they had agreed never to fight again.[50] The Woodvilles had triumphed in their foreign policy, and Warwick was reminded of his lessening influence over the king.

The Woodvilles cannot be given full credit, however. While they certainly pushed for the alliance, Edward was beginning to take a greater personal role in foreign policy. The early years of his reign had been spent fighting in England, suppressing Lancastrian rebellions, and as such he had entrusted Warwick with almost free rein in diplomacy. Now that the country was more settled, Edward had time to become involved in wider politics, and he shrewdly realised how unpopular a French alliance would be to the English public.[51]

The end of 1468 was filled with political intrigue and conspiracies. The *Croyland Chronicle* records 'many nobles and great men of the kingdom, as well as very many bishops and abbats, were accused before the king of treason', and it was true that there were murmurs against the king at all levels of society.[52] In January 1469, two prominent executions took place: those of Thomas Hungerford and Henry Courtenay, who was the heir of the Earl of Devon.[53] Rumours of plots to restore Henry VI and Lancastrian loyalists in England making contact with Queen Margaret, who had taken up residence in the French court, were not without credence.

Nonetheless, there was some good news for Edward this year. On 20 March, Elizabeth gave birth to their third child, another daughter, named Cecily after her paternal grandmother. After the birth of this 'very handsome daughter', Elizabeth travelled to Fotheringhay, around

10 miles west of Peterborough, to meet her husband.[54] The royal couple then travelled onwards to Norwich. Personally, they were a happy family unit, and even the rumours of plots against Edward were not enough to threaten them. Conspirators were executed and there were plenty of loyal nobles across the country to support them.

What Edward could not let himself acknowledge, however, was that Warwick's discontent was now dangerously high and that he had finally decided he would reclaim his power over the throne, one way or another. Warwick allied himself with Edward's younger brother George, Duke of Clarence, who had ambitions of his own, and the pair sailed to Calais in early July 1469. Here, they went against Edward's clear wishes by marrying Clarence to Warwick's daughter, Isabel. Warwick had now secured his place in the royal family, and his daughter was now married to a prince. If Edward could not be placated, then he now had options in Clarence.

During their absence, Warwick had orchestrated a rebellion in the north, led by a man called 'Robin of Redesdale' whose true identity is unknown. The rebellion had initially been quashed by Warwick's younger brother John Neville.[55] On 9 July, amid rumours and some evidence that Warwick and Clarence had been involved in the uprisings, Edward wrote letters to them both and the Archbishop of York summoning them to his presence, telling them that he did not believe the 'rumour here renneth, consederyng the trust and affeccion we bere in yow'.[56] He still could not believe that his family and closest friends would turn on him. He did not realise that Warwick and Clarence were already in Calais ready to betray him.

Warwick was now in open revolt. On 12 July, the day after Clarence and Isabel's wedding, he issued a document alongside Clarence and the Archbishop of York declaring his reasons.[57] Claiming he was acting on petitions from all across the realm which were decrying the 'deceivable covetous rule and guiding of certain seditious persons', the rebels therefore were depicted as being defenders of king and country. But who were these seditious people? None other than the Woodvilles, Warwick's competition for influence. The document specifically named Richard Woodville, Jacquetta and their sons Anthony and John. It also named some of their supporters, including the Earls of Pembroke and Devon. This was a very direct attack.

Warwick claimed that the Woodvilles and their allies had caused Edward and his kingdom to fall into great poverty, disturbing the administration of law, and cared only to promote and enrich themselves. The rest of the complaints were clearly Warwick's own feelings of isolation. He said that Edward had turned away great lords from his council and did not take their advice, instead taking it only from those 'not of their blood', suggesting the supposed upstart nature of the Woodvilles.

This was a very calculated document. Warwick could not start a rebellion for the real reason that he was losing power and influence at court, and so he had to make it look like the Woodvilles were evil advisors to the king. It is very important that Elizabeth was not named in the document – to attack the queen was to attack the king, something Warwick could lose his head for. It is interesting, however, that Jacquetta was also named in the document and was the only woman named.

On 26 July, the king's forces met with the rebels. Edward himself was waiting with a small force in Nottingham for reinforcements led by Devon and Pembroke, but their army met with the rebels before they could reach the king. The Battle of Edgecote Moor was a decisive rebel victory, aided by the presence of Warwick's own army. Devon and Pembroke were captured, and both were executed by Warwick.[58] He was going to make sure that his rivals were disposed of once and for all.

Elizabeth, meanwhile, had reached Norwich with her daughters. Here, huge celebrations and pageants were held for her, and on the surface all seemed normal. By the end of July Elizabeth had returned to London, and now she realised just what a dangerous position she was in.[59]

Jacquetta's husband, Richard, and sons John and Anthony had been with the king in Nottingham, but as Warwick's ire against the Woodvilles became clear, Edward had sent them away for their own safety. He sent Anthony to Norfolk, and Richard and John to Wales. His plan did not work, however, and Richard and John were seized by Warwick's men at Chepstow. Eventually Anthony was also captured. Meanwhile, Edward marched south with his small force, but most of them abandoned him. He had no further reinforcements after the defeat of Devon and Pembroke at Edgecote, and so he was easily captured by the Archbishop of York.

Warwick now seemed to have achieved all he wanted. The king was under his control, he had already dispensed of two of the enemies named in his manifesto, and he had another three – Woodvilles at that – in his control. On 12 August outside Coventry, Richard and John Woodville were put on a show trial and hastily (and illegally) executed.[60] Jacquetta had lost her beloved husband of thirty years and one of her sons, and Elizabeth had lost a father and brother. This was one of the greatest tragedies that could have befallen the family. They may have found some comfort, however, in the survival of Anthony who, for reasons unknown, Warwick had not executed.

When Richard and John were executed, Edward was being held at Warwick Castle. He had now been in Warwick's keeping for several weeks, and he must have wondered what Warwick's end game was going to be. Elizabeth, meanwhile, was suffering in London. The Milanese ambassador reported on 16 August that Elizabeth was 'keeping very scant state'.[61] Her father and brother were dead, another brother was in custody and could be killed any day, and her husband was captured and could even be deposed. The future looked bleak.

Now Warwick was to come for Jacquetta. When there were so many male members of the Woodville family in positions at court, it initially seems strange that Warwick would bother with the mother of the queen. In reality, it made great sense to target Jacquetta. It had already been proven by the accusations against Eleanor Cobham nearly thirty years previously that targeting a woman could bring down the men around her, and that was Warwick's goal here. He had perhaps by now realised how unwise it had been to murder Richard and John, and he needed justification for his actions. If he could prove that Jacquetta had been involved in nefarious deeds, then it would give proof to his accusations that the family were destroying the country and misleading the king.

A squire named Thomas Wake, who was a follower of Warwick's, made an accusation against Jacquetta.[62] He came into the presence of the king and various lords of the land at Warwick Castle, bringing an image of lead moulded to look like a man. The image was the length of a finger but had been broken in the middle and tied with a wire. Wake claimed that the image belonged to Jacquetta, and that she had used it for 'wichecraft and sorcerie'. He also said that a man called John

Daunger, who was a parish clerk in Stoke Bruerne, Northamptonshire, had found two other images made by Jacquetta of the king and queen. Although not explicitly said, the implication – especially considering later accusations against Elizabeth – was that Jacquetta had used these figures to perform love magic to make Edward fall in love with Elizabeth. The figure of the broken man could also be taken to suggest that Jacquetta had attempted to harm Edward or Warwick.

These were serious accusations. Although Warwick was carefully avoiding attacking the queen herself, by throwing in the possibility that the shocking marriage of Edward and Elizabeth had been procured by love magic, he was creating a chance to get rid of the Woodvilles once and for all. If he continued to have the power card of holding Edward in his custody, he might even be able to get Elizabeth and Edward's marriage annulled, just like Humphrey and Eleanor's a few decades previously. Warwick would have known that this was a very unlikely situation, but nonetheless the accusations of witchcraft provided proof that the Woodvilles were enemies of Crown and country.

As a result of the charges, Jacquetta was arrested and also brought to Warwick Castle.[63] In a shrewd move, Jacquetta decided to call in a favour. Remembering how she had saved London from attack by Margaret of Anjou back in 1461 and knowing the city's fondness for her, at the end of August Jacquetta wrote a letter to the mayor and aldermen of London. She reminded them of the service she had done them and appealed for them to help her now at her time of need. This the city was eager to do, and they sent a letter supporting Jacquetta to Warwick and Clarence.[64] Warwick would now have to tread carefully.

Despite this, Edward had been forced to order an inquest into Wake's accusations. He ordered the Bishop of Carlisle, the Earl of Northumberland, the Lords Hastings and Mountjoy and Master Roger Radcliff to examine Wake and Daunger. This was an authoritative group of people whose decisions could be trusted.

Under the slightest scrutiny, the accusations crumbled. When John Daunger was questioned about the image of a man, his story was entirely different from Wake's. Daunger said that the image had been found and subsequently left with an honest person in Stoke, who then delivered it to the clerk of the church as well as numerous neighbours. It was then passed around numerous towns, as well as a nunnery, eventually reaching Daunger. He said that he was then contacted by Wake who asked him to send him the image, 'at which time he heard no witchcraft of the lady of Bedford'.

Daunger said that the image had, in fact, been found in the house of a man named Harry Kingston after soldiers had departed. Daunger then went one step further and actually incriminated Wake. Daunger said that Wake had entreated him to say that there were two other images made by Jacquetta representing the king and queen, but that he had refused. This meant that the other images had never actually existed, and Wake was on record as having fabricated it.

In the meantime, Warwick was trying desperately to cling onto power. As he was claiming to be trying to save the king from his evil advisors, for a while he tried to rule in Edward's name. However, very few members of the nobility supported Warwick's rebellion, proving that the Woodvilles cannot have been as unpopular as has been claimed, and so he was already on shaky ground. Having Edward in custody instead led to a collapse of law and order in the country. Not having the authority of the king and the threat of repercussions meant that many family feuds were reignited.

London stayed loyal to the king, Elizabeth and the Woodvilles, while there were rebellions in the north. Noble families fought each other in petty squabbles and Warwick's cousin Humphrey Neville led a rebellion in the name of the still imprisoned Henry VI.[65] Warwick could not cling to power for much longer, and he could see that the country was collapsing.

On 10 September 1469, he was finally forced to free Edward. Edward immediately raised an army in his name and crushed Humphrey Neville's rebellion, executing him and his brother. The country quickly fell back into line, and law and order was restored for the time being. In October, Edward made a triumphant entry into London and was finally reunited with his family. Perhaps surprisingly, considering all that had happened, it was reported that the king was speaking well of Warwick and Clarence, 'seyng they be hys best frendys'.[66]

Jacquetta and Elizabeth had survived the rebellion, but it had cost them dearly. Now that Edward was free and putting everything back into order, it was necessary to exonerate Jacquetta officially. Such dangerous accusations could not be left to float around. Luckily, the inquest had already shown how shambolic the alleged charges were. On

20 January 1470, Jacquetta was cleared in front of the king and the lords of his council. On 10 February, in front of Parliament, Jacquetta also made sure that the results of the inquest were recorded for posterity.[67]

It is not recorded whether Wake was ever punished for his lies against Jacquetta. One can hardly imagine that he would have suffered no consequences, but considering Edward's forgiving nature that year, it may well be possible. There are records in the Inquisitions Post-Mortem of 1476–77 of the death of a Thomas Wake esquire, and it is reasonable to assume this is the same man.[68] If so, he certainly lived past his accusations.

The records in Parliament and in the Patent Rolls show that Jacquetta had learnt her lesson from Eleanor Cobham very well. She had seen at first hand how accusations of witchcraft and love magic could destroy a woman, and everything in the records point to the fact that Jacquetta – and the government – knew by now how important it was to refute accusations when necessary. The record in the Patent Rolls on 21 February states that it was being added 'at the supplication of Jacquetta, duchess of Bedford', while the record in Parliament explains that it is being written down 'so as the same her declaration may allway remaigne there of Record, and that she may have it exemplified undir your grete Seall'. Jacquetta was making sure that the highest institute in the land was recording her innocence, for the whole realm to see, and to have it recorded for years to come.

Unlike with Joan and Eleanor, the government was on Jacquetta's side and it too knew that it needed to stop the possibility of rumours of witchcraft spreading. In fact, the records themselves show how necessary this was, for Wake's accusations had already succeeded in part. The Parliament record recognises that Wake accused her, not only to hurt and impair her 'good name and fame' but also to cause the 'final destruction of her person'. In this, he had caused her to be 'brought in a common noise … of witchcraft throughout a great part' of the country. Already, then, rumours had circulated, and the idea had been seeded in some minds.

The accusations against Jacquetta were not without precedent. Beyond the earlier allegations against Joan and Eleanor, Jacquetta's position mirrored very well a case from the previous century in France. In 1316, Mahaut of Artois, who was the mother-in-law of

King Philip V, was accused of using love magic. Mahaut's daughter, Joan, and Philip had become estranged prior to Philip becoming king. They reconciled, and then King Louis X died, making Philip king and Joan queen. It was therefore alleged that Mahaut had used love magic to reconcile Joan and Philip, and then, once successful, poisoned Louis to guarantee their succession to the throne.[69] Jacquetta's position was not too dissimilar.

For the time being, the dust had settled. Jacquetta had her reputation restored and Edward was once again in power. Edward was remarkably forgiving towards Warwick and Clarence, considering all they had done. Both men returned to court without consequence, and Warwick was even present in Parliament when the refutation of the accusations against Jacquetta was announced. One can hardly begin to imagine the tension that must have been at court – it must have been extremely difficult for Elizabeth and Jacquetta to be around the man who had murdered members of their family.

Peace and reconciliation, therefore, seemed to be the order of the day. Tensions may have been simmering under the surface, but Edward must still have felt love and loyalty for his cousin, the man who had been his friend for so long and had helped put him on the throne, as well as for his brother. Despite their deep betrayal, it is somewhat understandable why Edward would not have wanted to punish them. Moreover, he may have felt that enough blood had already been spilt. The Woodvilles, meanwhile, were left to mourn. They had survived this attack, and could start to rebuild their lives. However, peace was not to reign for long.

12

THE MOTHER,
THE QUEEN AND
THE MISTRESS

UNEASY PEACE HAD been the atmosphere at court following the official refutation of the accusations against Jacquetta. At a Great Council held between November 1469 and February 1470, Warwick and Clarence had agreed to make peace with the king and the Woodvilles.[1] Despite Edward's desire to reconcile his estranged friend and brother, too much had now passed for things ever to go back to how they were before. In March, Warwick and Clarence once again rose up against Edward.

This month, there had been more rebellions in Lincolnshire.[2] As Edward moved north with an army, Warwick and Clarence sent Edward letters saying that they were raising an army to come and aid him. Warwick, in fact, planned to ambush him with his own army. Warwick's plan was thwarted, however, during the Battle of Losecoat Field on 12 March, when Edward's forces crushed those of the Lancastrian Lord Willoughby. Afterwards, Willoughby claimed that Warwick and George had been the ones who provoked him into his rebellion, and documents were found which showed that they were complicit.[3] Edward had unknowingly provided Warwick with his own rebel army.

Now that Edward had realised that Warwick was planning on betraying him again, Warwick and Clarence fled the country. Edward had gathered the support of many powerful nobles, whereas Warwick and Clarence had failed to gain any significant support beyond rebel commoners. Even members of their own family and known Lancastrian loyalists did not act to help them. They were forced to seek refuge at the court of Louis XI of France. Louis was Margaret of Anjou's cousin, and he had given her a home in France throughout her years of exile. Now, Warwick changed course drastically and Louis brought the former enemies together for a meeting. The two decided to put aside their differences and past strife to reach a common goal: defeating Edward IV and reinstating Henry VI as King of England.

On 23 July, Warwick was formally presented by Louis to Margaret: 'With great reverence Warwick went on his knees and asked her pardon for the injuries and wrongs done to her in the past.'[4] After numerous talks, the two came to a mutually beneficial agreement. Warwick's younger daughter, Anne Neville, was to be married to Margaret and Henry's son, Edward of Lancaster. In return, Warwick had to release Henry VI. The couple were certainly married by the end of the year, and although Margaret may have wished to wait to see the outcome of Warwick's success before committing to such an important marriage, it appears that Warwick did not want to leave for England before the wedding took place. As such, it seems the couple were married by the end of August.[5]

Warwick used his old tried and tested tactics and stirred uprisings in the north of England. When Edward IV marched to quell it, Warwick and Clarence set sail from France with a combined fleet of his and Margaret's ships, aided by the money of the French king. They landed at Dartmouth and Plymouth on 13 September 1470, and this time they found themselves gathering support from those who were discontented with Edward's regime.

In early June, Edward and Elizabeth had been residing in Canterbury with members of their family. Elizabeth was four months pregnant, and was most likely attended by Jacquetta. When Edward had to leave to deal with the rebellion Warwick had created in the north, he sent Elizabeth and his daughters to the Tower of London for their own safety.[6]

As soon as Warwick and Clarence landed in the south, Edward immediately rushed to meet their forces. Now, however, came more treachery against the king: John Neville, who had up to this point been staunchly loyal to Edward, finally turned on him. He led an army down behind Edward, who was now surrounded and outnumbered and could not hope to win. He must have realised that, this time, the terms of his imprisonment would not be so forgiving.

Edward's only option was to flee the country. Alongside his brother Richard, Duke of Gloucester, and Anthony Woodville, he travelled to Kings Lynn and then sailed to Flanders on 2 October. The journey was dangerous, with many of his men drowning on the way to Kings Lynn when they tried to cross the Wash in Lincolnshire.[7]

Edward intended to take refuge in the court of his brother-in-law, the Duke of Burgundy, but Burgundy would not receive him, not wishing to antagonise the French king. Edward and his small retinue of men were forced to wait in The Hague under the hospitality of Louis de Gruuthuse. They had nothing but the clothes on their backs and were completely reliant on Gruuthuse's generosity.[8] With Edward gone, Warwick now only had to secure London and the body of Henry VI. However, Elizabeth was still in residence in London and this was now a dangerous situation for her.

In the middle of the night of 1 October 1470, Queen Elizabeth Woodville, who was now eight months pregnant, took her three young daughters down to the dock at the Tower of London. Here, she secretly took a barge down the River Thames to Westminster Abbey, where she was met by her mother, Jacquetta of Luxembourg.[9] At the abbey they claimed the sacred right of sanctuary, as Eleanor Cobham had thirty years previously. This sanctuary was rock bottom for this once grand queen. Sanctuary was more used by petty criminals, not royalty, and as such the lodgings were small and cramped, located near a foul-smelling public latrine.[10] But she and her family were under the best protection left to them. Rumours had circulated that King Edward had died, and the heartbreak and worry Elizabeth must have felt at this news must have left her distraught.[11] Still, she had taken the best course of action she could.

Within a few days of Elizabeth's flight to sanctuary, the Earl of Warwick entered London all but unopposed. Fearing that Warwick would violate the sanctity of sanctuary and enter Westminster Abbey and kill her, Elizabeth ordered that the Tower of London be given over to the mayor and aldermen of the city. The Tower thusly surrendered on the condition that all those inside (loyal Yorkists and government servants) be allowed safe passage to sanctuary themselves.[12] Under a proclamation of Henry VI, the safety of sanctuary was strictly enforced, and many of those who had been part of Edward's government fled to sanctuary at St Martin's Church in London.[13]

Other nobles and members of government loyal to Edward did not escape so well, and Warwick imprisoned a huge contingent of Yorkists in the now Lancastrian-controlled Tower of London. Meanwhile, Henry was restored to the royal apartments of the Tower, ironically taking up residence in the sumptuous chambers which had been prepared for Elizabeth's imminent confinement. On 6 October, Henry VI was proclaimed King of England once more.

Elizabeth's protection in sanctuary was accepted by Henry's government. Henry himself, in his lucid moments, would have made sure of it, and Warwick could not afford to lose any credibility by violating such a sacred right, particularly against a pregnant woman. Thus, she, her mother and daughters were safe for the time being, which must have given some temporary relief, particularly considering Warwick's history of attacking her mother.

It was here in sanctuary that on 3 November 1470, the deposed Queen Elizabeth gave birth to her first son by the king.[14] The boy was named Edward, after his father. She had finally completed the most significant act of a queen, to produce a healthy male heir for her husband, but this must have come as little comfort. She was trapped in the grounds of the abbey, her enemies filling the streets of London all around her. It was only the respect for the Church that lay between her capture or possible death.

After Prince Edward's birth, he was christened in Westminster Abbey. Despite the illustrious location, the christening was simple. The child's godfathers were the abbey prior and Abbot Millyng – Millyng having become Elizabeth's protector and champion in sanctuary. His godmother was Elizabeth, Lady Scrope, who had been appointed by Henry VI's government to wait on Elizabeth.[15]

Elizabeth's one comfort during her time in sanctuary must have been that her mother was right there beside her. Her husband was in a foreign country and might never return, her family members were scattered across the country and so she was currently a single mother responsible for four children. Despite all this, her ever-constant mother was there to share in her despair and to provide courage whenever Elizabeth might feel at her lowest. This powerful mother and daughter had risen and fallen together, but through it all they stuck together.

Edward had not been complacent in exile, however. Although Burgundy had refused to grant him an audience, by 1471 the tides had changed. Tensions were rising with France, and an invasion of the duchy seemed ever more likely. In early January, Burgundy met several times with Edward in secret, one such instance being at Saint-Pol under the hospitality of Jacquetta's brother, Jacques of Luxembourg.[16] Finally, Burgundy – probably partially under the influence of his wife, Edward's sister, Margaret – agreed to secretly support Edward's reclamation of the English Crown. He gave Edward a very generous £20,000 and three of his own ships to fund the expedition, while in public he gave his verbal support to the newly restored Henry VI.

Meanwhile, in England, Warwick was having problems. Although he had imprisoned the most problematic Yorkist nobles, he knew that many on the Yorkist side would need to be reconciled to the Lancastrian regime to keep it in power. However, with Henry's restoration and the imminent return of Margaret and Edward of Lancaster, the Lancastrian nobles who had spent the past decade in exile with them would also be coming home. Many Yorkist nobles had been generously rewarded with sequestered Lancastrian estates, and great hostility and rebellion would be incurred if they were taken away again. Nonetheless, the returning Lancastrians would be wanting the restoration of their lands.

Five months after Elizabeth and her family had fled to sanctuary, Edward made his move. On 11 March, he set sail for England. The crossing to Norfolk was smooth, but Edward learnt it was controlled by Warwick's men. Instead, Edward decided to sail further north, but his ships got caught in a storm and separated. Edward's already small force was now depleted even further.[17] Edward instead landed on the Holderness coast in Yorkshire.

With just 500 men, he slowly made his way south under the pretence that he was merely returned to reclaim his lands owed as Earl of March and Duke of York. Remarkably, Edward travelled south unmolested. Although he gained very little active support in the north, no one attacked him on his journey – even those with Lancastrian leanings. As Edward's retinue reached further and further south, he started to gain greater support from the regions which had historically been loyal to him. His force was now looking more formidable.

Alarmed, Warwick left London for Coventry with a force of his own, made up of a mixture of Lancastrian and Yorkist men. Warwick sent for Clarence to bring reinforcements, and he duly made his way there. What Warwick had failed to recognise, however, was Clarence's growing realisation that the new regime was detrimental to his own position. Warwick could continue in Henry VI's government, particularly now that his daughter would eventually become Queen of England. Clarence, however, was a rival claimant to the throne and in control of vast territories and titles gifted to him by his brother Edward. Even though Margaret had agreed to make provisions for him, Clarence had at last realised that he would eventually be pushed out of government and perhaps even placed under suspicion.

Therefore, when Clarence arrived at Coventry and met with Edward's forces it did not go as Warwick expected. Clarence got on his knees before Edward, showing his humility. Edward bade him rise and kissed him several times, at which point Clarence shouted, 'Long live King Edward!'.[18] Edward had regained the loyalty of his brother and had his invasion force bolstered.

Warwick was now hesitant to attack the joint forces. Clarence attempted to negotiate a reconciliation between Warwick and Edward but, probably deciding that it was too late to go back, Warwick refused to meet.[19] At the same time, Edward learnt that London was all but undefended: the occupying Lancastrians had either joined Warwick or had now left to meet Queen Margaret who was expected to land any day. He therefore directed his army towards the capital.

Hearing of Edward's imminent arrival, the nobles who had been imprisoned in the Tower of London managed to overcome their captors and took control of the fortress once more.[20] On 9 April, Edward was confident enough in his success to send news of his arrival to Elizabeth, his lords and servants.[21]

Edward reached London and, despite attempts by the Archbishop of York to protect the city, the Londoners were loyal to Edward now.

The gates were opened to him, and he took the city without a battle on 11 April 1471. Although he must have been overwhelmingly anxious to meet with his forlorn queen, he had to follow protocol reiterating that he was the rightful king instead of Henry. He therefore rode straight to St Paul's Cathedral, where he gave thanks for his success and then had the crown placed on his head at Westminster Abbey.[22] At last, he could be reunited with his wife.

He rushed to meet Elizabeth and 'comfortyd hir', and finally he met his baby son, now 5 months old. Elizabeth had suffered 'right great trowble, sorow, and hevines [heaviness], whiche she sustayned with all mannar pacience that belonged to eny creature', and this was not missed by the citizens of London, nor the wider country. King Henry VI was found 'almoste alone' in the Bishop's Palace, abandoned by all of his men.[23] He was swiftly put back into the Tower of London. Edward was back on the throne.

Edward took Elizabeth and his children (and, presumably, Jacquetta) out of sanctuary and lodged them in Baynard's Castle in the city of London.[24] The castle had been rebuilt in the late 1420s by Humphrey, Duke of Gloucester, after a fire, but was now in the hands of Edward's mother, Cecily.[25] Edward could be assured of their safety there.

He was not able to rest long, however, because now Warwick made his move. Edward had to immediately march out of London with his forces to fight Warwick. They met at the Battle of Barnet, just north of London, in the early hours of Easter Sunday, 14 April.[26] Warwick's brother, John Neville, was killed in this fighting and, knowing the battle was being lost, Warwick attempted to flee. All signs point to Edward wanting Warwick apprehended alive, but somehow in his retreat Warwick was killed. The great Richard Neville, the Kingmaker, was dead.[27]

This victory must have been bittersweet for Edward. One of the greatest challengers to his rule had been destroyed once and for all, but this was no ordinary challenger. Warwick was his blood cousin, one of his best friends, and had been instrumental in giving him the Crown he was now defending. It can have come as no joy to hear news of his death. He had no time to ponder his feelings, however, for within a few days Queen Margaret and Prince Edward of Lancaster finally landed in England. For her safety, Edward placed Elizabeth and his family in the

Tower of London, leaving them in the trusted protection of her brother, Anthony. It was time once more for war.

Margaret and Edward of Lancaster had landed in Weymouth on the south-west coast of England, and although the news of the failure at Barnet made Margaret want to flee back to France, her son encouraged her to carry on the fight.[28] Her supporters had managed to raise an army in the West Country, and it was decided that they should march north to meet with Welsh forces led by Jasper Tudor. Her forces made it to Tewkesbury in Gloucestershire on 3 May, and the following day Edward's army met her in battle, having out-marched her.[29]

Margaret took up refuge in a nearby religious house. Her son Edward was now 17 years old and eager to fight for his Crown, so stayed for the battle. With King Edward also present on the battlefield, the mother and son would have known this was to be the battle that would decide their fate. Their parting must have been difficult.

The Battle of Tewkesbury was fought heavily and bloodily. Although the Lancastrians slightly outnumbered the Yorkist forces, King Edward's battle-hardened experience meant that he organised his troops better. The Lancastrian army started to flounder, with some of its leaders turning on each other.

The battle was won by King Edward. Many leading Lancastrians died in the fighting, but the most crucial death of all was that of Prince Edward of Lancaster. Later stories claim that Prince Edward was found alive and murdered after the battle; however, all the contemporary chronicles record that he was killed in battle, so this is the more likely reality.[30]

All of Margaret's hopes were now dashed. At 41 years old and with a husband who had sunk into an almost constant state of being unaware of his environment and unable to care for himself, she would not give birth to another child. Edward had been her sole heir, her only hope of ever reclaiming the Crown of England. Now all was lost. It was not long before she was found hiding in the religious community, and she was brought to Edward as a broken woman.

If news had reached Elizabeth and Jacquetta of Edward's victory, they did not have much chance to celebrate. Thomas Neville, Warwick's cousin, was in control of a contingent of ships off the coast of London, and in May he attacked. Hearing of this, Edward swiftly sent 1,500 men to defend the city and his family, but he was too far away for them to arrive in time.[31] Neville bombarded the city with artillery from his ships, while he ordered a multi-pronged attack on several fronts. Luckily for the Londoners, Edward had left one of his most trusted and experienced men, Anthony Woodville, to defend them. Anthony rallied the mayor and aldermen, who refused Neville access to the city. The Earl of Essex fought back across the river, while Anthony led the London citizens in fighting back on London Bridge. They were successful in their defence, but London Bridge was burnt in the assault.[32]

From Elizabeth's position at the Tower of London, she would have been able to view the fighting on London Bridge at first hand. It must truly have been terrifying watching the fighting from the windows, her children and young baby with her, knowing her brother was out in the midst of it defending them. Any moment the tide of battle could change and she might have been able to see Lancastrians advancing towards the Tower, coming for her. Jacquetta must surely have been standing beside her, perhaps offering comforting words.

However, the resistance of the Londoners was enough to make Neville retreat, and he was eventually defeated. On 21 May, King Edward IV once more made a triumphal entry to London, this time with a captured queen in his hands, as well as a king.[33] Margaret was sent to the Tower to join her husband, although they were not permitted to see each other. That night, King Henry VI of England, who had been king, even if just in name, for just less than fifty years, died. The official explanation was that the king had died of 'melancoly', but there were no pretences; everybody knew that Henry had been murdered by the Yorkist regime.[34] Most chronicles record that it was Richard, Duke of Gloucester, who killed him, although the real story of his death is lost to history.[35]

Edward had now removed the two rival claimants to his throne, and from now on his reign was generally secure. Margaret of Anjou was kept at the Tower for a time but soon she was moved to Windsor Castle, and then in early January 1472 she was taken to Wallingford in Oxfordshire.[36] Here, she was placed in the custody of the Duchess of Suffolk – the woman who had shared the position of Margaret's closest female attendant alongside Jacquetta all those decades ago.

It is intriguing that Margaret was placed in such a favourable household, particularly as there could be worries that Suffolk would help her escape. However, Margaret was no longer a threat. She now had no basis to raise an army, for she had no personal claim to the throne. It has been suggested that Margaret was moved to a friendly household under the influence of Elizabeth Woodville.[37] This could well be the case. Elizabeth had suffered for six months in the most unpleasant circumstances in sanctuary at Westminster and she may well have had sympathy for this deposed queen, who merely had the misfortune of being on the other side of the battlefield.

Now that the realm was once more secure, Edward set about organising his personal affairs. On 3 July, his firstborn son was invested as Prince of Wales, with all the nobles of the realm proclaiming allegiance to him as Edward's true heir. A Prince's Council was created for the baby, with Elizabeth appointed as its head. Thomas Millyng, the abbot who had protected Elizabeth in sanctuary, was greatly rewarded by being appointed chancellor to the young prince.[38]

In October, Parliament was summoned to restore order to the kingdom. This Parliament showed a genuine support for Elizabeth, which demonstrates just how popular she had become, despite her inauspicious start. Her decision to flee to sanctuary had not only possibly saved her family, but it had saved London from attack. Rather than having to repel the Lancastrians in the defence of the queen, they were able to let them into the city without a fight, saving much bloodshed. Elizabeth's stay in sanctuary as a helpless pregnant woman and then as the mother of the newborn prince was not only excellent propaganda for the newly restored Yorkist regime, but it clearly resonated deeply with the common people of the land. Elizabeth was seen as having suffered with them through the terrors of the brief restoration.

At the opening of Parliament, therefore, the Speaker of the House of Commons made a point to proclaim the 'desire of his Commons specially in the commendation of the womanly behaviour and the great constance of our Sovereign Lady the Queen'.[39] This certainly seems like a sincere accolade. In fact, a poem was composed not long after the restoration, written by someone who had clearly been in the city during the reclamation. The long poem tracks the recovery of the throne by Edward, but it is dedicated to Elizabeth and it recognises and celebrates her suffering alongside the people of the land: 'O quene Elizabeth, o blessid creature/ O glorius God, what payne had sche?/

What langowr and angwiche did sche endure?... to here of hir wepyng it was grett peté'.[40] Elizabeth had truly won the love of her people through her suffering. She had proven herself more queenly than ever.

Christmas 1471 was filled with huge festivities to demonstrate the wealth and power of the Yorkist regime. On Christmas Day, Edward and Elizabeth were crowned at Westminster Abbey, with the royal couple keeping great estate throughout the day. On New Year's Day, the couple took a procession through the city, followed by another procession on twelfth night. During this procession Edward wore his crown, but Elizabeth did not because 'she was grete with child'.[41] This baby was born on 19 April 1472 at Westminster, a girl named Margaret.[42] The name may well have been chosen to honour Edward's sister, who had been instrumental both in gaining Burgundy's support for Edward's invasion, and for persuading Clarence to return to Edward's side.

The joy of the birth of her seventh child, her fifth by Edward, was followed by tragedy. On 30 May 1472, Jacquetta of Luxembourg died, aged 56. This noble lady had survived the ravages of the Hundred Years War and the Wars of the Roses, had married a prince of England and then a humble knight, had given birth to fourteen children and seen her eldest daughter rise to queen. She had suffered through the execution of her husband and son, and survived the cruel accusations of witchcraft thrown against her. She had followed her Lancastrian mistress loyally until there was no choice but to support the Yorkists, where she then had to suffer seeing her former queen fighting against her daughter and son-in-law. She had stuck by her daughter, serving her during the highs of her reign and the lows of sanctuary. Educated, cultured, intelligent, affable – Jacquetta of Luxembourg had served England and its people to her death.

The deep loss that Elizabeth would have felt at the death of her mother is easy to imagine. Through every trouble that Elizabeth had experienced, she had always had her mother there to rely on. Jacquetta had taken her back in after the death of her first husband, and had facilitated her second marriage and thus her rise to the throne. She had shared in the joys of the birth of her children, and no doubt was always on hand to give her advice on how to proceed at court. To lose her just when troubles were settling down and she was preparing to live a calmer life must have been particularly poignant. Perhaps she took comfort in knowing that Jacquetta had lived to see her daughter restored to the throne and the birth of another grandchild.

While Elizabeth and the Woodville family were grieving the loss of their matriarch, Edward was having problems within his own family. Clarence was once more experiencing discontent. After Edward of Lancaster had been killed at Tewkesbury, his bride of just a few months, Anne Neville, was left a widow. Now, Gloucester wanted to marry her. The death of Warwick meant that his two daughters were now his joint heirs – and there was great wealth to be distributed.

Clarence was strongly against this marriage, for it would mean his brother became his rival in the inheritance. For this precise reason, Edward agreed to the marriage. He did not want Clarence to have access to so much wealth and power and Gloucester was a perfect balance.[43] On 12 July 1472, Gloucester and Anne Neville were married. Clarence's ambition and self-importance were growing, and not getting his way in the Neville marriages was another piece of fuel for his jealousy and discontent.

In September, Edward had a very special visitor on whom he wished to bestow all honour.[44] Louis de Gruuthuse, the man who had accommodated Edward and his small group of men when no one else would receive him, who had organised food and clothes and shelter when Edward did not have a penny to his name, was now to visit his court. Edward was going to make sure he showed his deep gratitude.

Gruuthuse was taken to Windsor Castle, where he was warmly greeted by both Edward and Elizabeth. Elizabeth was in her chamber, playing a game with her ladies called 'morteaulx', which was similar to bowls, while some of her other ladies were playing 'at the Closheys of yvery', a version of ninepin skittles or bowling. Touchingly, it is also described how the 'Kinge daunsed [with] my lady Elizabethe, his eldest doughter'.[45] By now, Princess Elizabeth was 6 years old. The scene described shows a heartwarming side to the family who had been through so much. It is also a rare insight to the everyday lives of the family, away from Yorkist, Lancastrian or Tudor propaganda. The feelings of the real people, their emotions and relationships shines through.

The following day, Edward gifted Gruuthuse with a cup of gold which had a piece of (what was believed to be) unicorn horn in it that was 7in long. Unicorn horn was believed to protect against poison. That night, Elizabeth hosted a banquet in her chamber attended by her husband, her eldest daughter, Anthony's wife Elizabeth Scales, Gruuthuse and numerous other members of the nobility. The final honour bestowed upon him was on St Edward's day when, in the chamber of Parliament, Edward created him Earl of Winchester.[46]

The year ended in more tragedy for Edward and Elizabeth when, on 11 December, their daughter Margaret died at just 8 months old. This was the first child that Elizabeth had lost – remarkable for the time, considering she was her seventh child – and coming the same year as the death of her mother, it must have hit her particularly hard. It must have been a sombre Christmas for the king and queen.

It was perhaps the death of baby Margaret that prompted Elizabeth and Edward to move their only son, Edward, to the Welsh border in March the following year. London was notoriously full of disease, and after all the strife of the previous years the family may have wanted a quieter upbringing for him and a time of rest for Elizabeth, who was now four months pregnant with another child. Prince Edward was nearing 2½ years old, and it was time for him to be properly established with his own household. Elizabeth took him to Ludlow Castle, which sat on the banks of the River Terne in Shropshire, south of Shrewsbury and north of Hereford.[47]

Elizabeth spent some time at Ludlow getting Prince Edward settled, and in June King Edward joined them. In July, Elizabeth moved to the nearby town of Shrewsbury to prepare for her confinement; it is not clear why she did not choose to stay at Ludlow Castle, but perhaps she wanted the luxuries, security and supplies of a town. On 17 August, Elizabeth gave birth to Edward's second son, Richard. It is possible that Edward was in the area for the birth of this son, and it must have been a joyous occasion. Although Prince Edward had been healthy up to now, he was still very young, and it was always reassuring to have a 'spare' heir. By autumn the following year, Prince Richard had joined his brother's household.

At the end of September, Edward sent a letter to Anthony Woodville and the Bishop of Rochester regarding the education of Prince Edward. Edward had assigned Anthony as his son's governor, and the rest of the prince's household was filled with his close relatives. Four of Elizabeth's brothers were in the household: as well as Anthony, her brother Lionel, who had taken the cloth, became her son's chaplain, while her brothers Edward and Richard were his counsellors. Numerous other relatives took up a variety of other positions, meaning the young prince was almost entirely surrounded by his mother's family.[48] King Edward's unwavering trust in Anthony was shown when he and the bishop were given full authority to move Prince Edward at any time should their discretion view it necessary.[49] This was quite a privilege.

The year 1474 arrived with few stirrings. Peace had settled reasonably quickly after the final defeat of the Lancastrians and Edward could now feel secure in his reign once more. His family with Elizabeth was ever growing and it is clear that the couple adored each other. Questions have been raised over time about their relationship, considering Edward's reputation for having extramarital affairs. The most well known of these was with Jane Shore, who was later to have potentially more of an important impact on Elizabeth's life. While it is impossible to know Elizabeth's feelings on the matter, particularly due to the different attitudes of the time, it is clear that Edward's desire for mistresses in no way diminished his love for Elizabeth. Elizabeth was never put under threat by mistresses gaining too much wealth or power, and Edward continued to bestow gifts and demonstrate his trust and love for Elizabeth until his death.

Edward continued to act on behalf of Elizabeth's family. That summer, Elizabeth's eldest son, Thomas Grey, had married his second wife, Cecily Bonville. Cecily was the stepdaughter of Lord Hastings – meaning the agreement made between Hastings and Elizabeth ten years previously had eventually been fulfilled – and one of the wealthiest heiresses in the country. This was an excellent marriage for both bride and groom, and Edward sorted out the inheritance for the couple to ensure their wealthy future together.[50]

In 1475, a royal marriage was in the air. Although Elizabeth's two eldest daughters were still unmarried, Edward drew up plans to have his third daughter, Cecily, betrothed to the son of the King of Scotland.[51] Prince James was just a few years old, while Cecily was only 6, but the marriage, if it were to come to fruition, would eventually make his daughter a queen. More importantly, however, war with France was on the horizon and Edward needed to shore up his northern borders before he could safely leave the kingdom. A marriage alliance was the perfect way to ensure peace with the Scots. The marriage agreed upon, it was time for Edward to gather an army.[52]

On 20 June, Edward drew up his will,[53] making provisions for the realm and his children upon the event of his death. Elizabeth featured heavily throughout. She was given control over the decision regarding the marriages of their daughters, to be shared with their son Edward if he had come of age. She was given all of the couple's moveable goods, including bedding, tapestries, items of their chapel, plates, jewels and books, and she was to be allowed to do whatever she wished with them without interference from the executors. Her rights to the goods and chattels that she currently owned was also confirmed, and his 'moost entierly beloved wiff Elizabeth the Quene' was named as the principal executor to the will. This was because, in her, he 'moost singulerly put oure trust'.

Edward had his army gathered and his affairs were set in order. Elizabeth can hardly have desired his departure; on top of the usual dangers of warfare, she was once more pregnant, due in just over four months. The heir to the throne was not yet 5 years old, which would result in a long and potentially dangerous regency were Edward to die. No time is a good one to lose your husband, but this was a particularly bad one.

In the end, Elizabeth had no need to fear. Although her brother Anthony and son Thomas Grey had joined Edward in his campaign, none of their lives were put in danger. King Louis had other problems on his mind and was not keen to start an expensive and bloody war with the English. He persuaded Edward to meet, and he offered very generous terms to the English: if they returned to England, leaving France in peace, then Louis would make them rich men. He would give Edward an up-front payment of £15,000 as well as an annual pension of £10,000 and would give extra monetary grants to his closest advisors. To seal the peace between them, he would marry his son and heir, the 5-year-old Dauphin Charles to Edward's eldest daughter, 9-year-old Princess Elizabeth.[54]

Edward, of course, seized upon this opportunity. The French king's money would make him a very wealthy man, solving many of his problems. It would also mean that a second daughter of his was now in line to become a queen. All of this could be obtained without long, drawn-out fighting. Edward returned home at the end September a very happy man.

His people were not so happy, however. They had wanted the glory of a great war, to reclaim land lost by Henry VI, and the soldiers were banking on getting wealthy through plunder. Instead, the ordinary members of the expedition left empty-handed.[55]

Edward was now home for the birth of his next child, Anne, on 2 November. Two weeks later, the French king made Edward another offer: he would pay a ransom to release Queen Margaret into his custody. Margaret was no longer a threat to Edward, and releasing her to the French king was both a kindness and meant Edward no longer had to pay to maintain her. He therefore agreed, and this once-great queen returned to her homeland.[56] However, if she had hoped to live out a comfortable retirement at the French court under the hospitality of her cousin, the king, then she was sadly mistaken. She was given a pittance to live on, and died in 1482 at the age of 52. Perhaps she might have preferred to have lived out the remainder of her life in England in the custody of her old friend.

In spring 1477, Elizabeth gave birth to a third son by Edward, a boy called George. However, his uncle and namesake, George, Duke of Clarence, was not part of the happy family. His discontent had been simmering for years. Now 28 years old, Clarence's burning jealousy and greed had never abated. All the time Warwick had spent whispering in his ear, suggesting that one day he might be king, had given him ideas above his station. Edward had constantly rewarded him, given him lands, title, positions and wealth, but nothing was enough to satiate him.

Clarence's wife, Isabel Neville, had died the previous year, and now he had his eyes on the new Duchess of Burgundy, the daughter and heir of the duke who had died in January. This would make him Duke of Burgundy through her. He would be rich and powerful, finally raised to the level he felt he deserved. Edward, however, did not want this match. Giving his younger brother so much power and the opportunity to antagonise France and Brittany and possibly endanger English interests would be unwise. Edward expressly forbade it and, to rub salt into the wound, even offered Anthony Woodville as an alternative husband.[57] Clarence was infuriated.

Rumours of treason were in the air once more. In May, two men were hanged on the charge of attempting to provoke a rebellion. Not long after their execution, Clarence came to the King's Council and had the men's declaration of innocence read to the assembled lords, promptly leaving afterwards.[58] He continued to have rumours spread across the realm that one of the men – his servant, Thomas Burdett – was innocent.[59] This was a very dangerous game. In these accusations, he was suggesting that the justice system had failed, or even that they had purposefully condemned an innocent man.

Left with no other option, Edward was forced to have Clarence arrested. For months, Clarence languished in the Tower of London. In the Parliament of January and February 1478, he was put on trial. The list of charges shows how deep Clarence's hatred had grown. He had his men spread all sorts of terrible rumours across the country, each as ridiculous as the next. Not only had he said that the two executed men were innocent, but he had claimed that Edward was, in fact, a bastard. This would make him ineligible to be king, and thus the Crown should pass to Clarence. Both of these were shocking, treasonous accusations, and there were many more in the document.

There was one particularly curious accusation. It was said that Clarence had spread rumours across the country that 'the King oure Sovereigne Lord, wrought by Nigromancy, and used Craft to poison his Subjects, such as him pleased'.[60] This is certainly a most intriguing accusation. In reality, it would be impossible to ever properly accuse a reigning king of such nefarious deeds, and there is no suggestion that Clarence tried anything to make the accusations seem credible. No charges were drawn up, no images produced, no witnesses found. No other sources apart from the Parliament papers record this accusation. Rather than being a serious accusation of malevolent magic, as with the women in this book, it seems more to be slander said in anger and frustration, as one of many attempts to blacken Edward's name.

The outcome of Clarence's trial by king and Parliament was inevitable, and he was found guilty of treason. The sentence was death. Despite all that Clarence had done, Edward could not bring himself to sign the death warrant. Eventually Parliament had to ask the House of

Lords to carry out the sentence themselves. On 18 February, Clarence was executed; legend says he was drowned in a barrel of Malmsey wine.[61] His death contrasted greatly with the fact that a month earlier, 4-year-old Prince Richard was married with great pomp and ceremony to the 5-year-old Anne Mowbray. Many would have been well aware of the ironies of the grand celebrations in London while, a stone's throw away, the king's brother was languishing in the Tower accused of treason.

Edward was now only left with Gloucester as a brother. He did have an ever-growing family with Elizabeth, however. Over the next few years, Elizabeth had two more children: Catherine, born August 1479, and Bridget, born November 1480. At the time of Bridget's birth, Elizabeth was 43 years old and had thus followed her mother in fecundity and continuing to give birth at a late age. She had produced twelve children in total, rivalling her mother's fourteen, and all but two had so far survived. Little Prince George had died in early 1479, possibly of plague, aged 2. Elizabeth was also a grandmother, her eldest son, Thomas Grey, by now having three children of his own.

As 1483 arrived, the York royal family was in a strong state. King Edward IV was only 40 years old, and there were plenty of healthy children ready to make foreign marriage alliances. Long gone were the days of strife against the Lancastrians or traitorous brothers. The men around the king were powerful but loyal, with trusted family members such as Gloucester or Anthony providing constant support and advice.

Christmas 1482 had been spent at the palace of Eltham. It was said that more than 2,000 people had been fed daily, showing the extravagance and wealth of the court.[62] This had penetrated other aspects of the royal government, as Edward now had the best finances he had ever had throughout his reign. He wore rich clothes in the newest fashion, giving him a 'new and distinguished air to beholders, he being a person of most elegant appearance, and remarkable beyond all others for the attractions of his person'.[63] As was the theme throughout Elizabeth's life, however, disaster was just around the corner.

At the end of March, after Parliament was dissolved, Edward, 'neither worn out with old age nor yet seized with any known kind of malady', took to his bed.[64] After a short period of unknown illness, King Edward IV of England died on 9 April 1483.[65] He had ruled for twenty-two years. Elizabeth, who was with him at Westminster, must have been devastated. The couple had been married for almost twenty years, and Edward had died as deeply in love with Elizabeth as he had been during their secret marriage in the summer of 1464. All of the challenges that had been put in their path they had weathered together and come out all the stronger for it. It was Elizabeth who Edward trusted above all others.

While Elizabeth was deep in mourning, she now had to stay strong and set about confirming the rights of her son, now King Edward V, to the throne. The security of child kings was always shaky, but there had now been numerous precedents of a child becoming King of England without being challenged by other claimants. Richard II had become king at the age of 10 a century before, and Edward IV's predecessor, Henry VI, had ruled since he was 9 months old. In theory, Edward V should have no bars to succeeding his father.

It seems that upon Edward's deathbed, he may have made some changes to the will he had left before the French expedition in 1475, giving Gloucester the regency of his son.[66] This is possible, although no records survive beyond hearsay in chronicles, and the dying wishes of a king were not always honoured. Regardless, Elizabeth began to make preparations for the coronation of her son and she sent word to Anthony and her son, Richard Grey, asking them to escort the king to London, for he was still residing at Ludlow.

As Anthony and Richard were bringing Edward V to London, Gloucester was marching south. The two parties met at Stony Stratford in Buckinghamshire at the end of April. That night, Gloucester sat for dinner with Anthony and Richard, the atmosphere amicable. Then, either at that dinner or the following morning, Gloucester shockingly arrested the two men. He then presented himself to young Edward V, giving him all due honours, and told him that there were men around him who 'had conspired against both his own honour and his very existence'.[67] He then dismissed the king's servants and took control of his person. Nonetheless, he continued to bring Edward to London for his coronation, which had been scheduled for May.

After news reached London of Gloucester's actions, Elizabeth suspected that she could be in danger. His actions were not the actions of a caring uncle looking to protect the rights of his nephew, as had been the case with Humphrey and Bedford earlier that century. The arrest of two of her family members also was a big warning sign. Taking her youngest son, Prince Richard, and her daughters with her, Elizabeth once more fled to sanctuary at Westminster Abbey.[68] This was not what she had imagined for this year when she had been celebrating Christmas in high estate just a few months before.

Gloucester reached London with the king in early May and lodged him in the royal apartments of the Tower of London, the traditional place for the king to stay prior to his coronation. Ostensibly, preparations were continuing for Edward's coronation, but it kept being delayed by Gloucester. On 27 May, the King's Council agreed that Gloucester should be declared Protector of the Realm during Edward's minority.[69]

What followed across the next month was a mess of confusion and treachery. The order of events seems difficult to unpick, but the most likely is as follows. The coronation of Edward V was set for 24 June.[70] Gloucester argued that Prince Richard needed to be brought out of sanctuary to prepare for the coronation, for how could Edward be crowned with his family in sanctuary, making it seem as though there was something amiss in the kingdom?

Gloucester therefore persuaded the Archbishop of Canterbury to go and talk to Elizabeth and entreat them to come out of sanctuary. After much persuasion and promises of Prince Richard's safety, Elizabeth gave him into the custody of the archbishop. However, she could not be so convinced to leave or give over her daughters.[71] Richard was conveyed to the royal apartments of the Tower to be alongside his brother, and preparations seemingly continued.

Then, on 10 June 1483, Gloucester wrote a letter to the mayor and citizens of York with the greatest sense of urgency. He requested that they come to London in all due haste, with as much money as they could, in order to:

> Aid and assist us against the Queen, her blood adherents and affinity, which have intended, and daily do intend, to murder and utterly destroy us and our cousin the Duke of Buckingham, and the old royal blood of this realm, and as it is now openly known, by their subtle and damnable ways forecasted the same, and also the final destruction and disinherison of you and all other inheritors and men of honour.[72]

This was a startling turn of events. Gloucester was now accusing Elizabeth, her family and her allies of trying to murder a prince of England. With Gloucester now Protector, it was essentially treason to kill him. It was a scandalous claim. By saying 'forecasted the same', it seems that Gloucester was suggesting that the Woodvilles had used astrological charts to predict, or even try and influence, his death. Their 'damnable ways' makes it seem that this was by using sorcery, rather than with a more scientific version of astrology.

Elizabeth's flight to sanctuary now seemed like an exceedingly wise idea. She and several of her children were safe from these accusations for the time being. She had, however, given up her second son by Edward, the heir to the throne were something to happen to Edward V.

Three days later, on 13 June, Gloucester called a meeting of the council to discuss the king's coronation. Present was Lord Hastings, Edward IV's great, loyal friend, who had now seemingly taken the side of Gloucester. According to sixteenth-century chroniclers, no one at the council was at all aware of what was to happen next.[73] Gloucester suddenly made an announcement that people had been plotting against his life.

Shocked to hear this, the lords waited for Gloucester to reveal who had been so conspiring. Here, he claimed, 'yonder sorceress, my brother's wife, and others with her'. Many lords of the council were still on Elizabeth's side, even if they supported a protectorate under Gloucester, and so they could not believe this news. Gloucester continued. He said, 'That sorceress [Elizabeth] and that other witch of her counsel, Shore's wife, with their affinity, have by their sorcery and witchcraft wasted my body.' Upon making these claims, Richard rolled up his left sleeve to show a small, withered arm, 'as if it were ever otherwise'.

Upon seeing this so-called evidence of sorcery on his arm which had been that way since his birth, the council believed that this was just an argument between Gloucester and Elizabeth. For they all knew that Elizabeth 'was too wise to go about any such folly' and if she were to, least of all would she choose to ally with her husband's mistress, Jane Shore, 'whom of all women she most hated'. Now, however, Gloucester turned to Hastings and accused him of being a traitor who had also been working against him. Gloucester's guards suddenly appeared and arrested him and he was swiftly beheaded.

This was the story as recalled by Tudor chroniclers, acting on hindsight and Tudor propaganda against Gloucester. The story seems apocryphal, embellished with later information. The excavation of Gloucester's skeleton in 2012 confirmed that he did not have a withered arm. Moreover, more contemporary chroniclers do not record Gloucester accusing Elizabeth or Jane Shore at this meeting, simply his arrest of Hastings. Apart from Gloucester's letter to the city of York, there is no other evidence that he openly accused Elizabeth of acting against his life. However, the story cannot be entirely discounted. Gloucester had already acted against Elizabeth and her family, and he was later to act against Jane Shore. Some accusations may well have been flung regarding them at this meeting.

Numerous other supporters of the Woodvilles and Edward IV's regime were arrested across the next few days. Although plans were ostensibly still on for Edward V's coronation, this was far from the reality. On Sunday 22 June, a preacher took to the stage at St Paul's Cross in London. Here, he gave a sermon known as 'Bastard Slips Shall Never Take Deep Root', where it was declared that Edward and Elizabeth's marriage was invalid for Edward had been pre-contracted in marriage to another woman. He also repeated Clarence's claims of six years previously that Edward IV was illegitimate.[74] Both of these were supposedly cases for their children to be illegitimate, and therefore incapable of taking the Crown of England. Several days later, Gloucester was asked by the Commons to take the throne for himself. Needless to say, he accepted.

On 23 June 1483, Anthony Woodville drew up his will at Pontefract Castle.[75] He knew his time was coming to an end. Gloucester had sent orders for the execution of Anthony and his nephew, Richard Grey.[76] He had the two heirs to the throne in his possession, he had taken control of London, and he had captured or disposed of obstacles to his plans. The Crown was within his grasp. He was now free to get rid of two powerful men who could cause considerable problems if they lived. By 25 June, both men had been executed without proper trial. Elizabeth had now lost her brother and her second eldest son. How distraught she must have been in sanctuary when she learnt of the news, knowing that two of her sons were still in the hands of the man who had ordered the executions.

On 6 July, Gloucester and his wife, Anne Neville, processed from the Tower of London to Westminster Abbey.[77] Gloucester was now King Richard III of England, and Warwick the Kingmaker finally had a daughter as queen, although he had not lived to see it. The wealth and expense of the coronation was as much as any before it, giving it as much legitimacy as possible. Some people may well have been content to see Richard become king, for a strong adult male was a far more preferable ruler than a child. However, many people still believed that Edward V was his father's legitimate heir and were not happy to bear witness to Richard's sly actions.

Not long after his coronation, Richard took action against an unlikely person: his brother's mistress, Jane Shore. Since at least 21 June, she had been imprisoned in the Tower of London.[78] For her crimes of being an adulteress she was made to perform a penance through London not dissimilar to that which Eleanor Cobham made forty years previously. Carrying a taper in her hand, she walked to St Paul's Cathedral wearing just a slip.[79] Why Richard chose to persecute her for her adultery is unclear, considering the many more important members of the government who were likely to oppose his rise to the Crown.

Throughout the summer, King Edward V and his brother Richard, Duke of York, had been seen playing in the grounds of the Tower of London, but sightings of the boys decreased. After the end of the summer, they were never seen again. It is overwhelmingly believed that the two boys, aged 12 and 10, were murdered, almost certainly on Richard III's orders or at least with his assent. The truth will never be known, but the chances that both died of accidental causes are almost none. Elizabeth had now lost two more children. She must have cursed the day she agreed to the archbishop's promises.

In October, Richard III faced his first great uprising. Many were still loyal to the Woodvilles and the memory of King Edward IV, and did not want to see Richard on the throne. Rumours of the deaths of the princes also lost him much support. Richard's cousin, the Duke of Buckingham, was named as the main instigator of the rebellion, but in reality many members of Edward IV's government were involved. The rising spread across most of southern England.[80]

Buckingham was married to Elizabeth's sister, Catherine, and it was perhaps under her encouragement for the protection of the rights of her nephews that he joined the fight. Elizabeth's son, Thomas Grey, joined the rebellion, and rumours had circulated certainly by the Tudor period that Elizabeth had been orchestrating support for the rebellion from her place in sanctuary. How possible this would have been in reality is limited.

Another key player who joined the rebellion was Henry Tudor, nephew of Jasper Tudor who had supported Henry VI and Margaret of Anjou for so long. Henry himself now had an, albeit weak, claim to the throne, since through his mother he was descended from the illegitimate line of John of Gaunt.

The aim of the rebellion is unclear. Initially, the plan may have been to restore Edward V to the throne, but by October the two princes had not been seen for at least a month, and rumours were already circulating of their deaths. The plan may then have been to place Henry Tudor on the throne, or perhaps there was no clear aim other than to remove Richard III. The rebellion was ultimately unsuccessful, but it had an important outcome: many important sections of the nobility had resolved that they would not support Richard III in his reign. Many, including Thomas Grey, evaded capture by Richard, and fled to Brittany where Henry Tudor was residing.[81] Buckingham was not so lucky, and he was executed for his crimes.[82]

At the end of October, rewards were issued for the capture of the main instigators of the rebellion. Intriguingly, the arrest warrant for Thomas Grey mentions that he had 'without Shame Devoured, Defloured, and Defouled, holding the unshapfull and myschevous Woman called Shores Wife in Adultry'.[83] Thomas' rebellion against Richard was already call enough for his arrest, so the fact that this charge of adultery with Jane Shore was included is intriguing. Had Thomas really taken his stepfather's mistress as his own? Or was this another ploy by Richard to show the evil morals of the Woodville family? For Jane Shore to be mixed up with the problems in government perhaps lends some credence to the sixteenth-century chronicles which show Richard going after her. She may well have been acting as a go-between for the rebel faction.

Elizabeth and her daughters spent the rest of the year in sanctuary, while steadily those who had supported them were executed, imprisoned, fled abroad or to sanctuary, or defected to Richard's regime.

On 23 January 1484, the newly summoned Parliament issued *Titulus Regius*, which proclaimed Richard as king.[84] Official reasons needed to be given as to why Richard had taken the throne, and the resulting document is filled with flimsy reasons justifying his accession.

The *Titulus* stated that Edward IV only followed the counsel of people who were 'insolent, vicious and of inordinate avarice', which meant that the 'prosperity of this land daily decreased, so that felicity was turned into misery, and prosperity into adversity'. This was clearly a reference to the Woodvilles and their followers. The document then went on to list all of the reasons why Edward's heirs were debarred from taking the throne, meaning Richard was the true king.

The reasons went as follows: Edward had a 'pretensed Marriage' to Elizabeth, under which the order of rule and the laws, customs and liberties of the Church and the country were perverted, broken, subverted and held in contempt. Their marriage was not legitimate because the marriage was undertaken without the assent of the lords of the land. More than that, it was caused 'by Sorcerie and Wichecrafte, committed by the said Elizabeth, and her Moder Jaquett Duchess of Bedford, as the common opinion of the people'. The marriage was further invalidated because the marriage had taken place in secret, and because at the time of the marriage Edward was already pre-contracted to a woman named Eleanor Butler. For these reasons, Edward and Elizabeth had been living together 'sinfully and damnably in adultery' and as such 'all th'Issue and Children of the seid King Edward, been Bastards, and unable to inherite' the throne.

These were astonishing accusations. In reality, almost none of these reasons were real claims for the marriage being invalid. While the Church in this period obviously preferred marriage to take place in public, in a church with many witnesses, time and again it had been shown to enforce marriages taken even as a promise between two people. Thus, many men who had seduced a woman with promises to marry her afterwards found themselves bound in marriage, despite no priest being present. That Elizabeth and Edward married in secret was no reason for the marriage to be invalid, particularly when there was a priest and witnesses present. For the same reasons, that it was undertaken without the assent of the lords of the land was not a reason for the marriage to be dissolved. While the king was expected to consult his lords on his choice of partner, there was no precedent that this was a requirement.

The issue of Edward's alleged pre-contract with another woman was a little more plausible. While no concrete evidence has been produced that Edward really had agreed to marry Eleanor Butler, if this were the case then the proceedings were unclear. Many medieval marriages were indeed declared invalid because one of the parties had already agreed to marry someone else. However, in terms of the nobility and royalty, marriages were often proposed that never came to fruition and a marriage as long as Edward and Elizabeth's, with so many children, would never in reality be annulled by the Church for this reason.

The last reason, therefore, was the alleged witchcraft of Elizabeth and Jacquetta. The case of Eleanor and Humphrey earlier this century had shown that it was possible for a marriage to be annulled when it had been procured by love magic. However, Richard provided no evidence for his claims, merely citing that it was the 'common opinion' of the land that this was the case and the accusations, 'if and as the case shall require, shall be proved sufficiently in time and place convenient'. Hardly convincing proof.

In reality, though, none of this mattered. Richard III had been king for six months, the direct male heirs to the throne were widely agreed to be dead, and he held great power, wealth and soldiers. Elizabeth was merely a 46-year-old woman hiding in sanctuary without a penny to her name, and with no one to fight for her. Richard did not need the reasons to be convincing because he had already won the battle. All he needed was to throw some accusations in the hope that one of them stuck.

That Jacquetta was brought in to the claims demonstrates the power that these accusations could have at this time. The first instance of Jacquetta's alleged witchcraft had occurred nearly fourteen years previously, and had been proven as entirely fabricated in the highest institution in the land – Parliament – and yet still rumours persisted. Still, it was enough now that it could be used to demonstrate the sorcery and guilt of her daughter. The label of witch would never truly go away.

Richard had all that he needed, and there was no need to formally charge and try Elizabeth. She was of no threat to him; in fact, she and her daughters could be an asset. He knew that he was still not completely secure on his throne, and there was now a plethora of exiled lords working with Henry Tudor to try and fight him. If he could bring the old Yorkist queen and her family to his side, it would give his reputation a great boost. As such, he began to find ways to persuade Elizabeth to leave her place of refuge.

After many months of persuasion (and possibly threats), Elizabeth Woodville and her daughters finally came out of sanctuary. This they only agreed to do after Richard had placed his hands on the relics of the Holy Evangelists and took a solemn oath in front of the Lords of England, the highest members of the Church, and the mayor and aldermen of London that he would fully protect Elizabeth and her daughters, he would not harm any of them or incarcerate them in any form of prison, and he would make provisions for suitable marriages for the girls.[85]

Elizabeth's movements after this point are unclear. She may have joined the residence of her sister, Catherine, who was being closely supervised in the London area after her husband's rebellion. It seems her daughters joined the court and may well have entered the household of Queen Anne. There were other plans afoot for Elizabeth's eldest daughter, however. In March, the exiled Henry Tudor was making solid designs on the English throne and Princess Elizabeth was key to this. After petitioning the pope, at the end of the month he received a papal dispensation authorising him to marry Princess Elizabeth. Now all he needed was a force.

Richard's victory at getting the Woodville women to come out of sanctuary was short-lived. In early April, Richard's only legitimate child, his 10-year-old son Edward, died after a short illness. Richard and Anne were grief-stricken at his death, 'his father and mother in a state almost bordering on madness, by reason of their sudden grief'.[86] Edward's death also put Richard in a difficult position, as he was now without heirs – not a situation any king wanted to find himself in. His wife was only 27 years old, so there was the chance for more children, but the couple had only had one child in twelve years of marriage, which made this reasonably unlikely.

The rest of the year passed without much incident. Christmas was spent at Westminster with great extravagance, to the chastisement of chroniclers, for 'far too much attention was given to dancing and gaiety'. Interestingly, it is also mentioned that there were 'vain changes of apparel presented to queen Anne and the lady Elizabeth, the eldest daughter of the late king, being of similar colour and shape'. This shows that Princess Elizabeth was indeed present at court and that she was being treated well. Anne may well have treated her fondly, for all she had been through, particularly after the loss of her own child. However, that Anne and Elizabeth received similar clothes 'caused the people to murmur and the nobles and prelates greatly to wonder thereat'.[87]

The reason for this murmur became clear a few months later. On 16 March 1485, Queen Anne died. Rumours began to circulate that Richard had had his wife poisoned. This was because it was believed he wanted to marry his niece, Princess Elizabeth. There were many reasons for this; it would prevent Henry Tudor trying to seize her for himself, and it would give Richard a more secure claim to the throne as she was now his brother's heir. Elizabeth was now 19 years old, and if the fertility of her mother and grandmother were anything to go by, she was a good option to give Richard another heir. These rumours were serious enough that Richard had to publicly refute that he had poisoned his wife and was considering marrying Elizabeth.[88]

Richard's regime was losing popularity, and Henry's ever-growing pool of Edward IV's old supporters was giving him greater strength. Now Henry gained the crucial support of the French.[89] Rumours of Richard's plans to marry Elizabeth not only upset the nobles in England, but it worried Henry. If the marriage happened, Henry's own designs on the throne would be threatened. Although he never openly admitted it, he needed Elizabeth's legitimacy as heir to secure his own place on the throne through a much weaker claim.

On 23 June, aware that invasion was imminent, Richard issued a proclamation against Henry Tudor, his uncle Jasper, Elizabeth's brother Edward Woodville, and others.[90] He called them traitors, known for open murders, adultery and extortion. In the proclamation, he reminded the country that Henry could not take the throne as he was descended from John of Gaunt's 'bastard' line with Katherine Swynford, which had been debarred from the line of succession 100 years ago. At the start of August, Henry Tudor and his army landed near Pembroke. War was coming once more.

Henry's army was not as substantial as the forces Richard had gathered, but he still had significant noblemen behind him. Throughout his journey through Wales and the English border he began to gather more troops. On 22 August 1485, King Richard III and Henry Tudor met at battle at Bosworth Field in Leicestershire. Bosworth was a 'battle of the greatest severity' and several contingents of noblemen who were present did not initially take part in the fighting, waiting to see which way the battle was going to go before they pledged their allegiance.[91] At one point, Richard and his vanguard charged at Henry, coming close to killing him. However, the soldiers under the command of the Stanleys, who had been observing up to now, now decided to come to Henry's aid. This finally pushed the battle in Henry's favour.

'While fighting, and not in the act of flight, the said king Richard was pierced with numerous deadly wounds, and fell in the field like a brave and most valiant prince.'[92] This is how Richard's death was described by the Croyland chronicler. Examinations of Richard's body in recent years showed that he suffered nine wounds to the head, with part of the rear of his skull having been sliced off.[93] It certainly was a brutal end for the man who had been king for scarcely two years. The male York bloodline had been all but extinguished.

However, Richard's body was not allowed to rest just yet. 'Not exactly in accordance with the laws of humanity', Richard's naked body was carried upon a horse to the nearby city of Leicester to prove to all that he had died. He was then quietly buried.[94]

Henry became King Henry VII of England on 30 October 1485 at his coronation in Westminster Abbey. He then set about summoning a Parliament to confirm many of the rights that people had held under Edward IV, undoing much that Richard III had done. Thomas Grey was recognised for the 'true service' he had given Henry. Richard III's attainder of high treason against him was reversed and his lands restored.[95] Business then turned to the two Elizabeths.

On 12 November, a petition was read from Queen Elizabeth Woodville requesting that she was given back all of her castles and other landed possessions that she had held under Edward IV.[96] This was not granted to her – Henry may have been wary of granting Elizabeth so much land when he might need some to grant to supporters. However, Elizabeth was given the right to 'enjoye from henceforth, all such Estate, Dignitee, Preemenence and Name' as if Richard III had never made an Act of Parliament against her. She was also given back the right to all of her goods and chattels that had been confiscated after Edward's death.[97] She may not have received any of her dower lands back yet, but she had been fully restored to her position of Queen Dowager without any impediments to what that entitled her to.

Matters now turned to her eldest daughter, the nearly 20-year-old Princess Elizabeth. The Speaker of the Commons reminded Henry VII of his promise to marry the princess. Many in the realm hoped 'to see the propagation of offspring from the stock of kings, to comfort the whole realm' and Henry agreed to this request.[98] Henry had repealed *Titulus Regius* and Elizabeth was now officially legitimate again. On 18 January 1486, the couple were married in Westminster Abbey. Elizabeth Woodville had survived to see her daughter rise to be Queen of England. It must have been bittersweet to see her daughter elevated to such a position, knowing that it only happened through the murder of her sons.

The marriage created an equal measure of problems and benefits to Henry. By marrying the Yorkist heir, he was preventing any other future claimants to the throne if she had married someone else and had children. It also confirmed the loyalty of those who had been part of Edward IV's government. However, it created problems and questions regarding his own legitimacy. His claim to the throne was weak because he was descended from a line that had been barred the throne.

Although England had not yet had a queen regnant, many indications show that by this point the country might not have been completely averse to the idea. It would be less than seventy years until the first queen regnant, Princess Elizabeth's granddaughter, Mary I, took to the throne. Moreover, with so much strife over the past few decades, and the fact that over the two years from 1483 to 1485 England had been ruled by four different kings, the idea of a woman ruling may no longer have seemed such a threat to stability. There is evidence that many people actually viewed Princess Elizabeth as Edward IV's true successor. Marrying her, therefore, secured Henry's position as king while simultaneously undermining it. Many would have seen him as a false king ruling through the right of his wife.

It was certainly for these reasons that Elizabeth's coronation did not occur shortly after their marriage as her mother's had. Elizabeth was quick to follow in her mother and grandmother's footsteps, however, for on 20 September that year she gave birth to a son, Arthur. Henry VII immediately had a male heir to succeed him, making his reign more secure. The birth of Arthur was received with joy by all and would clearly have been seen as a sign of divine blessing on the couple and the new regime. The baby seems to have been born about a month prematurely, assuming the royal couple had not had sex prior to their marriage. If this were a cause for concern, their fears were allayed, for both baby and mother were healthy.

The birth of Arthur allowed Henry to run with some myth-making for personal propaganda. The boy was named Arthur because Henry had got royal genealogists to trace his lineage back to the legendary king to add legitimacy to his own claim. Elizabeth had been sent to Winchester to give birth, because at this time Winchester was believed to have been the location of Camelot.[99] Henry was making a clear statement with the birth of this child.

The baby was baptised four days later at Winchester Cathedral, his grandmother Elizabeth Woodville serving as his godmother.[100] Elizabeth Woodville had witnessed much death. By the time of the birth of Arthur she had lost both her parents, four adult siblings, two husbands and six children. However, now she had four grandchildren, and she must have been cheered at his arrival, particularly as it now secured the position of her daughter on the throne.

At the start of March, Elizabeth Woodville had finally been compensated in part for the loss of her dower lands. Henry granted her six manors in Essex from the Duchy of Lancaster.[101] She had seemingly returned once more to Westminster Abbey – in a more comfortable capacity, this time. In early July, Elizabeth had made an agreement with the Abbot of Westminster to rent a mansion within the abbey called Cheyne Gate for forty years.[102] Elizabeth held no personal ties to the manors she had been granted and they were certainly not the royal palaces she had loved and called home with her husband. She had nowhere to truly call home. It is perhaps, then, understandable that she would want to make a home in the precinct of the place that had protected her during turmoil.

For some reason, however, Elizabeth was not to live at Cheyne Gate for long. In February 1487, she moved instead to Bermondsey Abbey, which stood on the banks of the Thames, just south-east of the Tower of London. The abbey had been on the site in its present form since the eleventh century and it was quite wealthy. Earlier that century, Queen Catherine of Valois, mother to Henry VI, had spent the last few months of her life at Bermondsey.[103]

Around this time, there was a rebellion surrounding a pretender to the throne named Lambert Simnel. Thomas Grey apparently had some involvement in the rebellion, spending some time in the Tower of London. It has been suggested that Elizabeth was involved in the rebellion and, as punishment, Henry sent her to Bermondsey. A few months afterwards, on 1 May, Henry also confiscated Elizabeth's properties, seemingly confirming this theory.[104]

In reality, this seems unlikely. Elizabeth would have had no motivation to join a rebellion against her son-in-law, especially when it would depose her daughter and disinherit her grandson. Elizabeth was shown to be fiercely loyal to her family throughout her life and had always done her best for her children. She had made a dangerous deal with Hastings back in 1464 to protect the inheritance of her Grey sons, and she had fled to sanctuary numerous times to save the lives of her children. Why, then, would she be involved in a conspiracy that would endanger her eldest daughter?

Elizabeth's move to Bermondsey may have been linked to the uprising, but perhaps for different reasons. Throughout her time as queen, Elizabeth had shown that when the realm was in turmoil she fled to the Church. A new rebellion, which potentially involved one of her sons, could well place doubt on her loyalty. There was no need to take the extreme of going to sanctuary, particularly when this would place suspicion on her, but if she wanted extra security then retiring to a quiet monastery which had a tradition of hosting women of the upper nobility would certainly dampen any questions of her loyalty.

Moreover, Elizabeth's lease of Cheyne Gate cannot be seen as confirmation that it was her long-term plan to live there. It was common to give long leases on properties of this level, so an agreement for forty years does not have to indicate Elizabeth was planning on never moving. Moreover, Elizabeth would hardly be the first person in history to have taken a lease on a property and decided a few months later it wasn't quite the place they wanted to live. Bermondsey may have simply been a more appealing place to be.

It was common in medieval England for high-status, wealthy, widowed older women to retire to monasteries or nunneries. The reasons for this were numerous: it meant they would not be forced to enter another marriage that they did not want; they would not be targeted for attack under suspicion of involvement in plots or by heirs who wanted to seize their property; it was a peaceful community to retire to; and very often the institutions they chose were very wealthy, meaning they could live out the last of their days in comfort. These religious institutions often had their own hospital on site, another benefit for an ageing woman.

For all these reasons, Bermondsey would certainly be appealing. It was close to the Tower of London if Elizabeth ever needed protection, and still near to the court for access to her daughter and other children. Elizabeth was turning 50 in this year, and she had lived quite the tumultuous life. She had witnessed great death, a long civil war, the reigns of numerous kings, and for much of it she had been deep in the fray, often fearing for her own life. Far from Henry exiling her from court, it is most likely that Elizabeth wanted to finally have some peace and simplicity in her life.

The confiscation of Elizabeth's properties in May is not as ominous as it first appears. When looking at the document, it is actually a transfer, giving her daughter Queen Elizabeth the properties instead. After the strife of the past decade, the royal purse was once more empty and Henry was almost certainly struggling to provide a dower for his wife as well as paying for the household of his new son. Not since Joan of Navarre and Catherine of Valois at the beginning of the century had the Crown had to finance a Queen Dowager and queen consort simultaneously. It has already been seen how Henry V dealt with this financial difficulty by having Joan sent away for alleged witchcraft; under this lens, Henry giving a mother's property to her daughter and recompensing the mother with an (albeit much reduced) annual salary hardly seems quite so malicious.

There may have been further reason behind it. On 28 November this year, an agreement was made between Henry and the King of

Scots, James III. They were organising a huge peace treaty between the two crowns. Several important marriages were agreed: Elizabeth and Edward's daughter, Catherine, was to marry the James III's second son, James Stewart; another unspecified daughter of Elizabeth and Edward was to marry his first son and heir, another James; and, perhaps most importantly, Queen Dowager Elizabeth Woodville was to marry the Scottish King James III himself.[105]

This would change Elizabeth's life; she would now have been both Queen of England and Queen of Scotland. What Elizabeth made of the match would be interesting to know. The Scottish king was only around 35 years old, making her fifteen years his senior. It would have returned her to the centre of courtly life, bringing her wealth and dignity which had been lost under the struggling English Crown. If, as suspected, Elizabeth was tired of this life and wanted a quiet retirement in a religious cloister, then the prospect of moving to a different country where she might not see any of her remaining children again and would have to be once more involved in official duties and court intrigue may have been quite unappealing. In the event, the marriage never came to fruition, for James III died in battle in June the following year.

At the end of 1487, Queen Elizabeth of York finally had her coronation. Intriguingly, Elizabeth Woodville is not recorded as having attended.[106] As it was traditional for the king not to attend, so too might it have been problematic to have a crowned queen attending the coronation of the next one. However, there surely would have been the possibility for Elizabeth to attend the following feast and celebrations, but she is conspicuously missing. This is certainly surprising, for one would expect that Elizabeth would have wanted to bear witness to her daughter's official coronation.

Across the next year, Elizabeth disappears from the record. At the end of October 1489, however, Queen Elizabeth entered confinement awaiting the birth of her second child. Eyewitnesses recount how, during her confinement, Elizabeth was attended by both her mother-in-law, Margaret Beaufort, and her own mother, Elizabeth Woodville.[107] Elizabeth was still involved in the activity of the court to some extent, then, even if it was just supporting her daughter in a personal aspect. During this confinement, she saw the birth of her granddaughter, Margaret, born at the end of November.

Once more, Elizabeth all but vanishes from the records. Across the last few years of her life she continued to have death follow her. In July 1488, her youngest brother, Edward Woodville, died in battle, aged 30, fighting for the Duke of Brittany. A year later almost to the day, her sister Anne Woodville died, aged 51. Finally, in March 1491, her brother Richard Woodville died. The title of Earl Rivers died with him, the earldom becoming extinct. The original Richard Woodville, Earl Rivers – Elizabeth's father – had risen to great heights, and despite his plethora of children, the memory of his title was now lost to history.

As 1492 started, Elizabeth Woodville was presumably happily settled at Bermondsey Abbey, her home for the past five years. However, it seems the former queen's health was beginning to fail. On 10 April, she drew up her will.[108] The will is a sorry affair, for she had no lands, wealth or possessions to give away. A far cry from the height of her power. The will begins, 'I Elsabeth by the grace of god Quene of Englond late wif to the most victoriouse prince of blessed memorie Edward the fourth'. Although this is a stylistic start to the will, it shows that Elizabeth still very much considered herself a queen. The blessed memory of her beloved husband must also surely betray that she still held deep love for the man she had lost nine years previously.

Elizabeth requested that she was to be buried alongside her husband at the chapel in Windsor Castle. She specified that she did not want the funeral performed with any pomp or under any great expense. As she had no worldly goods to bequeath to any of her remaining children, she asked God to bless them, and with 'as good hart and mynde as is to me posible', she gave her children her own blessing. She then asked that 'such smale stufe and goodes that I have' be given away as seen fit, giving preference to any of her blood who wished to have them. Thus, the will ends. Considering the pages upon pages of the 1475 will of her husband, even allowing for his greater responsibility, these small few sentences certainly show how simple a life Elizabeth lived in her last few years.

Queen Elizabeth Woodville, daughter of Jacquetta of Luxembourg, mother of Queen Elizabeth of York, died at Bermondsey Abbey on 8 June 1492. Her will was executed exactly as asked – to the dismay of one contemporary writer. They recorded the interment of Elizabeth and, although it had been her desire to be buried simply, considered that a once-noble queen should have been honoured more than the poor ceremony that occurred.[109]

A few days after her death, she was taken to Windsor by boat up the River Thames. Very few attended. Her eldest daughter, Elizabeth, was eight months pregnant with her fourth child, having given birth to a boy, the future Henry VIII, the previous summer. Queens tended to take to confinement a month prior to the birth and, as this fourth child was born on 2 July, it is almost certain that her absence from her mother's funeral is because she was already secluded away. The baby girl was, however, named Elizabeth in her honour.

Other attendees included an unnamed gentlewoman, Elizabeth's paternal cousin Edward Haute, and Grace, described as Edward IV's illegitimate daughter. No other mention is known of Grace, other than this entry, so no details about her age or life can be further inferred. Her presence does suggest at least a cordial, if not warm, relationship with her father's wife. Perhaps Grace had been living in Bermondsey with Elizabeth. It was not unusual for illegitimate daughters to take the cloth.

Elizabeth's hearse was 'such as they use for the common people', with a cloth of black and a cloth of gold over it.[110] On 12 June, closer family members arrived to honour Elizabeth. Her three unmarried daughters, Anne, Catherine and Bridget, attended, as well as other female members of her extended family. Elizabeth's son Thomas Grey also joined, alongside her nephew, Henry Bourchier. The funeral was performed with a requiem mass and a dirge sung during the night. In the morning, the Mass of Our Lady was sung, after which Elizabeth's family members made offerings of gold pieces. Her body was at last laid to rest next to her ever-loved husband, who was now reunited with his 'moost entierly beloved wiff'.

The two Woodville matriarchs had both experienced the great rises and deep lows of the wheel of fortune. Jacquetta had been born of noble family, with royal blood from numerous monarchies running through her veins. She had married the heir of England, a grand prince who tempered his skill in warfare with a love of books and culture. She then married a second time for love and had one of the most successful marriages one could hope for. She was blessed with many children, who she did her best to protect, but she could not stop the ravages of civil war and jealous courtiers from destroying many of them. She twice suffered the indignity of being accused of using witchcraft to further the grasp of her family, but she managed to survive with her life and her freedom. She died seeing her daughter at the heights of all power, ruling as Queen of England.

Elizabeth, meanwhile, had been born from humble beginnings. Although she had increased status due to the lineage of her mother, her father had come from a humble, knightly family and they had little wealth, living in their quiet manor house. Starting on one side of the civil war, chance saw her married to the leader of the opposite faction and vaulted to the most important woman in the country. Her life was marred with tragedy, with brothers, sons and a father murdered by political opponents. She may have been Queen of England, but she spent two long bouts in sanctuary fearing for her life. She lived long enough to see her daughter follow her as queen, but she ended her life in quiet obscurity, dying with hardly an object to her name. She, too, suffered from the witchcraft accusations that had chased her mother, but due to the virtue of her position and her usefulness as a political pawn, she was spared any trial, punishment or further harm from them. The blood of both of these royal witches has flowed in every subsequent English and British monarch since, including the current monarch, Queen Elizabeth II.

13

A ROYAL COVEN
OF WITCHES

'NOW VPPE NOWE downe as Fortune turnethe her whele'.[1] So writes the author of one poem in the 1460s. In the poem, the writer recounts the woes of the witch Eleanor Cobham, but this term fits neatly for all of the women in this book.

Eleanor Cobham truly experienced the greatest rise and fall of any of them. Born into the gentry to a respectable family, she fell in love with a prince of England and he loved her back. They lived a perfect life together until her fall from grace, which saw them never meet again.

Elizabeth Woodville had a very similar origin story, but her rise to queen still could not make her secure, and the ravages of the Wars of the Roses took almost all that she had. She too ended her life in relative obscurity.

Jacquetta of Luxembourg started high up the wheel, having what many contemporaries viewed as a fall when she fell in love with a humble knight. Through loyalty and hard work, the couple rose up once more to see a daughter placed on the throne, although it ultimately led to the murder of one of them and accusations of sorcery against the other.

Only Joan of Navarre came close to riding the wheel successfully, although the indignity, hurt and insult of being detained for years under suspicion of witchcraft must have been a great source of ire.

The court of England in the fifteenth century was not a welcoming place for many. The glories of the early wars of the noble Henry V soon fell apart under the extended infancy of his son. This was followed by his later lack of capability to rule, through both personality and mental health problems. This caused partisanship to grow at court, with the rise of powerful, warring factions and a battle to control the ear of the king. Casualties would always come as a result, and women at court were often vulnerable to the games played among men. As the country descended into civil war, the monarchy could not sustain itself and even at times of peace, intrigue, rebellion and plots abounded. Every man (and many women) tried to grab what power they could, and placed people of their own interest on the throne. No one was truly safe, not even the king himself.

In the battles at court, it was inevitable that some women would become targets. While men could raise armies to protect themselves, women's positions and their lack of formal role in government meant they were inherently weak. If a man was too well protected to bring down, then a woman close to him was a far easier target.

Across the course of the century, with each successful case the accusation of witchcraft became an invaluable weapon. While proof of treachery was more difficult to find, witchcraft, by its nature, was secretive. All one needed was to provide some witnesses and a few objects and the burden was placed on the victim to try to prove their innocence. When the accusation was often love magic, the women in this book discovered that proving their innocence was almost impossible. Eleanor and Elizabeth, daughters of knights, had married a prince and a king who had nothing to gain from the marriage – no wealthy dowry, no lands, estates or titles. Why would a man in his right mind marry such a woman? For them, the proof of the success of their witchcraft was that they had indeed married their targets.

These assumptions, of course, played into contemporary sexism and hatred of social upstarts. Both of these women were clearly intelligent, beautiful and charming, and were a perfect fit for their valorous, fun-loving husbands. The reasons for the marriages are obvious. However, women at court were always viewed with suspicion for the ways in which they could pull strings behind the scenes. In times of peace, this was seen as a positive; queens and royal women were a way for people across the kingdom to access the patronage and favour of the court. At times of war and conflict, such as during this century, however, their influence was viewed with more hatred and jealousy. Men such as Warwick, who found their influence waning, could quickly make these women their targets.

Despite the scandal of their lives, many of the women have spent time in obscurity. It is only in very recent years, with the interest in women's history on the rise, that their stories have begun to come to light. The medieval period was a man's world, but that does not mean that women did not continue to be of central importance and could not influence the course of history.

Joan of Navarre's huge dower from Henry IV put the queen in a greater place of honour and prominence, meaning that subsequent kings would have to match the expense lest their wives be viewed as less important. Eleanor Cobham's trial showed the failing in the justice system to not have a proper way to try women of such a significant rank, and it led to the creation of a new law to combat this.

Margaret of Anjou took the reins of government when her husband was no longer capable, and her refusal to give up the rights of her husband and son led to an extended civil war. Jacquetta of Luxembourg became the source of a new dynasty after falling in love and having children, for one of whom she secured the King of England through secret meetings.

Elizabeth Woodville, too, had great importance through her role as a mother, but her shrewd assessments of the turning tides of battle ultimately saved the lives of herself and her daughters, even if she could not save her sons. This preserved the York line so that it could eventually join to become the Tudor line.

All of these women shaped the world around them and changed the course of history. Yet, despite their huge achievements, all have been maligned by history. The Woodville women became grasping social climbers who destroyed any opponents, while Eleanor was a mistress who got so caught up in her own haughtiness and self-adoration that she grasped for the Crown but failed spectacularly. Joan of Navarre was the callous woman who abandoned her Breton children so that she could become queen, then became absorbed with wealth, clothes and jewels. However, in some ways, modern historians have occasionally gone too far in the other direction, making the women appear as saints in their attempts to save them from their evil legacy.

The reality is that these women were real, living, breathing human beings whose lives some 600 years ago we can touch through surviving documents. It is overwhelmingly certain that these women were not the wicked schemers they have been portrayed as across the centuries, and almost certainly they were all overwhelmingly good people. But they were human, and not caricatures, and each of them no doubt made mistakes, acted viciously at times and looked out for their own interests and those of their families. If they had high aspirations and wanted more power or wealth, then that merely makes them no differ- ent to any of the men alongside them at court. The fifteenth century saw four out of seven kings take the throne from another through vio- lence. Any judgements on these women for their desire for power must then be seen in the context of the time and not through modern eyes.

It is also important to remember that the women knew each other and lived among each other. Joan lived long enough to see both Eleanor and Jacquetta marry her stepsons. Eleanor and Jacquetta were part of the court for eight years together, were sisters-in-law through marriage and would have socialised often. Jacquetta was Elizabeth's mother and, if Elizabeth was indeed born in 1437, Eleanor may well have met the young girl numerous times before her exile. The women were all related to each other, even if just through marriage, and they lived together, shared presents with each other and passed in and out of each other's lives. More than that, each accusation against one woman informed the accusations against the next, as opponents learnt what made a successful allegation. In the same way, however, Jacquetta and Elizabeth learnt from the attacks on their predecessors and found ways to try and protect and restore themselves.

The truth of the use of witchcraft by Joan, Eleanor, Jacquetta and Elizabeth will never truly be known. It can be said with complete certainty that the religious Joan, who had nothing to gain through sorcery, did not act against Henry V, particularly when one of his dying acts all but admitted that he had fabricated the accusations.

Of all the women, Eleanor's guilt is most tangible. She does seem to have been involved in some level of astrological prediction, but when it is remembered that this was no unusual activity, even among royalty, and was often viewed with a scientific mind, whether fault lay with her for this is not so clear.

Eleanor may well have solicited the help of Margery Jourdemaine to conceive, or it may have been a lie intended to save her life. If she did try love potions to produce a child, she can hardly have been too different from many other women in her predicament at the time. Jacquetta and Elizabeth's sorcery is far less likely, but when it is so difficult to learn about royal women in a public sphere due to lack of records, it is even more impossible to know of their private lives. Maybe they did use traditional herbs and charms at their manor in Grafton Regis, following in a long-standing folk tradition. Even devout Christians, from peasants to kings, would use what we may consider superstitious means to protect themselves from poison or childbirth, to protect their crops from dying, to bring good fortune to their family and to cure ailments. The Woodville women may have followed in this tradition, and perhaps when Elizabeth gained the attention of the king, some spells were even used to try and secure his love. History will never know. Their stories, however, have now been rescued.

GENEALOGICAL TABLES

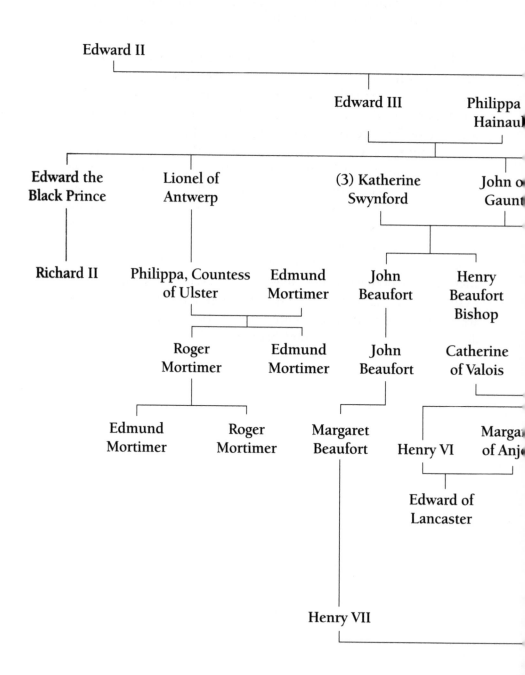

Edward II

Edward III — Philippa Hainau[l]

Edward the Black Prince   Lionel of Antwerp   (3) Katherine Swynford   John o[f] Gaunt

Richard II   Philippa, Countess of Ulster   Edmund Mortimer   John Beaufort   Henry Beaufort Bishop

Roger Mortimer   Edmund Mortimer   John Beaufort   Catherine of Valois

Edmund Mortimer   Roger Mortimer   Margaret Beaufort   Henry VI   Marga[ret] of Anj[ou]

Edward of Lancaster

Henry VII

A CONDENSED ENGLISH ROYAL FAMILY TREE

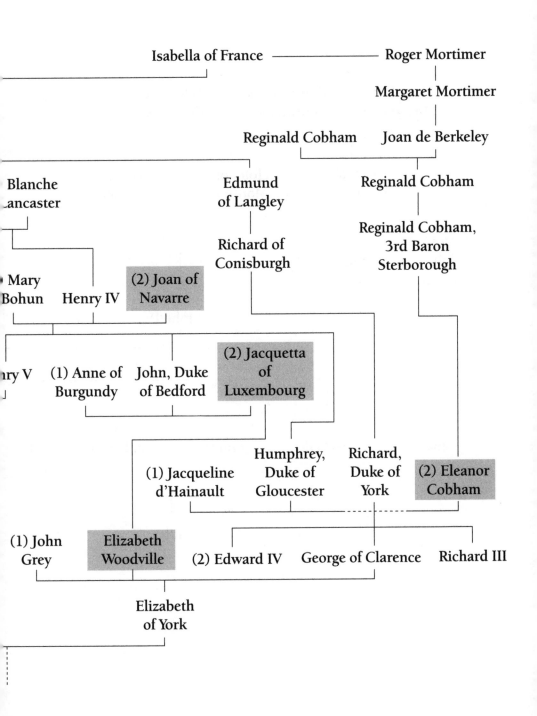

JOAN OF NAVARRE AND JOHN IV OF BRITTANY

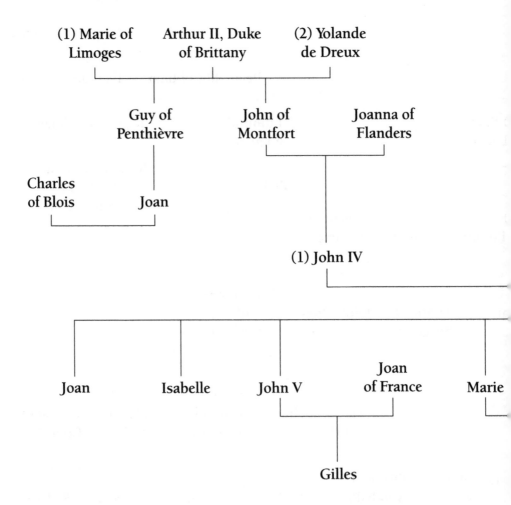

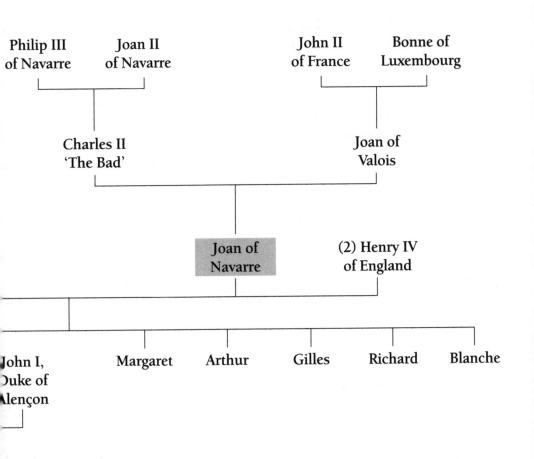

THE WOODVILLE FAMILY TREE

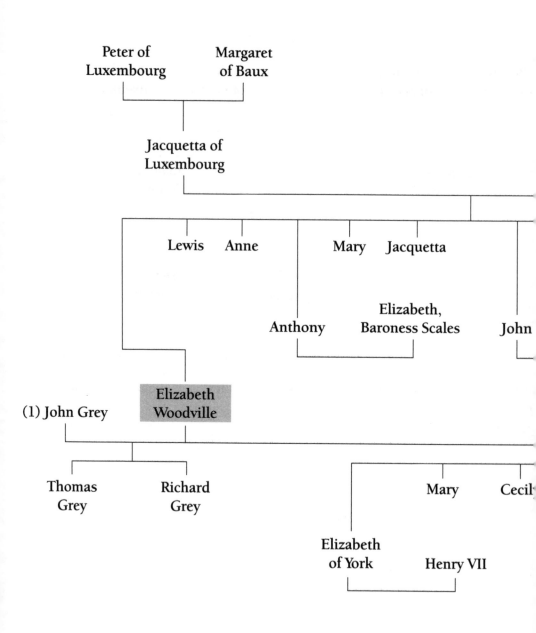

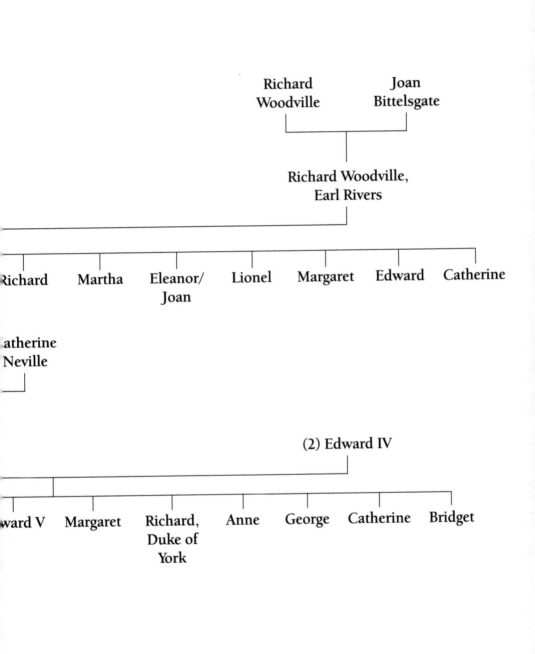

Richard
Woodville

Joan
Bittelsgate

Richard Woodville,
Earl Rivers

Richard   Martha   Eleanor/   Lionel   Margaret   Edward   Catherine
                      Joan

atherine
Neville

(2) Edward IV

ward V   Margaret   Richard,   Anne   George   Catherine   Bridget
                      Duke of
                      York

NOTES

Abbreviations

CCR	Calendar of the Close Rolls
CPR	Calendar of the Patent Rolls
Foedera	Rymer's *Foedera*
Oxford DNB	Oxford Dictionary of National Biography
PL	The Paston Letters
Privy Council	Proceedings and Ordinances of the Privy Council of England
RP	*Rotuli Parliamentorum*

Chapter 1

1   Michael Bailey, *Fearful Spirits, Reasoned Follies: The Boundaries of Superstition in Late Medieval Europe* (Ithaca: Cornell University Press, 2013), 75.
2   Bailey, *Fearful Spirits*, 115–16.
3   Richard Kieckhefer, *Magic in the Middle Ages* (Cambridge: Cambridge University Press, 2000), 127.
4   Charles Burnett, *Magic and Divination in the Middle Ages: Texts and Techniques in the Islamic and Christian Worlds* (Hampshire: Ashgate Publishing Limited, 1996), 133–5.
5   Philippa Gregory, David Baldwin & Michael Jones, *The Women of the Cousins' War: The Real White Queen and her Rivals* (London: Simon & Schuster, 2013), 57–8.
6   Burnett, *Magic and Divination*, 10.

7   Bailey, *Fearful Spirits*, 11; Burnett, *Magic and Divination*, 2–3; Karen Jolly, Catharina Raudvere and Edward Peters, *Witchcraft and Magic in Europe: The Middle Ages* (London: The Athlone Press, 2002), 59.

8   Kieckhefer, *Magic*, 6.

9   Hans Peter Broedel, *The* Malleus Maleficarum *and the Construction of Witchcraft: Theology and Popular Belief* (Manchester: Manchester University Press, 2003), 26.

10   Kieckhefer, *Magic*, 6, 108.

11   Broedel, *The* Malleus Maleficarum, 10, 26.

Chapter 2

1   R. Delachenal, *Deux prétendues lettres du régent fils aîné de Jean II au comte de Savoie Amédée VI* (Bibliothèque de l'École des chartes, 1911) Tome 72, 272; Lynn Thorndike, *A History of Magic and Experimental Science*, Vol. III (New York: Columbia University Press, 1934), 588.

2   Jonathan Sumption, *Divided Houses: The Hundred Years War III* (London: Faber and Faber, 2011), 338–9.

3   Geoffroy de la Tour-Landry, *The Book of the Knight of La Tour-Landry*, ed. Thomas Wright (London: Kegan Paul, Trench, Trubner & Co. Ltd, 1906), 18.

4   Christine de Pisan, *The Treasure of the City of Ladies*, trans. Sarah Lawson (London: Penguin Books, 1985), 76.

5   Michael Jones, *Ducal Brittany, 1364–1399: Relations with England and France During the Reign of Duke John IV* (London: Oxford University Press, 1970), 2–6.

6   *Ibid.*, 61, 93–6.

7   Details of Joan's journey to Brittany are from Michael Jones, *The Creation of Brittany: A Late Medieval State* (London: Hambledon, 1988), 175–91.

8   Jean Froissart, *Chronicles of England, France, Spain, and the Adjoining Countries*, Vol. 2, ed. Thomas Johnes (London: H.G. Bohn, 1857), 313–14.

9   Elena Woodacre, 'The Perils of Promotion: Maternal Ambition and Sacrifice in the Life of Joan of Navarre, Duchess of Brittany, and Queen of England', in *Virtuous or Villainess? The Image of the Royal Mother from the Early Medieval to the Early Modern Era* (New York: Palgrave Macmillan, 2016), 125–48.

10   Jones, *Ducal Brittany*, 105–6.

11   Translation via Woodacre, 'The Perils of Promotion', 128.

12   Jean Froissart, *The Chronicles of Froissart*, trans. John Bourchier (London: Macmillan and Co. Limited, 1899), 116.

13   Peter J. Begent and Hubert Chesshyre, *The Most Noble Order of the Garter: 650 Years* (London: Spink, 1999), 377.

14   Chris Given-Wilson, *Henry IV* (New Haven: Yale University Press, 2016), 118–19.

15   *Ibid.*, 121–2.

16   Frances Hingeston, *Royal and Historical Letters During the Reign of Henry the Fourth, Vol. I* (London: Longman, Green, Longman and Roberts, 1860), 19–20.

17   Great Britain Exchequer, *Issues of the Exchequer: Being a Collection of Payments Made Out of His Majesty's Revenue, from King Henry III to King Henry VI Inclusive* (London: John Murray, 1837), 285.

18   Given-Wilson, *Henry IV*, 234.

Chapter 3

1   Arthur Worthington Goodman, *The Marriage of Henry IV & Joan of Navarre in the Cathedral Church of S. Swithun, Winchester, Wednesday, 7 Feb. 1403* (Winchester: Warren & Son, 1934), 4.

2   Given-Wilson, *Henry IV*, 235.

3   Worthington Goodman, *The Marriage of Henry IV*, 5.

4   James Wylie, *History of England Under Henry IV*, Vol. 2 (London: Longmans, Green and Co., 1894), 287–8.

5   Great Britain Exchequer, *Issues of the Exchequer*, 292.

6   Worthington Goodman, *The Marriage of Henry IV*, 5–6.

7   *An English Chronicle of the Reigns of Richard II, Henry IV, Henry V, and Henry VI*, ed. Rev. John Silvester Davies (London: Nichols and Sons, 1856), 29.

8   Royal Archaeological Institute, 'Clarendon Palace, Wiltshire: Archaeology and History', *Notes for Visitors* (2017): 1.

9   *Two Fifteenth-Century Cookery-Books. Harleian ms. 279 (ab. 1430), & Harl. ms. 4016 (ab. 1450), with extracts from Ashmole ms. 1429, Laud ms. 553, & Douce ms. 55*, ed. Thomas Austin (London: N. Trübner & Co., 1888), 58–9.

10   Great Britain Exchequer, *Issues of the Exchequer*, 305.

11   Value calculated using 'Five Ways to Compute the Relative Value of a UK Pound Amount, 1270 to Present,' MeasuringWorth, 2018, www.measuringworth.com/index.php.

12   Great Britain Exchequer, *Issues of the Exchequer*, 295.

13   Ian Mortimer, *The Fears of Henry IV: The Life of England's Self-Made King* (London: Vintage Digital, 2013), accessed via the British Library.

14   Great Britain Exchequer, *Issues of the Exchequer*, 294.

15   *Ibid.*, 296.

16   Wylie, *History of England*, Vol. 2, 288.

17   *Cotton MS Julius E IV*, f.3r, the British Library; Mark Arvanigian, 'Henry IV of England,' in *Henry IV: The Establishment of the Regime, 1399–1406*, ed. Gwilym Dodd and Douglas Biggs (Woodbridge: York Medieval Press, 2003), 151.

18   CPR, Henry IV, Vol. 2, 213.

19   Christopher Dyer, *Standards of Living in the Later Middle Ages: Social Change in England, c. 1200–1520* (Cambridge: Cambridge University Press, 1998), 31.

20 A.R. Myers, *The Captivity of a Royal Witch: The Household Accounts of Queen Joan of Navarre, 1419–21*, Reprinted from the '*Bulletin of the John Rylands Library*', No. 1 (Manchester, 1940), 16.

21 Great Britain Exchequer, *Issues of the Exchequer*, 285–6.

22 CPR, Henry IV, Vol. 2, 241, 268, 347, 501.

23 CPR, Henry IV, Vol. 2, 473.

24 For example, the National Archives, SC 8/158/7900, SC 8/229/11420.

25 John V, *Lettres et mandements de Jean V, duc de Bretagne*, Vol. 2, No. 863, 11 July 1407, ed. René Blanchard (Nantes: Société des Bibliophiles Bretons, 1890), 75.

26 'Joan, Queen of England, letter to her stepson, John, Duke of Bedford, 10th November 1415,' quoted in *Letters of the Queens of England 1100–1547*, ed. Anne Crawford (Gloucestershire: Alan Sutton Publishing Ltd, 1994), 115–16.

27 Mortimer, *The Fears of Henry IV*.

28 *The Brut; or, The Chronicles of England*, Text H, ed. Friedrich Brie (London: K. Paul, Trench, Trübner & Co. Ltd, 1906), 549.

29 *The Brut*, Text H, 549.

30 Mortimer, *The Fears of Henry IV*; Stephen Broadberry et al, *English Medieval Population: Reconciling Time Series and Cross Sectional Evidence*, (University of Warwick, 2010), 22 (table 6).

31 Ian Mortimer, *The Time Traveller's Guide to Medieval England: A Handbook for Visitors to the Fourteenth Century* (London: Vintage, Random House, 2012), 10.

32 Andy King, '"They have the Hertes of the People by North": Northumberland, the Percies and Henry IV, 1399–1408', in *Henry IV: The Establishment of the Regime*, 161.

33 'A Northern Chronicle', in Charles Lethbridge Kingsford, *English Historical Literature in the Fifteenth Century* (New York: Burt Franklin, 1913), 282.

34 R.A. Brown, H.M. Colvin and A.J. Taylor, *The History of the King's Works, Volume 2: The Middle Ages* (London: H.M. Stationery Office, 1976), 933–6.

35 Given-Wilson, *Henry IV*, 389–90.

36 Mortimer, *The Fears of Henry IV*.

37 Douglas Biggs, 'The Politics of Health: Henry IV and the Long Parliament of 1406', in *Henry IV: The Establishment of the Regime*, 202; Great Britain Exchequer, *Issues of the Exchequer*, 304–5.

38 Biggs, 'The Politics of Health', 202.

39 Woodacre, 'The Perils of Promotion', 125–48.

40 'July 1418', *Foedera*, Vol. 9.

41 Great Britain Exchequer, *Issues of the Exchequer*, 306–7.

42 *Ibid.*, 307–8.

43 For a thorough investigation of Henry's illnesses and what they could have been, see Peter McNiven, 'The Problem of Henry IV's Health, 1405–1413' in *The English Historical Review*, Volume C, No. CCCXCVII (1985): 747–72.

44 John Nichols, *A Collection of all the Wills, Now Known to be Extant, of the Kings and Queens of England etc* (London: J. Nichols, 1780), 203–05.

45 CPR, Henry IV, Vol. 4, 455.

46 CPR, Henry IV, Vol. 4, 460.

47 'Parishes: Havering-atte-Bower', in *A History of the County of Essex*, Vol. 7, ed. W.R. Powell (London: Victoria County History, 1978), 9–17.

48 Christopher Allmand, *Henry V* (London: Methuen, 1992), 88; Benjamin Williams, *Henrici Quinti, Angliæ Regis, Gesta, cum Chronicâ Neustriæ* (London: Sumptibus Societatis, 1850), 46–60.

49 K.H. Vickers, *Humphrey, Duke of Gloucester: A Biography* (London: Archibald Constable and Company Limited, 1907), 20.

50 'On the Battle of Azincourt', in *Political Poems and Songs Relating to English History, Composed During the Period from the Accession of Edw. III. To that of Ric. III.* Volume 2, ed. Thomas Wright (London: Longman, Green, Longman and Roberts, 1861), 125.

51 Williams, *Henrici Quinti*, 59; Titus Livius Foro-Juliensis, *Vita Henrici Quinti, Regis Angliæ*, ed. Thomas Hearne (Oxford: E Theatro Sheldoniano, 1716), 20.

52 Perceval de Cagny, *Chroniques de Perceval de Cagny* (Paris: Librairie Renouard, H. Laurens, 1902), 21–2.

53 RP, Vol. 4, 79b.

Chapter 4

1 Raphael Holinshed, William Harrison and Richard Stanyhurst, *Chronicles of England, Scotland and Ireland,* Vol. 3, ed. Henry Ellis (London: J. Johnson, etc., 1808), 69; Privy Council, Vol. 2, 157.

2 *Foedera*, Vol. 9, 283.

3 E.g. CCR, Henry V, Vol.1: June 1418.

4 CPR, Henry V, Vol. 2, 271.

5 'Inventory of Queen Joan's valuables in the custody of Friar John Randolf, August 1419', in Myers, *The Captivity of a Royal Witch*, 15–21.

6 *The Brut*, Text D, 422–3.

7 *Issues of the Exchequer*, 365.

8 RP, Vol. 4, 118b.

9 *The Brut*, Text E, 444.

10 Edward Walford, 'Rotherhithe', in *Old and New London*, Vol. 6 (London: Cassell, Petter & Galpin, 1878), 134–42.

11 Information about John via Arthur Collins and Sir Egerton Brydges, *Peerage of England; Genealogical, Biographical, and Historical*, Vol. 5 (London: F.C. and J. Rivington [and others], 1812), 491–300; 'Pelham, John (d.1429), of Pevensey Castle and Laughton, Suss.', in *The History of Parliament: the House of Commons 1386–1421*, ed. J.S. Roskell, L. Clark and C. Rawcliffe (Suffolk: Boydell and Brewer, 1993).

12 Agnes Strickland, *Lives of the Queens of England*, Vol. 3 (Philadelphia: Lea & Blanchard, 1841), 108.

13 *Calendar of the Fine Rolls Preserved in the Public Record Office, Edward II Volume III 1319–1327* (Hereford: The Hereford Times Ltd, 1912), 300.

14 Broedel, *The Malleus Maleficarum*, 2.

15 *Chronicle of London, from 1089 to 1483*, ed. Edward Tyrrell and Sir N.H. Nicolas (London: Longman, Rees, Orme, Brown and Green, 1827), 107; *Chronicles of London, Julius B II*, ed. Charles Kingsford (Oxford: Clarendon Press, 1905), viii–ix.

16 *Concilia Magnae Britanniae et Hiberniae,* Vol. 3, ed. David Wilkins (London: Fleet Street, 1737), 392–3.

17 Myers, *The Captivity of a Royal Witch*, No. 1, 14.

18 The descriptions of costings of the first three months of her captivity come from 'Account-book ... of the household of Queen Joan of Navarre from Sunday, October 1st, to Friday, December 15th, 1419', in A.R. Myers, *The Captivity of a Royal Witch*, No. 2, 3–14.

19 Charles Wykeham Martin, *The History and Description of Leeds Castle, Kent* (Westminster: Nichols and Sons, 1869).

20 For details of her expenditure see 'Account-book of the household ... of Joan of Navarre ... at Leeds Castle (Kent) from Sunday, the 17th March, 1420, to Friday, the 7th March, 1421', in Myers, *The Captivity of a Royal Witch*, No. 2, 17–19.

21 Myers, *The Captivity of a Royal Witch*, 8, 16.

22 Records of Joan's visitors from 'Account-book of Joan at Leeds Castle', in Myers, *The Captivity of a Royal Witch*, 20.

23 Enguerrand de Monstrelet, *The Chronicles of Enguerrand de Monstrelet*, Vol. 1, trans. Thomas Johnes (London: George Routledge and Sons, 1867), 439.

24 *Foedera*, Vol. 9, 876 & 884.

25 Myers, *The Captivity of a Royal Witch*, 9.

26 CPR, Henry V, Vol. 2, 402.

27 *Ibid.*, 301.

28 RP, Vol. 4, 247–8.

29 See, for example, National Archives SC 8/194/9697.

30 Woodacre, 'The Perils of Promotion', 125–48; '*Traité d'Alliance entre le Duc de Bourgogne & les Etats de Bretagne* signed at Amiens April 18, 1423' in Hyacinthe Morice, *Memoirs pour servir de preuves a l'histoire ecclesiastique et civile de Bretagne*, Tome 2 (Paris: Charles Osmont, 1884), 125–6.

31 Woodacre, 'The Perils of Promotion', 146.

32 CPR, Henry VI, Vol. 1, 85.

33 'Humphrey, Duke of Gloucester: Canones pro tabulis ejus astronomicis secundum Fratrem Randolfe: 15th cent', *Sloane MS 407* (London, British Library, Western Manuscripts), ff. 224–6.

34 *Chronicles of London: Julius B II*, 80–1.

35 RP, Vol. 4, 299a.

36 *The Brut*, Text D, 423.

37 Michael Jones, 'Between France and England: Jeanne de Navarre, Duchess of Brittany and Queen of England (1368–1437)', in *Between France and England: Politics, Power and Society in Late Medieval Brittany* (Hampshire: Ashgate Publishing, 2003), 22.

38 Johanne Amundesham, *Chronica Monasterii S. Albani, Annales Monasterii S. Albani (1421–1440)*, Vol. 1 (London: Longmans, Green & Co., 1870), 8, 16, 19.

39 *Ibid.*, 28–9.

40 *Ibid.*, 61–2.

41 Myers, *The Captivity of a Royal Witch*, 12.

42 For example, Robert Fabyan, *The New Chronicles of England and France*, ed. Henry Ellis (London: Printed for F.C. & J. Rivington [etc.], 1811), 611; *Chronicles of London, from 1089 to 1483*, 123; Privy Council, Vol. 5, 56.

43 Privy Council, Vol. 5, 56.

Chapter 5

1 Peter Fleming, 'Cobham, Reynold, first Lord Cobham of Sterborough', *Oxford Dictionary of National Biography*.

2 *Cotton MS Nero D VII*, British Library.

3 Jean de Wavrin, *Recueil des croniques et anchiennes istories de la Grant Bretaigne, a present nomme Engleterre*, ed. William Hardy (London: Longman & Co., 1879), 176–7.

4 For information about Jacqueline's life, see Vickers, *Humphrey*, 91–5; Alison Weir, *Britain's Royal Families: The Complete Genealogy* (London: Penguin Random House, 2011), 127–8.

5 R. Stein, 'De Brabantse Leeuw sluimert (1356–1430),' in *Geschiedenis van Brabant, van het hertogdom tot heden*, ed. R van Uytven et al (2004), 165–6.

6 Monstrelet, *Chronicles*, Vol. 1, 495; Alessandra Petrina, *Cultural Politics in Fifteenth Century England: The Case of Humphrey, Duke of Gloucester* (Leiden: Brill Academic Publishers, 2004), 120.

7 Vickers, *Humphrey*, 126–30.

8 Joseph Stevenson, *Letters and Papers Illustrative of the Wars of the English in France During the Reign of Henry the Sixth, King of England*, Vol. 2, Part 2 (London: Longman, Green, Longman and Roberts, 1861), 388–409.

9 Petrina, *Cultural Politics*, 122; Great Britain Exchequer, *Issues of the Exchequer*, 403.

10 Monstrelet, *Chronicles*, Vol. 1, 517–21.

11 For example, *Royal 15 E VI f2v* and *Cotton MS Nero D VII*, British Library.

12 Aeneas Sylvius Piccolomineus, *De Viris Illustribus* (Stuttgardiæ: Sumtibus Societatis literariæ stuttgardiensis, 1842), 52.

13 Leopold Devillers, *Cartulaire des comtes de Hainault de l'avènement de Guillaume II à la mort de Jacqueline de Bavière*, Vol. 4 (Brussels: Bruzelles F. Hayez, 1889), 648.

14 Johanne Amundesham, 'Chronicon Rerum Gesterum in Monasterio Sancti Albani (AD 1422–1431),' in *Chronicles and Memorials of Great Britain and Ireland During the Middle Ages* (London: Master of the Rolls, 1857), 20.

Chapter 6

1 'Primus compotus Johannis Bugge Armigeri', Accounts of John Bugge, treasurer and receiver general of Joan, Queen Consort of Henry IV, from 4 Apr. 5 Hen. VI (1427) to 4 Apr. 1428. SAL/MS/216, National Archives fols 56–9.

2 Amanda Richardson, 'Greenwich's First Royal Landscape: The Lost Palace and Park of Humphrey of Gloucester', *Southern History: A Review of the History of Southern England*, 34 (2012): 54.

3 RP, Vol. 4, 498b–99a.

4 Details of the composition of the house come from the comprehensive article by Richardson, 'Greenwich's First Royal Landscape', 51–72.

5 W.M. Ormrod, 'Edward III', *Oxford DNB*, 2004.

6 National Archives, C 143/448/2.

7 Richardson, 'Greenwich's First Royal Landscape', 61.

8 Vickers, *Humphrey*, 212, 280, 375.

9 For information on the court they cultivated, see Petrina, *Cultural Politics*; for a list of some of the scholars in their service see Rutilius Palladius, *The Middle-English Translation of Palladius De re rustica, Part 1*, ed. Mark Liddell (Berlin: E. Ebering, 1896), 22.

10 *Theological Treatises by St Athanasius*, trans. Antonio Beccaria, British Library, Royal MS 5 F.ii, f.91v.

11 Jane Kelsall, *Humphrey Duke of Gloucester, 1391–1447* (St Albans: Friends of St Albans Abbey, 2000), 2–3.

12 Hilary Carey, *Courting Disaster: Astrology at the English Court and University in the Later Middle Ages* (Hampshire: Macmillan Academic and Professional Ltd, 1992), 49.

13 Palladius, *De re rustica*, 22, 66, 85, etc.

14 John Lydgate, *Fall of Princes*, ed. Henry Bergen (Washington: The Carnegie Institution of Washington, 1923), 11–12.

15 William Page, F.S.A., *St Alban's Cathedral and Abbey Church, A Guide* (London: George Bell and Sons, 1898), 76.

16 *Book of Benefactors of St Albans Abbey*, trans. David Preest, unpublished, 310.

17 Kelsall, *Humphrey*, 7.

18 *Ibid.*

19 Petrina, *Cultural Politics*, 132.

20   *Ibid.*

21   Information about the Ladies of the Garter from James L. Gillespie, 'Ladies of the Fraternity of Saint George and of the Society of the Garter', in *Albion: A Quarterly Journal Concerned with British Studies*, 17, No. 3 (1985): 259–78.

22   Privy Council, Vol. 4: xix, 21 May 1432.

23   Gillespie, 'Ladies of the Fraternity', 272.

24   CPR, Henry VI, Vol. 2, 505.

25   'July–December 1436', *Foedera*, Vol. 10, 658.

26   National Archives, C 67/37A.

27   National Archives, SC 1/57/97.

28   *Excerpta historica: or, Illustrations of English history*, ed. Samuel Bentley (London: Samuel Bentley, 1831), 148–50.

29   Vickers, *Humphrey*, 256.

30   Leonard Walker, *To Dine With Duke Humphrey* (Romford: Ian Henry, *c.* 1987), 9.

31   CPR, Henry VI, Vol. 3, 430; 'Protest of Humphrey, Duke of Gloucester, against the liberation of the Duke of Orleans, 1440', in Stevenson, *Letters and Papers*, 440–51.

32   'Statement, by the council, of the king's reason for liberating the duke of Orleans, 1440', in Stevenson, *Letters and Papers*, Vol. 2, part 2, 451–60.

33   Gillespie, 'Ladies of the Fraternity', 272.

34   *Chronicle of Henry VI*, 'Second Unerased Version', ed. Giles, recorded in Kingsford, *English Historical Literature*, 340.

Chapter 7

1   'On the mutability of worldly changes', in Kingsford, *English Historical Literature*, 396 (written *c.*1460); *An English Chronicle 1377–1461: A New Edition*, ed. William Marx (Rochester: Boydell Press, 2003), 64.

2   Barbara Hanawalt and Kathryn Reyerson, *City and Spectacle in Medieval Europe* (Minneapolis: University of Minnesota Press, 1994), 173–4.

3   *Chronicle of Henry VI*, 'Second Unerased Version', ed. Giles, recorded in Kingsford, *English Historical Literature*, 341.

4   Kingsford, *English Historical Literature*, 156.

5   Ralph Griffiths, 'The Trial of Eleanor Cobham: An Episode in the Fall of Duke Humphrey of Gloucester,' in *King and Country: England and Wales in the Fifteenth Century*, ed. Ralph Griffiths (London: The Hambledon Press, 1991), 236.

6   CCR, Henry VI, Vol. 3, 422.

7   Petrina, *Cultural Politics*, 146.

8   All of Thomas' education and preferments are recorded in Elizabeth Biggs, *The College and Canons of St Stephen's, Westminster, 1348–1548*, Vol. 2 (PhD, University of York, 2016), 318.

9   *The Brut*, Text D, 478; George Lyman Kittredge, *Witchcraft in Old and New England* (New York: Russel & Russel, 1956), 81.

10 *An English Chronicle*, 61–2; *Chronicles of London Cleopatra*, 148; *The Brut*, Text F, 478.

11 See numerous examples in *Memorials of London and London Life in the XIIIth, XIVth, and IVth Centuries*, trans. Henry T. Riley (London: Longmans, Green and Co., 1868), such as pp. 600, 601, 623 and 646.

12 Griffiths, 'The Trial of Eleanor Cobham,' 238–9; Petrina, *Cultural Politics*, 146.

13 William Worcester, 'Wilhelmi Wyrcester Annales Rerum Anglicarum', in Stevenson, *Letters and Papers,* Vol. 2, part 2, 763.

14 *An English Chronicle*, 62; *The Brut*, Text F, 478.

15 *An English Chronicle*, 62.

16 'Prebendaries: Nonnington', in *Fasti Ecclesiae Anglicanae 1300–1541: Volume 2, Hereford Diocese*, ed. Joyce M. Horn (London: Institute of Historical Research, 1962), pp.37–8; Griffiths, 'The Trial of Eleanor Cobham', 238–9; Fabyan, *The New Chronicles*, 614.

17 *An English Chronicle*, 62–3.

18 *An English Chronicle*, 62.

19 CPR, Henry VI, Vol. 3, 559.

20 For example, Griffiths, 'The Trial of Eleanor Cobham', 243.

21 *The Brut*, Text F, 480; *An English Chronicle*, 63; *Chronicle of London, from 1089 to 1483*, 129.

22 Privy Council, Vol. 4, xix and 114.

23 Jessica Freeman, 'Sorcery at Court and Manor: Margery Jourdemayne, The Witch of Eye Next Westminster', *Journal of Medieval History*, 30, No. 4 (2004), 346.

24 The indictment files for the trial are held at the National Archives, KB 9/72.

25 *Chronicle of London, from 1089 to 1483*, 129; Fabyan, *The New Chronicles*, 614.

26 *An English Chronicle*, 64; *The Brut*, Text F, 481.

27 *An English Chronicle*, 63.

Chapter 8

1   Accounts of Eleanor's penance can be found across many chronicles, for example: *An English Chronicle 1377–1461*, 63; *The Brut*, 481, 508; *Chronicle of London, from 1089 to 1483*, 129.

2   See for example a 1516 case recorded in Jeremy Goldberg, *Women in England, c. 1275–1525: Documentary Sources* (Manchester: Manchester University Press, 1995), 227–8, No.12.

3   Vickers, *Humphrey*, 172.

4   *The Brut*, Text F, 481.

5   *An English Chronicle 1377–1461*, 63.

6   R.H. Helmholz, *Marriage Litigation in Medieval England* (Cambridge: Cambridge University Press, 1974), 90–4; Chris Given-Wilson, *An Illustrated History of Late Medieval England* (Manchester: Manchester University Press, 1996), 67–8.

7   *Foedera*, Vol. 10, 852.

8   Value calculated using 'Five Ways to Compute the Relative Value of a UK Pound Amount, 1270 to Present', MeasuringWorth, 2018, www.measuringworth.com/index.php.

9   Richard Hill, 'Lament of the Duchess of Gloucester', in *Political Poems and Songs*, 207.

10   Sir Henry Ellis, *Original Letters, Illustrative of English History: Including Numerous Royal Letters; from Autographs in the British Museum, and One Or Two Other Collections*, Vol. 1 (Harding and Lepard, 1827), 105–7.

11   The National Archives, E 101/71/3/873; Douglas Richardson, *Magna Carta Ancestry: A Study in Colonial and Medieval Families*, 2nd Edition (Salt Lake City: Douglas Richardson, 2011), 90–1; Hannah Ann Bullock, *History of the Isle of Man* (London: Longman, Hurst, Rees, Orme and Brown, 1816), 60.

12   Bullock, *History of the Isle of Man*, 27–9.

13   Ronald Stewart-Brown, 'The Imprisonment of Eleanor Cobham, Duchess of Gloucester', *Lancs Historic*, LXXXV (1933), 90.

14   Great Britain Exchequer, *Issues of the Exchequer*, 441.

15   *Ibid.*, 447–8.

16   Griffiths, 'The Trial of Eleanor Cobham', 248.

17   Great Britain Exchequer, *Issues of the Exchequer*, 441; Stewart-Brown, 'The Imprisonment of Eleanor Cobham', 91.

18   Griffiths, 'The Trial of Eleanor Cobham', 251.

19   Kelsall, *Humphrey*, 19.

20   Kelsall, *Humphrey*, 22; Maude C. Knight, 'Humphrey, Duke of Gloucester', *St Albans and Hertfordshire Architectural and Archaeological Society Transactions*, 2, No. 1 (1903–04), 86.

21   'July–December 1443', *Foedera*, Vol. 11, 45.

22   For details on works done to Kenilworth see John H. Harvey, 'Side-Lights on Kenilworth Castle', *The Archaeological Journal*, 101 (1944): 91–107.

23   Adrian Pettifer, *English Castles: A Guide by Counties* (Woodbridge: Boydell and Brewer, 2002), 257.

24   Christine Carpenter, *The Wars of the Roses: Politics and the Constitution in England, c. 1437–1509* (Cambridge: Cambridge University Press, 1997), 142.

25   *The Brut*, Text F, 483.

26   *Ibid.*, 484.

27   *Foedera*, Vol. 11, 45.

28   The National Archives, DDK/1/11.

29   Great Britain Exchequer, *Issues of the Exchequer*, 447–8.

30 John Ashdown-Hill, *The Secret Queen: Eleanor Talbot, the Woman Who Put Richard III on the Throne* (Stroud: The History Press, 2009), 50.

31 Ralph Griffiths, *The Reign of King Henry VI: The Exercise of Royal Authority, 1422–1461* (London: Ernest Benn Limited, 1981), 281.

32 Petrina, *Cultural Politics*, 150.

33 Vickers, *Humphrey*, 284.

34 Vickers, *Humphrey*, 258.

35 Vickers, *Humphrey*, 286; Fabyan, *The New Chronicles*, 617.

36 Polydore Vergil, *Three Books of Polydore Vergil's English History* (London: J.B. Nichols & Sons, 1844), 72.

37 Stevenson, *Letters and Papers*, Vol. 2, part 2, 116–23.

38 Privy Council, Vol. 6, 51.

39 *An English Chronicle*, 65.

40 Johannes Whethampstede, 'Registrum Abbatiae Johannis Whethamstede, Abbatis Monasterii Sancti Albani', in *Chronicles and Memorials of Great Britain and Ireland during the Middle Ages* (London: Master of the Rolls, 1857), 179.

41 See, for example, *An English Chronicle*, 65; For rumours of his murder, see Fabyan, *The New Chronicles*, 619 and *Chronicles of London, Vitellius A XVI*, 157.

42 'Brief notes of occurrences under Henry VI and Edward IV', from MS. Lambeth, 448, recorded in John Stowe, *Three Fifteenth-Century Chronicles* (Westminster: Camden Society, 1880), 149.

43 For example, 'Brief notes of occurrences', 150.

44 Petrina, *Cultural Politics*, 150; Fabyan, *The New Chronicles*, 619; Vickers, *Humphrey*, 292–93.

45 Ellis, *Original Letters*, 108–9.

46 CPR, Henry VI, Vol. 5, 74, 104, 110, 112.

47 National Archives, SC 8/85/4240.

48 Fabyan, *The New Chronicles*, 619.

49 *Ibid.*

50 Kelsall, *Humphrey*, 22.

51 Ralph Griffiths, 'Richard, Duke of York and the Royal Household in Wales, 1449–50', *Welsh History Review Cylchgrawn hanes Cymru*, 8, No. 1 (1976–77), 23–4.

52 *Ibid.*, 24.

53 RP, Vol. 5, 135b.

54 *Foedera*, Vol. 5, 171.

55 Vickers, *Humphrey*, Appendix C, 442–3.

56 Griffiths, 'Richard, Duke of York and the Royal Household in Wales', 24.

57 National Archives, DL 28/1/11.

58 Richard Hill, 'Lament of the Duchess of Gloucester', in *Political Poems*, 205–8.

Chapter 9

1   Juliet Barker, *Conquest: The English Kingdom of France, 1417–1450* (Massachusetts: Harvard University Press, 2012), 189.

2   Guy Perry, *The Briennes: The Rise and Fall of a Champenois Dynasty in the Age of the Crusades, c. 950–1356* (Cambridge: Cambridge University Press, 2018), 13.

3   Barker, *Conquest*, 147.

4   Gregory et al., *The Women of the Cousins' War*, 52.

5   Vita Sackville-West, *Saint Joan of Arc* (London: Penguin Random House, 2018).

6   Enguerrand de Monstrelet, *La Chronique d'Enguerran de Monstrelet: En Deux Livres, Avec Pièces Justificatives 1400–1444*, Vol. 5 (Paris: Jules Renouard, Libraire de la Société de l'Histoire de France, 1861), 44–5.

7   Monstrelet, *La Chronique*, 55–6.

8   Gregory et al, *The Women of the Cousins' War*, 56.

9   Great Britain Exchequer, *Issues of the Exchequer*, 425.

10   Henri Sauval, *Histoire et Recherches des Antiquités de la Ville de Paris*, Tome 2 (Paris: Charles Moette, 1724), 208–11.

11   Gregory et al, *The Women of the Cousins' War*, 58.

12   British Library, MS Harley 4431.

13   Monstrelet, *La Chronique*, 57–8.

14   'Henry VI: July 1433', in *Parliament Rolls of Medieval England*, ed. Chris Given–Wilson et al. (Woodbridge: Boydell & Brewer, 2005), accessed via British History Online.

15   *Ibid.*

16   Gregory et al, *The Women of the Cousins' War*, 59.

17   RP, Vol. 4, 439a; National Archives, SC 8/121/6031.

18   Gillespie, 'Ladies of the Fraternity', 272.

19   Susan Higginbotham, *The Woodvilles: The Wars of the Roses and England's most Infamous Family* (Stroud: The History Press, 2013), 11.

20   CPR, Henry VI, Vol. 2, 489, 518.

21   John Leland, *Joannis Lelandi antiquarii De rebvs Britannicis Collectanea*, Vol. 2 (London: Apud Benj. White, Fleet Street, 1774), 490–1.

22   Higginbotham, *The Woodvilles*, 12.

23   Nichols, *A Collection of all the Wills*, 270–6.

24   Great Britain Exchequer, *Issues of the Exchequer*, 436.

25   CPR, Henry VI, Vol. 2, 516.

26   Monstrelet, *La Chronique*, 272.

27   RP, Vol. 4, 498.

28   CPR, Henry VI, Vol. 3, 53.

29   Michael Hicks, *Richard III and his Rivals: Magnates and their Motives in the War of the Roses* (London: The Hambledon Press, 1991), 210.

30   See for example a grant of lands in CPR Henry VI, Vol. 3, 479.

31 *Foedera*, Vol. 10, 677.

32 CPR, Henry VI, Vol. 3, 426.

33 'Grafton Regis', in *A History of the County of Northampton: Volume 5, the Hundred of Cleley*, ed. Philip Riden and Charles Insley (London: Victoria County History, 2002), 142–76.

34 Higginbotham, *The Woodvilles*, 13.

35 Wm. E. Baumgaertner, *Squires, Knights, Barons, Kings: War and Politics in Fifteenth Century England* (Victoria: Trafford Publishing, 2010), accessed via Google Books.

36 Barker, *Conquest*, 290.

37 *Chronicles of London, Cleopatra C IV*, 146.

38 Gregory et al, *The Women of the Cousins' War*, 70–1.

39 Higginbotham, *The Woodvilles*, 65.

40 See for example John Matthews, *King Arthur: Dark Age Warrior and Mythic Hero* (New York: Rosen Publishing Group, 2008), 104–7; Jean Flori, 'The Plantagenet Court and the World of King Arthur', in *Eleanor of Aquitaine: Queen and Rebel*, ed. Jean Flori (Edinburgh: Edinburgh University Press, 2007).

Chapter 10

1   Matthew Lewis, *The Wars of the Roses* (Stroud: Amberley Publishing, 2015), accessed via the British Library..

2   Higginbotham, *The Woodvilles*, 15–16.

3   RP, Vol. 5, 176–7.

4   *Chronicles of London, Vitellius A XVI*, 158–9; Alison Hanham, *John Benet's Chronicle, 1399–1462: An English Translation with New Introduction* (Basingstoke, Hampshire: Palgrave Macmillan, 2016), 26–7.

5   *Chronicles of London, Vitellius A XVI*, 159; Hanham, *John Benet's Chronicle*, 27–29.

6   Lewis, *The Wars of the Roses*.

7   Higginbotham, *The Woodvilles*, 16.

8   *Chronicles of London, Vitellius A XVI*, 159.

9   *Ibid.*, 161; Lewis, *The Wars of the Roses*.

10 Hanham, *John Benet's Chronicle*, 30.

11 Higginbotham, *The Woodvilles*, 16.

12 Griffiths, 'Richard, Duke of York and the Royal Household in Wales', 14.

13 Lewis, *The Wars of the Roses*.

14 *The Gascon Rolls, C 61/138*, the National Archives, accessed via www.gasconrolls.org/en/ Richard's order is Membrane 15, No. 11, 27 October 1450.

15 Hanham, *John Benet's Chronicle*, 32.

16 Douglas Richardson, *Plantagenet Ancestry: A Study in Colonial and Medieval Families*, Second Edition, Vol. 1 (Utah: Salt Lake City, 2011), 163.

17 David Baldwin, *Elizabeth Woodville: Mother of the Princes in the Tower* (Stroud: Sutton, 2002), 4.

18 Lewis, *The Wars of the Roses*.

19 Lewis, *The Wars of the Roses*.

20 PL, Vol. 2, 296.

21 Joseph Hunter, *Three Catalogues: Describing the Contents of the Red Book of the Exchequer, of the Dodsworth Manuscripts in the Bodleian Library, and of the Manuscripts in the Library of the Honourable Society of Lincoln's Inn* (London: Pickering, Chancery Lane, 1838), 277–8.

22 PL, Vol. 2, 297.

23 Lewis, *The Wars of the Roses*.

24 Hanham, *John Benet's Chronicle*, 37.

25 Lewis, *The Wars of the Roses*.

26 *Chronicles of London, Vitellius A XVI*, 165.

27 Hanham, *John Benet's Chronicle*, 38.

28 Richardson, *Plantagenet Ancestry*, 164.

29 Baldwin, *Elizabeth*, 5.

30 Fabyan, *The New Chronicles*, 631; Higginbotham, *The Woodvilles*, 19.

31 Mary Dormer Harris, *The Coventry Leet Book: Or Mayor's Register* (London: Kegan Paul, Trench, Trübner & Co., 1907), 300.

32 Baldwin, *Elizabeth*, 5.

33 *Chronicles of London, Vitellius A XVI*, 168.

34 Hanham, *John Benet's Chronicle*, 43; *Chronicles of London, Vitellius A XVI*, 168.

35 *Chronicles of London, Vitellius A XVI*, 168; Fabyan, *The New Chronicles*, 633.

36 Hanham, *John Benet's Chronicle*, 45; *Chronicles of London, Vitellius A XVI*, 170.

37 *Chronicles of London, Vitellius A XVI*, 169–70; Fabyan, *The New Chronicles*, 634–5

38 PL, Vol. 3, 203–5; *Chronicles of London, Vitellius A XVI*, 170.

39 PL, Vol. 3, 204–5.

40 Hanham, *John Benet's Chronicle*, 46–7.

41 *Chronicles of London, Vitellius A XVI*, 171; Fabyan, *The New Chronicles*, 636.

42 *Chronicles of London, Vitellius A XVI*, 171.

43 *An English Chronicle*, 100–6.

44 Baldwin, *Elizabeth*, 199.

45 Higginbotham, *The Woodvilles*, 23; *Chronicles of London, Vitellius A XVI*, 172–3.

46 *An English Chronicle*, 109.

47 *Chronicles of London, Vitellius A XVI*, 173; *An English Chronicle*, 107–8.

48 *Chronicles of London, Vitellius A XVI*, 173; *An English Chronicle*, 109.

49 *Chronicles of London, Vitellius A XVI*, 173–5.

50 Bertram Wolffe, *Henry VI* (New Haven: Yale University Press, 2001), 331.

51 Higginbotham, *The Woodvilles*, 23–4.

52 Baldwin, *Elizabeth*, 9.

53 CPR, Edward IV, Vol. 1, 97.

54 'Venice: 1461–1470', in *Calendar of State Papers Relating To English Affairs in the Archives of Venice*, Volume 1, 1202–1509, ed. Rawdon Brown (London, 1864), No. 385, 30 August, 92–126.

55   *Chronicles of London, Vitellius A XVI*, 176.
56   CPR, Edward IV, Vol. 1, 81, 83.

Chapter 11

1   National Archives, C 1/27/268.
2   Baldwin, *Elizabeth*, 10.
3   CCR, Edward IV, Vol. 1, 179.
4   CPR, Edward IV, Vol. 1, 169–70.
5   Higginbotham, *The Woodvilles*, 28; Charles Ross, *Edward IV* (London: Eyre Methuen, 1974), 89.
6   Baldwin, *Elizabeth*, 10–11.
7   Baldwin, *Elizabeth*, 10–11; *The Coronation of Elizabeth Wydeville ... On May 26th, 1465. A Contemporary Account Now First Set Forth from a XV Century Manuscript*, ed. George Smith (London: Ellis, 1935), 31.
8   Jean de Wavrin, *Anchiennes cronicques d'Engleterre*, Vol. 2 (Paris: Jules Renouard, 1859), 325–8.
9   J.L. Laynesmith, *The Last Medieval Queens: English Queenship 1445–1503* (Oxford: Oxford University Press, 2004), 60.
10   Baldwin, *Elizabeth*, 14.
11   See for example: John Warkworth, *A Chronicle of the First Thirteen Years of the Reign of King Edward the Fourth*, ed. James Halliwell (London: John Bowyer Nichols and Son, 1839), 3; Fabyan, *The New Chronicles*, 654; Thomas More, *The History of King Richard the Third*, 53–4, accessed via www.thomas-morestudies.org.
12   John Giles, 'Hearne's fragment of an old chronicle, from 1460–1470', *The Chronicles of the White Rose of York* (London: James Bohn, 1845), 15.
13   More, *The History of King Richard the Third*, 54.
14   One of the earliest coming from Antonio Cornazzano, 'La Regina d'Ingliterra', in *De Mulieribus Admirandis, 1466–1468*.
15   Higginbotham, *The Woodvilles*, 31.
16   Ross, *Edward IV*, 84.
17   Baldwin, *Elizabeth*, 17.
18   *Ibid*.
19   Weir, *Britain's Royal Families*, 126; CPR, Edward IV, Vol. 1, 311–12.
20   PL, Vol. 4, 217.
21   *Calendar of Letter-Books of the City of London: L, Edward IV–Henry VII*, ed. Reginald R. Sharpe (London, 1912), Folio 37b.
22   Arlene Okerlund, *Elizabeth Wydeville: The Slandered Queen* (Stroud: Tempus, 2006), 61.
23   Higginbotham, *The Woodvilles*, 37; Okerlund, *Elizabeth Wydeville*, 61–2.
24   Following details from *The Coronation of Elizabeth Wydeville*, 14–25.
25   Okerlund, *Elizabeth Wydeville*, 66; Baldwin, *Elizabeth*, 19.

26 CPR, Edward IV, Vol. 1, 433–4, 525; CPR, Edward IV & Henry VI, 64.
27 Okerlund, *Elizabeth Wydeville*, 69.
28 *Ibid.*, 70.
29 Ross, *Edward IV*, 106–7.
30 Henry Riley, *Ingulph's Chronicle of the Abbey of Croyland with the Continuations* (London: H.G. Bohn, 1854), 439; Higginbotham, *The Woodvilles*, 50.
31 CPR, Edward IV, Vol. 1, 516.
32 Ross, *Edward IV*, 95.
33 For details of the various marriages see Higginbotham, *The Woodvilles*, 34–5.
34 J.R. Lander, *Crown and Nobility, 1450–1509* (London: Edward Arnold Ltd, 1976), 112.
35 Ross, *Edward IV*, 115; Hannes Kleineke, *Edward IV* (London: Routledge, 2009), 92.
36 Higginbotham, *The Woodvilles*, 40.
37 The following account comes from Malcolm Letts, *The Travels of Leo of Rozmital through Germany, Flanders, England, France, Spain, Portugal and Italy 1465–1467* (Abingdon: Taylor & Francis, 2017), 45–7.
38 Strickland, *Lives of the Queens of England*, Vol. 2, 214; Ross, *Edward IV*, 89.
39 Ross, *Edward IV*, 109.
40 'Milan: 1467', in *Calendar of State Papers and Manuscripts in the Archives and Collections of Milan 1385–1618*, ed. Allen B. Hinds (London, 1912), 117–22.
41 *Ibid.*
42 For the full account see *Excerpta historica*, 171–222.
43 *Ibid.*, 205–6.
44 CCR, Edward IV, Vol. 1, 456–7.
45 'Milan: 1467', 117–22.
46 Ross, *Edward IV*, 119.
47 Higginbotham, *The Woodvilles*, 55–6.
48 Okerlund, *Elizabeth Wydeville*, 99.
49 *Excerpta historica*, 227.
50 PL, Vol. 4, 298.
51 Kleineke, *Edward IV*, 88.
52 Riley, *Ingulph's Chronicle*, 439.
53 Kleineke, *Edward IV*, 95.
54 'Milan: 1469', 128–34; Okerlund, *Elizabeth Wydeville*, 109.
55 Kleineke, *Edward IV*, 95.
56 PL, Vol. 5, 35–6.
57 Warkworth, *A Chronicle*, 46.
58 Kleineke, *Edward IV*, 97.
59 Higginbotham, *The Woodvilles*, 59–60.
60 'Milan: 1469', 128–34.
61 *Ibid.*
62 RP, Vol. 6, Appendix, 232; CPR, Edward IV & Henry VI, 190.

63 Anne F. Sutton, 'Sir Thomas Cook and his "Troubles": An Investigation', *Guildhall Studies in London History*, Vol. 3, No. 2 (1978): 103.

64 *Ibid.*, 103–4.

65 Higginbotham, *The Woodvilles*, 61.

66 PL, Vol. 5, 62–3.

67 RP, Vol. 6, 232; CPR, Edward IV & Henry VI, 190.

68 National Archives, C 140/56/45; *Calendarium Inquisitionum Post Mortem, Volume IV* (Tower of London: Robert Lemon, 1828), 376, No. 45.

69 William Jones, 'Political Uses of Sorcery in Medieval Europe', *The Historian*, 35, No. 4 (1972): 679.

Chapter 12

1   Kleineke, *Edward IV*, 100.

2   Warkworth, *A Chronicle*, 8.

3   Kleineke, *Edward IV*, 102.

4   'Milan: 1470,' 134–45.

5   *Ibid.*

6   David MacGibbon, *Elizabeth Woodville: A Life* (Stroud: Amberley, 2013), 82.

7   *Chronicles of London, Vitellius A XVI*, 181.

8   MacGibbon, *Elizabeth Woodville*, 83.

9   *Chronicles of London, Vitellius A XVI*, 182; Fabyan, *The New Chronicles*, 658–9.

10 Okerlund, *Elizabeth Wydeville*, 120.

11 Kleineke, *Edward IV*, 109.

12 MacGibbon, *Elizabeth Woodville*, 84.

13 PL, Vol. 5, 85; *Chronicles of London, Vitellius A XVI*, 182.

14 Fabyan, *The New Chronicles*, 659; *Chronicles of London, Vitellius A XVI*, 183.

15 *Chronicles of London, Vitellius A XVI*, 183.

16 Kleineke, *Edward IV*, 110.

17 *Ibid.*, 112–13.

18 'Lettre de Marguerite d'York' in Wavrin, *Anchiennes cronicques*, Vol. 3, 210.

19 Giles, *White Rose*, 52.

20 *Ibid.*, 59–60.

21 John Bruce, *Historie of the Arrivall of Edward IV in England and the finall recouerye of his kingdomes from Henry VI* (London: J.B. Nichols & Son, 1838), 15.

22 Giles, *White Rose*, 60; Fabyan, *The New Chronicles*, 660.

23 Bruce, *Historie of the Arrivall*, 17; Fabyan, *The New Chronicles*, 660–1.

24 Bruce, *Historie of the Arrivall*, 17; MacGibbon, *Elizabeth Woodville*, 90.

25 John Stow, 'Of Towers and Castels: Baynard's Castle', in *A Survey of London. Reprinted From the Text of 1603*, ed. C.L. Kingsford (Oxford, 1908), 44–71.

26 *Chronicles of London, Vitellius A XVI*, 184; Warkworth, *A Chronicle*, 16.

27 Warkworth, *A Chronicle*, 16.

28   Bruce, *Historie of the arrivall*, 23.
29   Warkworth, *A Chronicle*, 18; Fabyan, *The New Chronicles*, 661.
30   Warkworth, *A Chronicle*, 18; Fabyan, *The New Chronicles*, 662; *Chronicles of London, Vitellius A XVI*, 184; Bruce, *Historie of the Arrivall*, 30.
31   Bruce, *Historie of the Arrivall*, 34.
32   Bruce, *Historie of the arrivall*, 33–5; *Chronicles of London, Vitellius A XVI*, 185; Warkworth, *A Chronicle*, 19.
33   Kleineke, *Edward IV*, 121; Warkworth, *A Chronicle*, 21.
34   Bruce, *Historie of the Arrivall*, 38; 'Milan: 1471', 145–62.
35   Fabyan, *The New Chronicles*, 662; *Chronicles of London, Vitellius A XVI*, 185; Warkworth, *A Chronicle*, 21.
36   PL, Vol. 5, 131.
37   Okerlund, *Elizabeth Wydeville*, 132.
38   *Ibid.*, 130–1.
39   'The Record of Bluemantle Pursuivant 1471–1472', in Kingsford, *English Historical Literature*, 382.
40   'On the Recovery of the Throne by Edward IV', in *Political Poems and Songs*, 281.
41   'The Record of Bluemantle Pursuivant', 379.
42   PL, Vol. 5, 137.
43   Kleineke, *Edward IV*, 91; Okerlund, *Elizabeth Wydeville*, 133–4.
44   'The Record of Bluemantle Pursuivant', 384.
45   *Ibid.*, 386.
46   *Ibid.*, 386–8.
47   PL, Vol. 5, 179.
48   Okerlund, *Elizabeth Wydeville*, 148.
49   James Orchard Halliwell, *Letters of the Kings of England*, Vol. I (London: Henry Colburn, 1848), 136–44.
50   RP, Vol. 6, 106–8.
51   *Excerpta historica*, 369.
52   Okerlund, *Elizabeth Wydeville*, 160.
53   *Excerpta historica*, 366–79.
54   'Milan: 1475', No. 303, 308, 312–13.
55   *Ibid.*, no. 316.
56   CPR, Edward IV & Henry VI, 571; RP, Vol. 12, 51.
57   MacGibbon, *Elizabeth Woodville*, 103; Riley, *Ingulph's Chronicle*, 478.
58   Riley, *Ingulph's Chronicle*, 479.
59   RP, Vol. 6, 193.
60   *Ibid.*, 193–4.
61   Fabyan, *The New Chronicles*, 666; *Chronicles of London, Vitellius A XVI*, 188.
62   John Stow, *Annals of England to 1603* (via Princeton Theological Seminary Library), 720.
63   Riley, *Ingulph's Chronicle*, 481–2.
64   *Ibid.*, 483.

65 *Chronicles of London, Vitellius A XVI*, 189; Riley, *Ingulph's Chronicle*, 483; Fabyan, *The New Chronicles*, 667.

66 Riley, *Ingulph's Chronicle*, 484.

67 Riley, *Ingulph's Chronicle*, 484–5; *Chronicles of London, Vitellius A XVI*, 190.

68 *Chronicles of London, Vitellius A XVI*, 190; Fabyan, *The New Chronicles*, 668.

69 Sarah Gristwood, *Blood Sisters: The Women Behind the Wars of the Roses* (New York: Basic Books, 2013), 177.

70 Riley, *Ingulph's Chronicle*, 488.

71 *Chronicles of London, Vitellius A XVI*, 190; Fabyan, *The New Chronicles*, 668; Riley, *Ingulph's Chronicle*, 489.

72 Robert Davies, *Extracts from the Municipal Records of the City of York, During the Reigns of Edward IV, Edward V, and Richard III* (London: J.B. Nichols and Son, 1843), 149–50.

73 For the following account see Polydore Vergil, *Anglica Historia 1555*, ed. Dana F. Sutton (The University of California: Irvine, 2010), Chapter 25; More, *Richard the Third*, 41–2.

74 Fabyan, *The New Chronicles*, 669; Riley, *Ingulph's Chronicle*, 489.

75 A transcript of his will can be found in Higginbotham, *The Woodvilles*, 181.

76 *Chronicles of London, Vitellius A XVI*, 190; Fabyan, *The New Chronicles*, 668; Riley, *Ingulph's Chronicle*, 489.

77 *Chronicles of London, Vitellius A XVI*, 191; Riley, *Ingulph's Chronicle*, 490.

78 Charles Lethbridge Kingsford, *The Stonor Letters and Papers, 1290–1483*, Vol. 2 (London: Offices of the Royal Historical Society, 1919), 160–1.

79 Paul Murray Kendall, *Richard the Third* (New York: W.W. Norton & Company, 2002), 550.

80 Charles Ross, *Richard III* (London: Eyre Methuen, 1981), 105; Riley, *Ingulph's Chronicle*, 490–1.

81 Riley, *Ingulph's Chronicle*, 490–1.

82 *Chronicles of London, Vitellius A XVI*, 192.

83 *Foedera*, Vol. 12, 204; CPR, 1476–85, 371.

84 'Titulus Regius', in RP, Vol. 6, 240–2.

85 Gristwood, *Blood Sisters*, 206; Ross, *Richard III*, 101.

86 Riley, *Ingulph's Chronicle*, 496–7.

87 Ibid., 498–9.

88 Ibid., 499–500.

89 PL, Vol. 6, 82.

90 Ibid.

91 Riley, *Ingulph's Chronicle*, 503.

92 Ibid., 504.

93 For information about the finding and examination of Richard's remains, see Philippa Langley and Michael Jones, *The King's Grave: The Search for Richard III* (London: John Murray, 2013).

94 Riley, *Ingulph's Chronicle*, 504; *Chronicles of London, Vitellius A XVI*, 193.

95   RP, Vol. 6, 315.
96   'Henry VII: November 1485', in Given-Wilson, *Parliament Rolls*.
97   RP, Vol. 6, 288b.
98   'Henry VII: November 1485, Part 1', in Given-Wilson, *Parliament Rolls*, No. 9.
99   Bonnie Wheeler, Robert L. Kindrick, Michael Norman Salda, *The Malory Debate: Essays on the Texts of Le Morte Darthur* (Cambridge: D.S. Brewer, 2000), 377.
100 Higginbotham, *The Woodvilles*, 162.
101 'Henry VII: November 1485', in Given-Wilson, *Parliament Rolls*.
102 Joseph Armitage Robinson, *The Abbot's House at Westminster* (Cambridge: Cambridge University Press, 1911), 22–3.
103 Walford, 'Bermondsey: The Abbey', *Old and New London*, 117–33.
104 Higginbotham, *The Woodvilles*, 163.
105 *Foedera,* Vol. 12, 328.
106 *Chronicles of London, Vitellius A XVI*, 194; Higginbotham, *The Woodvilles*, 167.
107 Higginbotham, *The Woodvilles*, 172.
108 Transcript of the will found in Higginbotham, *The Woodvilles*, 186.
109 Arundel MS 26, f.29v, British Library.
110 Arundel MS 26, f.29v.

Chapter 13

1   'On the mutability of worldly changes', in Kingsford, *English Historical Literature*, 395.

BIBLIOGRAPHY

Primary

Amundesham, Johanne. *Chronica Monasterii S. Albani, Annales Monasterii S. Albani (1421–1440)*, Vol. 1. London: Longmans, Green & Co., 1870.

Amundesham, Johanne. '*Chronicon Rerum Gesterum in Monasterio Sancti Albani* (AD 1422–1431)'. In *Chronicles and Memorials of Great Britain and Ireland during the Middle Ages*. London: Master of the Rolls, 1857.

An English Chronicle 1377–1461: A New Edition. Edited by William Marx. Rochester: Boydell Press, 2003.

An English Chronicle of the Reigns of Richard II, Henry IV, Henry V and Henry VI. Edited by Rev. John Silvester Davies. London: Nichols and Sons, 1856.

Book of Benefactors of St Albans Abbey. Translated by David Preest, unpublished.

'Brief notes of occurrences under Henry VI. And Edward IV', from Lambeth MS, 448. Recorded in John Stowe, *Three Fifteenth-Century Chronicles*. Westminster: Camden Society, 1880.

British Library:
  Arundel MS 26, f.29v.
  Cotton MS Julius E IV, f.3r.
  Cotton MS Nero D VII.
  Lambeth MS.
  MS Harley 4431.
  Royal MS 15 E VI f.2v.
  Sloane MS 407.

Cagny, Perceval de. *Chroniques de Perceval de Cagny*. Paris: Librairie Renouard, H. Laurens, 1902.

Calendarium Inquisitionum Post-Mortem, Volume IV. Tower of London: Robert Lemon, 1828.

Calendar of the Close Rolls. London: HMSO:
  Henry V, Volume 1, 1413–19.
  Henry VI, Volume 3, 1435–41.
  Edward IV, Volume 1, 1461–68.

Calendar of the Fine Rolls Preserved in the Public Record Office, Edward II Volume III 1319–27. Hereford: The Hereford Times Ltd, 1912.

Calendar of the Patent Rolls. London: HMSO:
  Henry IV, Volume 2, 1401–05.
  Henry IV, Volume 4, 1408–13.
  Henry V, Volume 2, 1416–22.
  Henry VI, Volume 1, 1422–29.
  Henry VI, Volume 2, 1429–36.
  Henry VI, Volume 3, 1436–41.
  Henry VI, Volume 5, 1446–52.
  Edward IV, Volume 1, 1461–67.
  Edward IV & Henry VI, 1467–77.
  Edward IV, Edward V, Richard III, 1476–85.

Calendar of Letter-Books of the City of London: L, Edward IV–Henry VII. Edited by Reginald R. Sharpe. London, 1912.

Calendar of State Papers and Manuscripts in the Archives and Collections of Milan 1385–1618. Edited by Allen B. Hinds. London, 1912.

Calendar of State Papers Relating to English Affairs in the Archives of Venice, Volume 1, 1202–1509. Edited by Rawdon Brown. London, 1864.

Chronicles of London. Edited by Charles Kingsford. Oxford: Clarendon Press, 1905.

Chronicle of London, from 1089 to 1483. Edited by Edward Tyrrell and Sir N.H. Nicolas. London: Longman, Rees, Orme, Brown and Green, 1827.

Concilia Magnae Britanniae et Hiberniae, Volume 3. Edited by David Wilkins. London: Fleet Street, 1737.

Cornazzano, Antonio. 'La Regina d'Ingliterra'. In *De Mulieribus Admirandis, 1466–1468*.

Extracts from the Municipal Records of the City of York, During the Reigns of Edward IV, Edward V, and Richard III. Edited by Robert Davies. London: J.B. Nichols and Son, 1843.

Cartulaire des comtes de Hainault de l'avènement de Guillaume II à la mort de Jacqueline de Bavière, Volume 4. Edited by Leopold Devillers. Brussels: Bruzelles F. Hayez, 1889.

The Coventry Leet Book: Or Mayor's Register. Edited by Mary Dormer Harris. London: Kegan Paul, Trench, Trübner & Co., 1907.

Original Letters, Illustrative of English History: Including Numerous Royal Letters; from Autographs in the British Museum, and One or Two Other Collections, Volume 1. Edited by Sir Henry Ellis. London: Harding and Lepard, 1827.

Excerpta Historica: Or, Illustrations of English History. Edited by Samuel Bentley. London: Samuel Bentley, 1831.

Fabyan, Robert. *The New Chronicles of England and France*. Edited by Henry Ellis. London: Printed for F.C. & J. Rivington [etc.], 1811.

Fleming, Peter. 'Cobham, Reynold, first Lord Cobham of Sterborough'. *Oxford Dictionary of National Biography*.

Foro-Juliensis, Titus Livius. *Vita Henrici Quinti, Regis Angliæ*. Edited by Thomas Hearne. Oxford: E Theatro Sheldoniano, 1716.

Froissart, Jean. *Chronicles of England, France, Spain, and the adjoining countries*, Vol. 2. Edited by Thomas Johnes. London: H.G. Bohn, 1857.

Froissart, Jean. *The Chronicles of Froissart*. Translated by John Bourchier. London: Macmillan and Co. Ltd, 1899.

The Paston Letters, A.D. 1422–1509, Volumes 1–6. Edited by James Gairdner. London: Chatto & Windus, 1904.

Gascon Rolls, via www.gasconrolls.org/en/.

The Chronicles of the White Rose of York, 'Hearne's fragment of an old chronicle, from 1460–1470'. Edited by John Giles. London: James Bohn, 1845.

Great Britain Exchequer. *Issues of the Exchequer: Being a Collection of Payments Made Out of His Majesty's Revenue, from King Henry III to King Henry VI Inclusive*. London: John Murray, 1837.

John Benet's Chronicle, 1399–1462: An English Translation with New Introduction. Edited by Alison Hanham. Basingstoke: Palgrave Macmillan, 2016.

Royal and Historical Letters During the Reign of Henry the Fourth, Volume 1. Edited by Frances Hingeston. London: Longman, Green, Longman and Roberts, 1860.

Historie of the Arrivall of Edward IV in England and the Finall Recouerye of his Kingdomes from Henry VI. Edited by John Bruce. London: J.B. Nichols & Son, 1838.

Holinshed, Raphael, William Harrison and Richard Stanyhurst. *Chronicles of England, Scotland and Ireland*, Volume 3. Edited by Henry Ellis. London: J. Johnson, etc., 1808.

Three Catalogues: Describing the Contents of the Red Book of the Exchequer, of the Dodsworth Manuscripts in the Bodleian Library, and of the Manuscripts in the Library of the Honourable Society of Lincoln's Inn. Edited by Joseph Hunter London: Pickering, Chancery Lane, 1838.

'Joan, Queen of England, letter to her stepson, John, Duke of Bedford, 10th November 1415'. In *Letters of the Queens of England 1100–1547*. Edited by Anne Crawford. Gloucestershire: Alan Sutton Publishing Ltd, 1994.

John V. Lettres et mandements de Jean V, duc de Bretagne, Volume 2, No. 863, 11 July 1407. Edited by René Blanchard. Nantes: Société des Bibliophiles Bretons, 1890.

English Historical Literature in the Fifteenth Century. Edited by Charles Lethbridge Kingsford. New York: Burt Franklin, 1913.

Kingsford, Charles Lethbridge. *The Stonor Letters and Papers, 1290–1483*, Volume II. London: Offices of the Royal Historical Society, 1919.

Leland, John. *Joannis Lelandi antiquarii De rebvs britannicis collectanea*, Volume II. London: Apud Benj. White, Fleet Street, 1774.

Letters of the Queens of England 1100–1547. Edited by Anne Crawford. Gloucestershire: Alan Sutton Publishing Ltd, 1994.

The Travels of Leo of Rozmital through Germany, Flanders, England, France, Spain, Portugal and Italy 1465–1467. Edited by Malcolm Letts. Abingdon: Taylor & Francis, 2017.

Lydgate, John. *Fall of Princes.* Edited by Henry Bergen. Washington: The Carnegie Institution of Washington, 1923.

Monstrelet, Enguerrand de. *La Chronique d'Enguerran de Monstrelet: En Deux Livres, Avec Pièces Justificatives 1400–1444,* Volume 5. Paris: Jules Renouard, Librairie de la Société de l'Histoire de France, 1861.

Monstrelet, Enguerrand de. *The Chronicles of Enguerrand de Monstrelet,* Volume 1. Translated by Thomas Johnes. London: George Routledge and Sons, 1867.

More, Thomas. *The History of King Richard the Third.* Edited by George Logan. Bloomington: Indiana University Press, 2005; also accessed via www.thomas-morestudies.org.

National Archives:
> C 1/27/268.
> C 61/138.
> C 67/37A.
> C 140/56/45.
> C 143/448/2.
> DDK/1/11.
> DL 28/1/11.
> KB 9/72.
> SAL/MS/216.
> SC 1/57/97.
> SC 8/85/4240.
> SC 8/121/6031.
> SC 8/158/7900.

A Collection of all the Wills, Now Known to be Extant, of the Kings and Queens of England, etc. Edited by John Nichols. London: J. Nichols, 1780.

Letters of the Kings of England, Volume I. Edited by James Orchard Halliwell. London: Henry Colburn, 1848.

Palladius, Rutilius. *The Middle-English Translation of Palladius De re rustica, Part 1.* Edited by Mark Liddell. Berlin: E. Ebering, 1896.

Parliament Rolls of Medieval England. Edited by Chris Given-Wilson et al. Woodbridge: Boydell & Brewer, 2005. Accessed via British History Online.

Piccolomineus, Aeneas Sylvius. *De Viris Illustribus.* Stuttgardiæ: Sumtibus Societatis literariæ stuttgardiensis, 1842.

Pisan, Christine de. *The Treasure of the City of Ladies.* Translated by Sarah Lawson. London: Penguin Books, 1985.

Political Poems and Songs relating to English History, composed during the period from the accession of Edw. III. To that of Ric. III, Volume 2. Edited by Thomas Wright. London: Longman, Green, Longman and Roberts, 1861.

'Prebendaries: Nonnington'. In *Fasti Ecclesiae Anglicanae 1300–1541: Volume 2, Hereford Diocese*. Edited by Joyce M. Horn. London: 1962.

Proceedings and Ordinances of the Privy Council of England. London: The Public Records Office:
12 Henry IV to 10 Henry V, Volume 2.
8 Henry VI to 14 Henry VI, Volume 4.
15 Henry VI to 21 Henry VI, Volume 5.
22 Henry VI to 39 Henry VI, Volume 6.

Ingulph's Chronicle of the Abbey of Croyland with the Continuations. Edited by Henry Riley. London: H.G. Bohn, 1854.

Rotuli Parliamentorum, ut et petitiones, et placita in Parliamento. Great Britain, Parliament:
Volume 4, Henry V.
Volume 5, Henry VI.
Volume 6, Edward IV.

Rymer, Thomas. *Foedera*, Volumes 5, 9, 10.

Letters and papers illustrative of the wars of the English in France during the reign of Henry the Sixth, King of England, Volume 2, part 2. Edited by Joseph Stevenson. London: Longman, Green, Longman, and Roberts, 1861.

Stow, John. *Annals of England to 1603*. Digitised by Princeton Theological Seminary Library.

The Brut; or, The Chronicles of England. Edited by Friedrich Brie. London: K. Paul, Trench, Trübner & Co. Limited, 1906.

The Coronation of Elizabeth Wydeville ... On May 26th, 1465. A Contemporary Account Now First Set Forth from a XV Century Manuscript. Edited by George Smith. London: Ellis, 1935.

Theological Treatises by St Athanasius. Translated by Antonio Beccaria. The British Library, Royal MS 5, F.ii.

'Traité d'Alliance entre le Duc de Bourgogne & les Etats de Bretagne' signed at Amiens April 18 1423. In Hyacinthe Morice 'Memoirs pour servir de preuves a l'histoire ecclesiastique et civile de Bretagne', Tome 2. Paris: Charles Osmont, 1884.

Tour-Landry, Geoffroy IV de la. *The Book of the Knight of La Tour-Landry*. Edited by Thomas Wright. London: Kegan Paul, Trench, Trübner & Co. Ltd, 1906.

Two Fifteenth-century Cookery-books. Harleian Ms. 279 (Ab. 1430), & Harl. Ms. 4016 (Ab. 1450), with Extracts from Ashmole Ms. 1429, Laud Ms. 553, & Douce Ms. 55. Edited by Thomas Austin. London: N. Trübner & Co., 1888.

Vergil, Polydore. *Anglica Historia 1555*. Edited by Dana F. Sutton. Irvine: The University of California, 2010.

Vergil, Polydore. *Three books of Polydore Vergil's English History*. London: J.B. Nichols & Sons, 1844.

Warkworth, John. *A Chronicle of the First Thirteen Years of the Reign of King Edward the Fourth*. Edited by James Halliwell. London: John Bowyer Nichols and Son, 1839.

Wavrin, Jean de. *Anchiennes cronicques d'Engleterre*, Volume II. Paris: Jules Renouard, 1859.

Wavrin, Jean de. *Recueil des croniques et anchiennes istories de la Grant Bretaigne, a present nomme Engleterre.* Edited by William Hardy. London: Longman & Co., 1879.

Whethampstede, Johannes. '*Registrum Abbatiae Johannis Whethamstede, Abbatis Monasterii Sancti Albani*'. In *Chronicles and Memorials of Great Britain and Ireland during the Middle Ages*. London: Master of the Rolls, 1857.

Henrici Quinti, Angliæ Regis, Gesta, cum Chronicâ Neustriæ. Edited by Benjamin Williams. London: Sumptibus Societatis, 1850.

Secondary

Allmand, Christopher. *Henry V*. London: Methuen, 1992.

Armitage Robinson, Joseph. *The Abbot's House at Westminster*. Cambridge: Cambridge University Press, 1911.

Ashdown-Hill, John. *Eleanor the Secret Queen*. Stroud: The History Press, 2009.

Bailey, Michael. *Fearful Spirits, Reasoned Follies: The Boundaries of Superstition in Late Medieval Europe*. Ithaca: Cornell University Press, 2013.

Baldwin, David. *Elizabeth Woodville: Mother of the Princes in the Tower*. Stroud: Sutton, 2002.

Barker, Juliet. *Conquest: The English Kingdom of France, 1417–1450*. Massachusetts: Harvard University Press, 2012.

Baumgaertner, W.E. *Squires, Knights, Barons, Kings: War and Politics in Fifteenth-Century England*. Victoria: Trafford Publishing, 2010. Accessed via Google Books.

Begent, Peter J. and Hubert Chesshyre. *The Most Noble Order of the Garter: 650 Years*. London: Spink, 1999.

Biggs, Elizabeth. *The College and Canons of St Stephen's, Westminster, 1348–1548*, Volume 2. PhD, University of York, 2016.

Broadberry, Stephen et al. *English Medieval Population: Reconciling Time Series and Cross Sectional Evidence*. University of Warwick, 2010.

Broedel, Hans Peter. *The Malleus Maleficarum and the Construction of Witchcraft: Theology and Popular Belief*. Manchester: Manchester University Press, 2003.

Bullock, Hannah Ann. *History of the Isle of Man*. London: Longman, Hurst, Rees, Orme, and Brown, 1816.

Burnett, Charles. *Magic and Divination in the Middle Ages: Texts and Techniques in the Islamic and Christian Worlds*. Hampshire: Ashgate Publishing Limited, 1996.

Carey, Hilary. *Courting Disaster: Astrology at the English Court and University in the Later Middle Ages*. Hampshire, Macmillan Academic and Professional Ltd, 1992.

Carpenter, Christine. *The Wars of the Roses: Politics and the Constitution in England, c. 1437–1509*. Cambridge: Cambridge University Press, 1997.

Collins, Arthur and Sir Egerton Brydges. *Peerage of England; Genealogical, Biographical, and Historical*, Volume 5. London: F.C. and J. Rivington [and others], 1812.

Delachenal, R. *Deux prétendues lettres du régent fils aîné de Jean II au comte de Savoie Amédée VI*. Tome 72. Paris: Bibliothèque de l'École des chartes, 1911.

Dyer, Christopher. *Standards of Living in the Later Middle Ages: Social Change in England, c. 1200–1520*. Cambridge: Cambridge University Press, 1998.

'Five Ways to Compute the Relative Value of a UK Pound Amount, 1270 to Present'. MeasuringWorth, 2018. www.measuringworth.com/index.php.

Flori, Jean. 'The Plantagenet Court and the World of King Arthur'. In *Eleanor of Aquitaine: Queen and Rebel*. Edinburgh: Edinburgh University Press, 2007.

Freeman, Jessica. 'Sorcery at Court and Manor: Margery Jourdemayne, The Witch of Eye Next Westminster.' *Journal of Medieval History*, 30, No. 4 (2004): 343–57.

Gillespie, James L. 'Ladies of the Fraternity of Saint George and of the Society of the Garter'. *Albion: A Quarterly Journal Concerned with British Studies*, 17, No. 3 (1985): 259–78.

Given-Wilson, Chris. *An Illustrated History of Late Medieval England*. Manchester: Manchester University Press, 1996.

Given-Wilson, Chris. *Henry IV*. New Haven: Yale University Press, 2016.

Goldberg, Jeremy. *Women in England, c. 1275–1525: Documentary Sources*. Manchester: Manchester University Press, 1995.

'Grafton Regis'. In *A History of the County of Northampton: Volume 5, the Hundred of Cleley*. Edited by Philip Riden and Charles Insley. London, 2002.

Gregory, Philippa, Baldwin, David & Jones, Michael. *The Women of the Cousins' War: The Real White Queen and her Rivals*. London: Simon & Schuster, 2013.

Griffiths, Ralph. 'Richard, Duke of York and the Royal Household in Wales, 1449–50.' *Welsh History Review* [*Cylchgrawn Hanes Cymru*], 8, No. 1 (1976–77), 14–25.

Griffiths, Ralph. *The Reign of King Henry VI: The Exercise of Royal Authority, 1422–1461*. London: Ernest Benn Limited, 1981.

Griffiths, Ralph. 'The Trial of Eleanor Cobham: An Episode in the Fall of Duke Humphrey of Gloucester'. In *King and Country: England and Wales in the Fifteenth-Century*. Edited by Ralph Griffiths. London: The Hambledon Press, 1991.

Gristwood, Sarah. *Blood Sisters: The Women Behind the Wars of the Roses*. New York: Basic Books, 2013.

Hanawalt, Barbara and Reyerson, Katherine. *City and Spectacle in Medieval Europe*. Minneapolis: University of Minnesota Press, 1994.

Harvey, John H. 'Side-Lights on Kenilworth Castle'. *The Archaeological Journal*, 101 (1944): 91–107.

Helmholz, R.H. *Marriage Litigation in Medieval England*. Cambridge: Cambridge University Press, 1974.

Henry IV: The Establishment of the Regime, 1399–1406. Edited by Gwilym Dodd and Douglas Biggs. Woodbridge: York Medieval Press and The Boydell Press, 2003.

Hicks, Michael. *Richard III and his Rivals: Magnates and their Motives in the War of the Roses*. London: The Hambledon Press, 1991.

Higginbotham, Susan. *The Woodvilles: The Wars of the Roses and England's Most Infamous Family*. Stroud: The History Press, 2013.

Jolly, Karen, Raudvere, Catharina, and Peters, Edward. *Witchcraft and Magic in Europe: The Middle Ages*. London: The Athlone Press, 2002.

Jones, Michael. 'Between France and England: Jeanne de Navarre, Duchess of Brittany and Queen of England (1368–1437)'. In *Between France and England: Politics, Power and Society in Late Medieval Brittany*. Hampshire: Ashgate Publishing, 2003.

Jones, Michael. *Ducal Brittany, 1364–1399: Relations with England and France During the Reign of Duke John IV*. London: Oxford University Press, 1970.

Jones, Michael. *The Creation of Brittany: A Late Medieval State*. London: Hambledon, 1988.

Jones, William. 'Political uses of sorcery in medieval Europe'. *The Historian*, 35, No. 4 (1972): 670–87.

Kelsall, Jane. *Humphrey Duke of Gloucester, 1391–1447*. St Albans: Friends of St Albans Abbey, 2000.

Kieckhefer, Richard. *Magic in the Middle Ages*. Cambridge: Cambridge University Press, 2000.

Kittredge, George Lyman. *Witchcraft in Old and New England*. New York: Russel & Russel, 1956.

Kleineke, Hannes. *Edward IV*. London: Routledge, 2009.

Knight, Maude C. 'Humphrey, Duke of Gloucester.' *St Albans and Hertfordshire Architectural and Archaeological Society Transactions*, 2, No. 1. (1903–04), 51–86.

Lander, J.R. *Crown and Nobility, 1450–1509*. London: Edward Arnold Ltd, 1976.

Langley, Philippa and Jones, Michael. *The King's Grave: The Search for Richard III*. London: John Murray, 2013.

Laynesmith, J.L. *The Last Medieval Queens: English Queenship 1445–1503*. Oxford: Oxford University Press, 2004.

Lewis, Matthew. *The Wars of the Roses*. Stroud: Amberley Publishing, 2015, accessed via the British Library.

MacGibbon, David. *Elizabeth Woodville: A Life*. Stroud: Amberley, 2013.

Matthews, John. *King Arthur: Dark Age Warrior and Mythic Hero*. New York: Rosen Publishing Group, 2008.

McNiven, Peter. 'The Problem of Henry IV's Health, 1405–1413'. *The English Historical Review*, Volume C, No. CCCXCVII (1985): 747–772.

Mortimer, Ian. *The Fears of Henry IV: The Life of England's Self-Made King*. London: Vintage Digital, 2013. Accessed via the British Library

Mortimer, Ian. *The Time Traveller's Guide to Medieval England: A Handbook for Visitors to the Fourteenth Century*. London: Vintage, Random House, 2012.

Murray Kendall, Paul. *Richard the Third*. New York: W.W. Norton & Company, 2002.

Myers, A.R. *The Captivity of a Royal Witch: The Household Accounts of Queen Joan of Navarre, 1419–21*, Reprinted from the *Bulletin of the John Rylands Library*, Nos 1 & 2. Manchester, 1940.

Okerlund, Arlene. *Elizabeth Wydeville: The Slandered Queen*. Stroud: Tempus, 2006.

Ormrod, W.M. 'Edward III.' *Oxford DNB*, 2004.

Page, William. *St Alban's Cathedral and Abbey Church, A Guide*. London: George Bell and Sons, 1898.

'Parishes: Havering-atte-Bower'. In *A History of the County of Essex*, Volume 7. Edited by W.R. Powell. London, 1978.

'Pelham, John (*d*.1429), of Pevensey Castle and Laughton, Suss.' In *The History of Parliament: the House of Commons 1386–1421*. Edited by J.S. Roskell, L. Clark and C. Rawcliffe. Suffolk: Boydell and Brewer, 1993.

Perry, Guy. *The Briennes: The Rise and Fall of a Champenois Dynasty in the Age of the Crusades, c. 950–1356*. Cambridge: Cambridge University Press, 2018.

Pettifer, Adrian. *English Castles: A Guide by Counties*. Woodbridge: Boydell and Brewer, 2002.

Petrina, Alessandra. *Cultural Politics in Fifteenth Century England: The Case of Humphrey, Duke of Gloucester*. Leiden: Brill Academic Publishers, 2004.

Richardson, Amanda. 'Greenwich's First Royal Landscape: The Lost Palace and Park of Humphrey of Gloucester'. In *Southern History: A Review of the History of Southern England*, 34 (2012), 51–72.

Richardson, Douglas. *Magna Carta Ancestry: A Study in Colonial and Medieval Families*, Second Edition. Salt Lake City: Douglas Richardson, 2011.

Ross, Charles. *Edward IV*. London: Eyre Methuen, 1974.

Ross, Charles. *Richard III*. London: Eyre Methuen, 1981.

Royal Archaeological Institute. 'Clarendon Palace, Wiltshire: Archaeology and History'. *Notes for Visitors* (2017): 1.

Sackville-West, Vita. *Saint Joan of Arc*. London: Penguin Random House, 2018.

Sauval, Henri. *Histoire et Recherches des Antiquités de la Ville de Paris*, Tome 2. Paris: Charles Moette, 1724.

Stewart-Brown, Ronald. 'The Imprisonment of Eleanor Cobham, Duchess of Gloucester'. *Lancs Historic*, LXXXV (1933), 89–97.

Strickland, Agnes. *Lives of the Queens of England: From the Norman Conquest*, Volumes 1–3. Philadelphia: Lea & Blanchard, 1842.

Stow, John. 'Of Towers and Castels: Baynards Castle'. In *A Survey of London. Reprinted From the Text of 1603*. Edited by C.L. Kingsford. Oxford, 1908.

Sumption, Jonathan. *Divided Houses: The Hundred Years War III*. London: Faber and Faber, 2011.

Sutton, Anne F. 'Sir Thomas Cook and his "troubles": An Investigation'. *Guildhall Studies in London History*, Volume 3, No. 2 (1978), 85–108.

Thorndike, Lynn. *A History of Magic And Experimental Science*, Volume 3. New York: Columbia University Press, 1934.

Vickers, K. H. *Humphrey, Duke of Gloucester: A Biography*. London: Archibald Constable and Company Limited, 1907.

Walford, Edward. *Old and New London*, Volume 6. London: Cassell, Petter & Galpin, 1878.

Walker, Leonard. *To Dine With Duke Humphrey*. Romford: Ian Henry, *c*. 1987.

Weir, Alison. *Britain's Royal Families: The Complete Genealogy*. London: Penguin Random House, 2011.

Wheeler, Bonnie, Robert L. Kindrick and Michael Norman Salda. *The Malory Debate: Essays on the Texts of Le Morte Darthur*. Cambridge: D.S. Brewer, 2000.

Wolffe, Bertram. *Henry VI*. New Haven: Yale University Press, 2001.

Woodacre, Elena. 'The Perils of Promotion: Maternal Ambition and Sacrifice in the Life of Joan of Navarre, Duchess of Brittany, and Queen of England', in *Virtuous or Villainess? The Image of the Royal Mother from the Early Medieval to the Early Modern Era*. Edited by Carey Fleiner and Elena Woodacre. New York: Palgrave Macmillan, 2016.

Worthington Goodman, Arthur. *The Marriage of Henry IV & Joan of Navarre in the Cathedral Church of S. Swithun, Winchester, Wednesday, 7 Feb. 1403*. Winchester: Warren & Son, 1934.

Wykeham Martin, Charles. *The History and Description of Leeds Castle, Kent*. Westminster: Nichols and Sons, 1869.

Wylie, James. *History of England Under Henry IV*, Volume 2. London: Longmans, Green and Co., 1894.

INDEX

The History Press

The destination for history
www.thehistorypress.co.uk